GRADUS

BOOK I

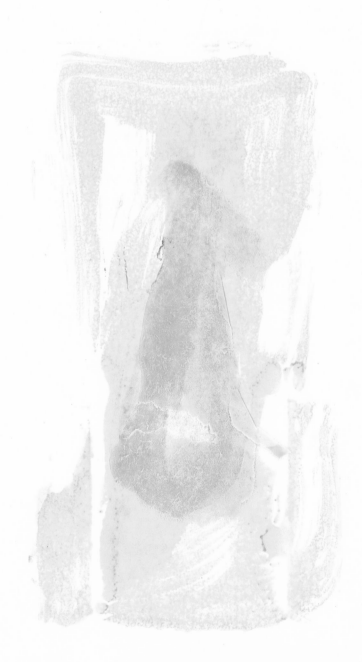

GRADUS

AN INTEGRATED APPROACH TO HARMONY, COUNTERPOINT, AND ANALYSIS

BOOK I

by Leo Kraft

PROFESSOR OF MUSIC, QUEENS COLLEGE OF THE CITY UNIVERSITY OF NEW YORK

W·W·Norton & Company·Inc·New York

to the memory of Paul Klapper

Library of Congress Cataloging in Publication Data

Kraft, Leo.
  Gradus.

  Includes bibliographies.
  — —Music anthology.
  1. Music—Theory. 2. Music—Analysis, appreciation.
I. Title.
MT6.K877G7 Class suppl: MT6.K877G7Suppl. 781 75–40207

ISBN 0 393 09180 5

Printed in the United States of America

3 4 5 6 7 8 9

CONTENTS

ACKNOWLEDGMENTS

It is a pleasant duty to acknowledge the help of many kind friends and colleagues whose suggestions have been useful to me in writing this book.

In the endless search for the perfect musical example I have benefitted from the advice of Edward Lerner, Paul Maynard, and Mark Lindley. Raymond Erickson read the section on medieval music and offered a number of constructive comments. Rosette Lamont and Serge Sobolevitch provided translations of difficult texts. Joseph Raben illuminated for me the meanings of *So Light Is Love*.

Two of my younger colleagues, Drora Pershing, and Bruce Saylor, used various parts of this text in syllabus form and provided frank and valued comments.

My debt is very great to the several generations of Queens College students who worked their way through the several versions of this material. It was their response, positive or negative, that guided me in the shaping and reshaping of my ideas until they reached the present form.

I must add that it is hardly possible to work with such colleagues as Charles Burkhart, Saul Novack, George Perle, Henry Weinberg, and Hugo Weisgall over a period of years without learning a good deal from them. I cheerfully acknowledge that our many conversations and meetings have been a considerable source of intellectual stimulus and have opened up many lines of thought. Naturally, it is not possible to recall the details of this learning process, which took place on so many occasions and at so many levels. But my sense of obligation is none the less real.

Douglass Green and Robert Morgan read the manuscript and offered many constructive suggestions.

Work on this book, particularly in regard to the musical examples, was greatly facilitated by the capable staff of the Queens College Music Library. My special thanks go to Barbara Greener and Julia Rosenfeld for their help.

I also wish to express my thanks to the music editor of W. W. Norton and Company, Claire Brook. Her understanding of the particular nature of *Gradus* and her work in finding the best forms in which to embody its content have materially aided the successful publication of this book. The advice and encouragement she and her assistant Hinda Keller Farber have offered are deeply appreciated.

LEO KRAFT

GRADUS

BOOK I

Musicians in the orchestra by Edgar Degas (1834-1917) (Louvre, Paris: Photographie Giraudon).

PRELUDE

As a serious student of music, you know that one of the subjects to be learned is called "theory." But if theory means the opposite of practice, the truth is that there is little theory in a good music course. Nor should there be. For what you have to learn is how music is put together, a very practical matter indeed. And this book is devoted to the investigation of one practical problem: how sounds are organized into a coherent musical whole, which we call a piece of music.

Conventional music pedagogy has formulated separate courses of study in which different aspects of music are studied. These are usually called harmony, counterpoint, analysis, and so on. But music involves all these, and more. How is anyone to learn the connections between harmony and counterpoint? Where do you study all the factors that make a piece work? And don't the various elements of music interact with each other? Doesn't voice leading influence orchestration, and doesn't modulation have something to do with the form of a piece? In order to answer some of these questions and offer a view of music as a whole, this book presents a unified approach to the subject. Topics that have been taught in isolation from each other are brought together in one comprehensive whole.

The goal is total musicianship. It may take many years to achieve or may never be fully attained, but it is our ideal. To progress toward that goal, specific skills must be developed. We may summarize those skills or competencies as follows:

listening skills—knowing what you hear in a piece of music;

analytic skills—understanding how a piece works, both from hearing it and from studying the score;

writing skills—developing mastery of the materials and processes of music through exercises and creative work;

performing skills—projecting the aesthetic and emotional content of music in stylistically valid performances;

historical skills—placing a piece in a frame of reference so as to understand its relation to other works and to significant artistic and intellectual currents.

It is your responsibility to acquire these skills. It is the responsibility of this book and of the instructor to present the material in such a way that the skills can be learned most efficiently. With the intention of making this volume as useful as possible, the book is organized more like a course than a treatise. You will find many short sections, each a lesson or two in itself, each focusing on one topic. Some of the material requires class discussion. Some can be studied independently.

The key to success is your own personal effort and involvement. The book is written in a way that demands your active participation rather than passive reading. You will find:

blanks in the text, which you fill in;

worksheets at the end of various sections with exercises to develop writing and analytical skills;

projects in tonal composition in which you build upon the skills learned in the exercises and develop your ability to express musical ideas;

music examples for you to learn, study, analyze, and perform.

While the acquisition of skills is indispensable, it is not sufficient to make a total musician. To develop intelligent musical behavior you must also understand the connections between skills, areas, topics. Connections are sometimes seen as similarities and sometimes as differences. The difference

2

between one piece of music and another, for instance, is usually an easy thing to perceive. Similarities require a higher degree of generalization. It takes some thought to realize that there are elements in common among many different kinds of music. If you never learn those common elements, you are forced to consider each piece as a special case, and your grasp of musical process remains rudimentary. This book identifies, in as many ways as possible, the common elements in tonal music.

Those interested in the pedagogical method of the book will soon realize that a small nucleus of principles and processes is introduced in the opening section in a simple way, then studied in contexts of gradually increasing complexity. Rules—that is, generalizations based on actual musical practice—are few. Each discussion begins with a piece of music. Therefore, an essential part of the course is your study of the music itself, both in class and on your own. Out of your musical experiences will come the realization of the common principles of tonal music.

For a better understanding of the musical and pedagogical thought that animates this book you should read the sections entitled "Why Study Counterpoint?" (page 115) and "Music and the Rules" (page 118). They may be read at any time,

but you will probably get more out of them if you first read them early in the course, then reread them later. They are included because of the author's conviction that an intelligent music student is interested not only in the subject matter, but also in how it is presented.

Finally, total musicianship must include the historical dimension, for no human activity exists in isolation. While the course is not organized along historical lines, discussion of historical and stylistic aspects of the music studied is integrated into the text. Every musician must be his or her own historian. Instead of waiting until you take a formal course in music history you would do well to look up in a reference book such as *Grove's Dictionary of Music and Musicians* each composer whose music you study. Follow through by writing a short summary of the composer's life and work in your notebook. You should also take advantage of the suggestions that appear from time to time under the heading "For further study." These will enable you to expand your horizon beyond what is contained in the course. All of which is only the beginning of a lifetime study, for music is an inexhaustible universe, offering limitless possibilities for personal growth and development.

Numbers in this book are used in the following way:

6̲ means music example number 6.

6 means the sixth degree of a scale.

6̲ means measure number 6 in a music example.

6th means the interval of a sixth.

VI means the triad built on the sixth degree of a scale.

VI⁶ means the first inversion of that triad, also known as the ⁶₃ position.

3

A page from an Italian book of chants (second half of the fourteenth century).

PART ONE
MELODY

1

Introduction to Melody

One way to begin the study of music is through melody. At its simplest, *melody* is a heightened form of speech. Where words are inadequate to express human emotions the voice is raised and music is born. When we try to speak emphatically or expressively the exaggerated rise and fall of the voice foreshadows the curve of a melodic line. Although it is but a single line, melody can convey a world of meaning. Many musical cultures consist of nothing but melody. Our study of tonal music begins with melodies that are self-sufficient and that can be investigated fully without reference to other dimensions of music.

Specifically, the body of music on which Part One is based consists largely of folk songs and chants, [1] through [37] . Not only are such melodies beautiful and enjoyable in themselves, they also embody the musical impulses of many peoples, many faiths. As beginning students, you will find much to learn from these melodies. Later you will also find that they may serve as the basis for larger musical compositions.

FOLK SONG A folk song is the work of many hands; its origin is usually lost in the distant past. It belongs to the people who use it and who con-

stantly refashion it. This reworking process occurs naturally when songs are handed down from one generation to another by oral tradition. Once a melody is written down it becomes fixed in one version, which is not necessarily an advantage. Just as the spread of literacy and the communication of spoken language by means of radio, cinema, and television have reduced regional variations in spoken language, so have these same media inhibited the evolution of a genuine folk music. In studying melodies that stem from an oral tradition, we should not be surprised to find that many tunes exist in a number of different versions, all equally authentic. The well-known ballad *Barbara Allen* appears in Cecil Sharp's rich collection *English Folk Songs of the Southern Appalachians* in no less than sixteen variants. You may know other versions of some of the tunes included in this book.

CHANT Those songs used in the services of different religions and known as chants also originated in the distant past and almost certainly took on different forms at different times. But the tendency of an institution is to codify its material in a systematic way and to settle on one version as the official one, which parallels the fixing of religious worship into established forms. The best-known chant to our Western ears is that of the Roman Catholic church, known as plainchant or Gregorian chant. The official version of that chant may be found in the *Liber Usualis*, the complete collection of melodies for the liturgical year.

MELODY AND SPEECH We start to study the relation between the spoken word and song by examining an American folk song, ☐1. Say the words aloud, following their natural accent. Listen to the rise and fall of your own voice. Did you speak on one level from beginning to end? Did you speak without any pause, or did you stop at some points? Do those stops come at some particular places? How is the text divided up? Does the rise and fall of the voice have any connection with the phrases of the text?

Sing the melody with the words. What happens to the words when they are sung? The vowels are lengthened and certain syllables are emphasized. We may say that singing is an intensified form of speech. And just as the text is grouped into phrases, so we sense that the music falls into groups of notes that we also call phrases. Just as the voice rises and falls in speaking the lines, so does the melodic inflection rise and fall. How can we be more specific about the ups and downs in the tune? Can we learn more about their shape if we use some note as a reference point for the others?

2

Tonality 1: The Major Mode

Since we perform a piece before studying it, sing ☐4 with the words and be familiar with it. In singing the piece, listen for the breathing places. These help define the natural divisions of the melody into smaller units. You may feel that the first part of the tune consists of two four-measure units, or you may hear it as one eight-measure group. What we are beginning to discuss here is the musical *phrase*. It is investigated in detail at a later point (page 22), but we must at least say that the melody is formed in phrases, and that we will think of eight measures as constituting the phrase. Within that framework, do any notes have a special function?

THE TONIC The first note is E♭, heard as an *upbeat;* the next note is A♭, the *downbeat*. The first two measures rise and fall, creating what we might call a small arch. The dotted lines in the example show this arch and the next two melodic groups as well. The first arch ends on A♭, the third

emphasizes A♭, and the phrase ends on the same note. The second phrase repeats the first, with the emphasis again on A♭. While the third phrase highlights different notes, the fourth again affirms A♭. We might describe A♭ as the center of gravity in this melody, with all the other notes in motion about it. Such a referential note is called a *tonic*. Since the name of that note, in ☐4, is A♭, we say that the melody is in the *key* of A♭.

THE MAJOR SCALE Can we arrange the pitches used in *The Ash Grove* in any kind of order? One way is to list the pitches, starting with the tonic and continuing until the tonic is reached again. But one problem arises immediately. Both D and D♭ are in the melody. Are they both to be included? Looking through the tune, we notice that D is heard only once, at the point where E♭ is emphasized, and that D♭ is heard in all other parts of the tune. Let us set aside the D, for this discussion, and list all other pitches in the melody (see example below).

A♭-major scale

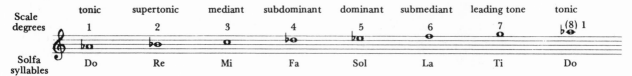

This list is called a *scale* (Italian: *scala,* "ladder"), and the particular scale written above is that of A♭ major. A scale is a collection of those notes used most often in a piece, arranged from the tonic to the tonic and usually written in ascending order. Each letter name appears only once, except for the repetition of the tonic. The notes of a scale, such as the major, are called the *diatonic* notes of the key. There are always five notes that are not in the diatonic scale but that may appear in a piece of music. These are known as the *chromatic* notes. Even a simple folk song may have chromatic notes. The D in *The Ash Grove* is a chromatic note; it is not in the A♭-major scale, but it certainly is in the tune.

SCALE DEGREES In speaking of the scale, the various steps of the ladder are known as the *degrees of the scale.* These are identified three different ways: (1) by names, (2) by Arabic numerals, and (3) by sol-fa syllables. All three are to be found in the scale shown above, and you should know them, since all are widely used. In this text, a scale degree is indicated by an Arabic numeral.

Returning to *The Ash Grove,* we now can see that the formulation of the major scale enables us to define the rise and fall of the melodic line more precisely. We observe that the tonic is the center of gravity, that the melody rises quickly to 5, finds its way down to the lower 5, and ends the eight-bar phrase on 1; that the second phrase has the same shape; that the third emphasizes 5 (the D has something to do with that); and that the last phrase literally repeats the first. Tonic and dominant are the goals. Tonic is repose, stability. But just how much stability? That depends partly on the rhythmic placement. The last note of the piece seems very stable, falling on the downbeat and lasting two beats. But another A♭ one bar earlier, on a weaker beat, had very little stability. The opposite of stability is activity or motion, which the dominant embodies. Now we need more precise ways of measuring melodic rise and fall and of knowing the distance between one note and another.

TONAL AND ATONAL Music that revolves around a central note is called *tonal,* not because it has anything to do with "tone" but because it has a tonic. All the notes in the piece are related to that tonic, and what we have begun to study is the operation of those relationships. But there is also music that has no tonic. The relationships that connect the notes to each other have nothing to do with a particular key center, or tonic. Thus, the music is called *atonal,* without a tonic. The term *atonal,* being negative, tells us nothing about the way in which the piece is put together, and other concepts will have to be developed for that purpose.

3

Intervals and the Scales

Is it possible to express the distance between pitches in a specific way? Yes, if we can agree on a unit of measure. Then we can measure the distance from one note to another by adding together the number of times the unit occurs. The smallest unit normally used in Western music is the *semitone or half step.* All distances between notes, whether heard simultaneously or successively, are measured by the number of half steps they comprise. We call these distances *intervals.* We should also be aware of the fact that smaller intervals than the semitone may be sung or played. They occur in the music of some Eastern cultures as well as in that modern music called "microtonal."

NAMES OF THE INTERVALS One way to measure the size of an interval is to count the number of semitones it includes. Another is by the usage it has acquired in tonal music. Since such music is the chief concern of this text, traditional tonal terminology is most often used. But in talking about atonal music, composers and theorists often prefer to denote an interval by a number showing its semitone content.

In the major mode, from scale degree 3 to 4 is an example of a minor 2nd or half step.

1 to 2	= major 2nd or whole step
2 to 4	= minor 3rd
1 to 3	= major 3rd
1 to 4	= perfect 4th
1 to 5	= perfect 5th
3 to 8	= minor 6th
1 to 6	= major 6th
2 to 8	= minor 7th
1 to 7	= major 7th
1 to 8	= octave
4 to 7	= augmented 4th ⎫ both called
7 (up) to 4	= diminished 5th ⎬ "tritone"

DIATONIC AND CHROMATIC SEMITONES

A further distinction may be made between two kinds of semitones. Those that occur in the diatonic scale are the *diatonic semitones*. Those that involve any of the five notes not in the diatonic scale are *chromatic semitones*. In 90A, 65–66, the interval from D to D♯ is a chromatic semitone.

INTERVAL STRUCTURE OF THE SCALE

A scale lists a series of pitches in a specific order which may be defined as a series of intervals, read from tonic to tonic. In this way we can find a general formulation for the major scale, independent of any particular key. The only intervals that need be used are whole steps and diatonic half steps, or major (M) and minor (m) 2nds.
The major scale:

M 2nd	M 2nd	m 2nd	M 2nd	M 2nd	M 2nd	m 2nd
1	2	3	4	5	6	7 8 (1)

AUGMENTED AND DIMINISHED INTERVALS

Any perfect, major, or minor interval may be enlarged by a semitone (*augmented*) or decreased by a semitone (*diminished*). This operation does not change the name of the interval, but it does change the size. Thus if a minor 3rd is diminished, the result must be some kind of 3rd—namely, diminished. If a perfect 4th is augmented the result must be some kind of 4th—namely, augmented.

An interval may be augmented or diminished in two ways—from its upper note or from its lower note:

perfect 5th   becomes augmented 5th   another way

To summarize the pitches that are available in the Western system, those pitches are listed below as the chromatic scale. The system of tuning on which Western music is based divides the octave into twelve equal parts, called semitones or minor 2nds. The chromatic scale belongs to no particular key, but provides the raw material out of which the other scales are made. As we have just seen, the major scale uses a collection of seven notes out of the twelve, those being the diatonic notes in a given key. The remaining five notes are the chromatic notes. Reading the chromatic scale, you can see that the same note may be spelled in two different ways. Two different spellings of the same note are said to be *enharmonically* equivalent. The use of double sharps and double flats adds still additional spelling possibilities. The spelling that is actually used depends on the musical context: the tonic of D♭ major is spelled D♭, but 7 in D major is spelled C♯.

Spell each of these notes in two other ways:

F = ——— or ———,

C♯ = ——— or ———,

B♭ = ——— or ———,

B = ——— or ———.

The chromatic scale

It is essential that you

1. know the names of the intervals,
2. can find them on the piano readily,
3. recognize their sound,
4. sing them,

for intervals are the building blocks of music.

ANOTHER VIEW OF THE MAJOR SCALE

Is the familiar listing of the major scale, stepwise from tonic to tonic, the only one possible? Not at all. Other formulations exist and have at least a speculative interest. As one possibility, is there a single interval that can generate a major scale? Yes, the perfect 4th and the perfect 5th, both of which yield the same sequence of notes but in reverse order.

8

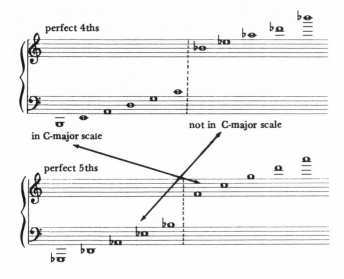

perfect 4ths

in C-major scale

not in C-major scale

perfect 5ths

First, observe that from any given note the next note in the series may be derived either by counting up a perfect 4th or down a perfect 5th. If this series is called a "circle of 5ths" remember that the 5ths are descending. Second, the practical application of the series may be heard in many tonal compositions, usually in the lowest part, which will be called the bass line. But if more than six perfect 5ths are heard in succession, the music must introduce notes that are not in the key, as the example above shows. To stay within the key, one of the 5ths must be diminished, or one of the 4ths augmented. In the series as shown, the diminished 5th or augmented 4th would have to occur between scale degrees 4 and 7, which suggests that those two scale degree are in some sense the boundaries of the key.

KEY AND SCALE It is important to clarify the difference between key and scale. Key refers to all those intervallic relationships within a piece that define one pitch as the tonic. All other pitches function in relation to that tonic. Thus a key involves a network of relationships, while a scale is simply a list of the diatonic pitches of a key.

OCTAVE EQUIVALENCE What is the difference between the A♭ that began our scale and the A♭ that completed the list? An intuitive answer might be that the second A♭ is the same as the first, but higher. In many ways this is correct, for even at this early stage of the study we can see that both belong to the same pitch class and both represent the same scale degree. This is true no matter which A♭ is played, no matter how high or low.

PITCH CLASS We have referred to the letter names commonly used to specify pitches. Now we must define them more precisely. Just what are A, B♭, and C♯? The letters denote pitches, but not any particular level for those pitches. If you ask someone to play A on the piano he might play a high A, a low A, any of the available As. All of them are indeed A. By definition, then, we say that by A we mean all the possible locations of A. A represents an entire class of pitches. In our tempered system of tuning, there are _____ different pitch classes.

TRANSPOSITION From the scale used in ④ we were able to generalize a succession of major and minor seconds called the major scale. That formula may start on any pitch class. The process by which a group of notes, whether it be a scale, a chord, or even an entire piece, is reproduced exactly at a higher or lower pitch level is known as *transposition*.

KEY SIGNATURE Higher or lower, C–D–E–F–G–A–B will not yield any major scale but a C major scale. How are other keys spelled out? When the major-scale pattern is transposed and starts on a pitch class other than C, sharps or flats must be added to give the desired array of whole and half steps. The particular group of sharps or flats that defines the pitches of a particular scale is called the *key signature*. It is printed at the beginning of every line in a piece of tonal music. You must know the signature of every key—that is, to recognize it when you see it, remember the key signature of each key, and be able to play all major scales on the piano.

REGISTER The various levels at which pitches may be heard in a piece of music are called *registers*. These do not have hard and fast boundaries. We speak of high and low registers, and often of the middle register. Folk song and chant are usually restricted to a single register, but compositions with more than one voice may use more than one register.

COMPOUND INTERVALS If an octave is added to an interval, how is that interval changed? No new pitch class is added, but a higher or lower register may be introduced. Adding an octave to a major 3rd makes it a major 10th. Both are major and have the same pitch classes. Intervals larger than an octave are called *compound intervals*. Intervals smaller than an octave are called *simple intervals*.

INVERSION An octave can be added to an interval; an interval may also be subtracted from an octave. Since an octave contains twelve semitones, subtracting (let us say) the interval of four semitones yields the interval of eight semitones. Another way to say this is that the inversion of a major 3rd is a minor 6th. The inversion of a major interval is always a minor interval and vice versa. The inversion of an augmented interval is always a diminished interval and vice versa.

☞ Worksheet 1

Illustrations of interval inversion

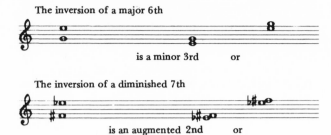

The inversion of a major 6th

is a minor 3rd   or

The inversion of a diminished 7th

is an augmented 2nd   or

4

Melodic Structure 1

TONIC AND DOMINANT The scale provides us with a list of notes, but it tells us nothing about how those notes are used in a piece. In building a melodic line, what is the function of each note? We have already found that the note called the tonic is stable and serves as a reference point for the other notes. Is there another note that also plays an important part in the structure of the melody?

Sing the melody of the Kyrie, 35. The first short move consists of a rise from the tonic to the dominant. Then the last syllable of "Kyrie" is extended in time by a florid passage known as a *melisma*. It circles around one note, the dominant, rising once to the higher tonic but not stopping there, circling again around the dominant. On "eleison" there are two descending moves, one quicker, one a bit slower. The first, from dominant down to tonic, touches upon the goal but doesn't bring the momentum to a halt. The second, falling a shorter distance, arrives at the tonic more gradually and uses up the musical energy of the melody. In summary, a curve may be described rising from 1 to 5, maintaining its activity around 5, and descending to the starting point, 1.

It is as if there were some law of musical gravity at work here. The rising inflection builds tension, which makes the listener expect release in the form of a falling inflection. But the descent has to wait, and part of the melody's interest lies in the way that the tension is kept up while we await the inevitable descent. The dominant represents the op-

posite pole to the tonic. Between the two, active tones move to keep the melody alive.

SONG AND SPEECH Looking again at our comparisons with spoken language, the tonic may be compared with the low pitch from which most sentences start and to which they return. The higher pitch at which most of a sentence is spoken may be compared to the dominant of the scale. Significantly, in talking about chant, the note of tension is called the *reciting tone,* suggesting again the link between song and speech. The overall shape of many chants, such as 25, may be seen as several extensions of the reciting tone and descents to the tonic.

THE PERFECT 5TH Play a perfect 5th on the piano. Which note sounds like the tonic and which like the dominant? Almost invariably the lower note of the 5th sounds stable. The perfect 5th has a power that no other interval has. It can define a key center. Musics from many of the world's cultures, differing from each other in a great many ways, use the 5th as the basic key-defining interval.

ANOTHER ILLUSTRATION Melodic motions of the same kind as we found in the Gregorian Kyrie (35) are heard in all types of music, including the American folk song with which we began our study, 1. The very first two notes in 1 are 5 and 1. Here the dominant may be described as a prefix. We hear the interval of a 4th, the inversion of a 5th. Which note sounds like the tonic? Probably the upper one, but by itself the 4th is not as convincing as the 5th. The rise up to the dominant is not as quick as in the chant (35). The curve first reaches 3, then falls back, then reaches up to 5. There are three different descents from 5, and, as in the chant, the tonic is touched on briefly on the way to the concluding note. Within the framework of motion from tonic to dominant, the number of pathways that a line can take seems to be infinite. What arouses our admiration is the skill and sense of play in the material, as well as the clear sense of direction given to the melody.

We will find other forms of basic melodic motion, but all center around the tonic (part of the definition of tonal music) and most play upon the tension between tonic and dominant. With this in mind we should be able to find a more specific answer to a question previously asked and to which we had an intuitive response—namely, how do we know what key a piece is in? The answer is not necessarily to be found by looking at a key signa-

ture or even by looking at the last note, but rather by listening for the intervals that determine the structure of the melody and thus define the key. As soon as we hear the opening 4th in ⊡, we suspect that F is the dominant and B♭ the tonic. This is confirmed by the way in which the whole melody is built around the B♭–F polarity. In ②, the D–A relationship takes a few measures to make itself felt, but it emerges as you sing through the entire melody. The 5-1 axis is even less obvious in the beginning of ③, yet it is as much in control of the line as can be. In ④, the tonic-dominant relationship is readily apparent, as it is in ⑤. ⑥ starts with a descent from 5 to 1, but something is different. The key is E, but the mode is not major.

For study

Identify all the folk songs that are in the major mode, and write the name of the key at the beginning of each.

5

Tonality 2: The Minor Mode

MAJOR AND MINOR In singing ⑥, we hear the way in which the melody circles around the dominant, then curves down to the tonic. These are the same scale degrees around which melodic motion centered in the other songs. Yet the sound of the Spanish song is different from that of the other songs. The reason is that the tune is based on a different scale. Starting with the tonic, write the pitches of the melody on the staff at the bottom of this page.

Between the scale degrees write the interval, either a half step or a whole step. Compare the result with the major scale, page 6 . In the major mode the half steps fall between scale degrees _____ and _____; in the minor mode the half steps fall between _____ and _____.

The names of the scale degrees are the same in major and minor with the single exception of 7. The difference is significant. The leading tone has a strong impulse to move to the tonic. The minor's

E-minor scale

	tonic	supertonic	mediant	subdominant	dominant	submediant	subtonic	tonic
Scale degrees	1	2	3	4	5	6	7	8
Solfa syllables	Do	Re	Me	Fa	Sol	Le	Te	Do

7 usually moves down and is simply the note below the tonic, or the subtonic. There are more differences in the sol-fa syllables of the two modes, and these should be compared now.

RELATIVE MINOR There is a close relationship between a major key and the minor key whose tonic is a minor 3rd below the major's tonic—for example, G major and E minor. They both have the same key signature and hence the same pitch classes. We say that E minor is the *relative minor* of G major, and G major is the *relative major* of E minor. Since the key signature of a major key and its relative minor are the same, you must examine the music (look for key-defining intervals) to determine the mode.

The letter name, then, describes the key, and the mode must be defined too. The key of 19 is ____; the mode is ____. The key of 21 is ____; the mode is ____.

PARALLEL MINOR When a major and minor scale have the same tonic, they are said to be *parallel*. The parallel major of G minor is ____. The parallel minor of E major is ____.

MODE MIXTURE Is every piece of music limited to a single mode, major or minor? Consider 8. The key is ____, the mode ____. The third note of the melody, F♯, is not the 7 of G minor; it is the 7 of G major. Although the prevailing mode is minor, a note from the parallel major is part of the melody. This particular note is the leading tone, whose drive toward the tonic adds so much to the direction of a melody that it is often used in the minor mode. Thus it is a chromatic note. We call the procedure by which notes from one mode are used in a piece largely in another mode *mode mixture*. Mode mixture is found in 48, ____, ____, ____, and ____.

Although a thorough investigation of mode mixture comes much later (Book II), its importance should be stressed even at this early stage. You will find mode mixture in many works of many styles, from the Middle Ages to the present. The reason is that mixture is a way of getting beyond the limits of the diatonic scale, enabling the composer to use the chromatic notes while keeping the tonic unchanged.

OTHER MINOR MODES (?) Many theorists affirm the existence of not one, but three minor scales:

The differences lie in the distribution of whole steps and half steps in the upper part of the scales. What is gained by this threefold distinction? Can it be said that a piece is in the harmonic-minor mode? Hardly. A piece is in the minor mode. Pieces in the minor mode almost always use notes borrowed from the parallel major, starting with but not limited to the leading tone. It is not necessary to invent new scale formulations to explain the different versions of 6 and 7 in minor-mode music since they are readily understandable as the result of mode mixture. The "natural minor" is the minor, and mode mixture is a basic fact of musical life.

6

Tonality 3: Other Modes

Most of the tonal music you know, the music written between 1600 and 1900, is in either the major or the minor mode. But much of the music written before 1600, some of the music written

discussed. There is a family of modes used in Near Eastern, Greek, and Balkan music that is characterized by the interval of an augmented 2nd. In [20], the tonic is _____, as the 5th relationship shows. Write the scale starting with the tonic.

The first interval in the scale is _____. There are two versions of the fourth scale degree, and it is difficult to say that one is diatonic and one is chromatic. This mode should be thought of as just one variant of a group of modes that uses the augmented 2nd, has elements of major and minor, and stands somewhere between Eastern and Western music.

ANOTHER MODE MIXTURE The humorous Greek wedding song, [7], is in two sections. In the first half, the bridegroom's friends urge him to start the festivities, in F major. Then he expresses his reluctance in a mode that sounds like the minor but has a raised 4, creating the interval of _____ between 3 and 4. Moreover, the top half of the scale, from 5 up to 8, is neither major nor minor, but more like Dorian. The scale used in the second part of the tune is another variant of the Near Eastern type that is popular in Hungarian, Armenian, and Turkish music.

TRANSPOSED MODES In principle, any mode may be transposed so as to start with any pitch class as tonic. But medieval and Renaissance music, which used Dorian, Phrygian, and Mixolydian, limited itself to what we now think of as the white notes on the piano, with an occasional B♭ and a rare E♭, F♯, or C♯ in the Middle Ages and a gradually increasing number of other sharps and flats in the Renaissance. The transpositions were limited to a 4th up from the original pitch location (D for Dorian, E for Phrygian, G for Mixolydian) and, infrequently, two 4ths up or a _____ down. The only purpose of these transpositions was to bring the music within the range of certain vocal combinations. The flat that looks like a key signature in Renaissance music is not. It is simply the sign that the mode has been transposed up a 4th.

What mode? The only way to tell is to examine the music for the intervals that define tonality. But this is also true of music without the flat.

The mode of the Hungarian melody set by Bartók, [73], is _____.

The melody of [76] is in the _____ mode.

The melody of [72E] is in the _____ mode.

NONTONIC ENDINGS It remains to be said that just as some melodies do not begin with the tonic note, a few do not end with the tonic. [72C] is in C major. It ends with a G which may sound somewhat inconclusive to our ears. The problem lies with our ears, not with the melody.

AFTERTHOUGHT During the seventeenth century, the difference between Dorian and minor gradually disappeared, although in the eighteenth century, due to the conservatism of musicians, we find many pieces in the minor mode that are missing one flat in the signature. Thus [65], [66], and [67] are in D minor, but lack the key signature of one flat. A later work, [81], is in F minor but has only three flats in its key signature. All of these examples look Dorian but sound minor.

The Mixolydian was absorbed by the major, as was any remnant of the Lydian. The Phrygian maintained its identity longest of all, since the half step between 1 and 2 could not be reconciled with either major or minor. But to all intents and purposes there were only two modes by 1700. No doubt a certain variety of sound was lost, but the rich possibilities of the major-minor language begged for exploration in the eighteenth and nineteenth centuries. Early in the twentieth century many composers who were seeking a fresh approach to tonality rediscovered the modes, put them to new uses, and developed new modes as well.

For study

Identify the key or mode of each melody not previously defined, including the top line in [65] through [76].

☞ Worksheet 2

7

Melodic Structure 2: Embellishing Tones

MELODIC MOTION   We have described the rise and fall of a melodic line in general terms. We found points of stability, represented by the tonic, and more active notes centering around the dominant or linking tonic and dominant. Now we must learn more about how a melody moves, how notes are joined together in specific ways. We begin the study by examining melodies. What we learn from those melodies can then be applied to other tonal music.

NT   We may describe the opening of $\boxed{8}$ in a general way as a rise from 1 to 5. But a melody that simply rose in a straight line might not be very interesting. Part of the charm of the tune lies in the way the detail moves down even as the overall motion is upward. As soon as 1 is heard it is followed by the closest note below it and is then repeated. These three notes form a small unit. The F♯ embellishes the G, adding to its life but subordinate to it. The same kind of pitch movement is heard in the next measure, in which A might be called the main note and G the decorative one. Such a move to an adjacent note and back is a basic operation in tonal music. The embellishing note is called a *neighbor tone* (NT) or auxiliary tone. The NT in the first measure is chromatic, the F♯ resulting from mixture with the major mode, while in 2 we hear a diatonic NT. Another NT may be found in _____. Is it diatonic or chromatic? Another melody that includes a chromatic NT is _____. A chant that begins with a diatonic NT is _____.

IN   We located the NT in the center of a three-note group. An abbreviated form that also uses the principle of the neighboring note is a two-note group. Either the first or the second note is the main note and the other is the embellishment. In $\boxed{13}$, 7 , the melody moves from E to D, completing the scale descent 2–1. As an expressive detail, the E is decorated with an F. That note is a neighbor but

does not return to the main note, E. Thus it is an *incomplete neighbor*, IN. An example in which the first note of the two-note group is the neighbor is in $\boxed{8}$, 4 . The E♭ is the main note, and the rising line overshoots, going beyond the E♭ to F. The F shows its function by falling back to the E♭ immediately. It is an IN.

DN   A more extended type of neighbor or auxiliary note occurs in $\boxed{8}$, 10–11 . We hear a four-note group, B♭–A–C–B♭. B♭ seems to be the center of the group, while the other two notes act as neighbors, circling around the main note. Perhaps we should consider example (a) below an abbreviation of example (b). The four-note group is a *double neighbor,* DN.

STEPS AND SKIPS   Consecutive notes in a melody may be connected in one of two ways. If the two notes are a half step or a whole step apart, we speak of *stepwise or conjunct motion.* If two consecutive notes are separated by an interval larger than a step, we speak of a *skip or disjunct motion.*

S   The lively Hungarian tune $\boxed{15}$ begins with a four-measure phrase. Its overall shape is a rise from 1 to 4 and a descent back to 1. The melodic curve is quite straightforward except for two notes. In 3 , D and A break the straight line of the descent. The notes that embody the descent are F and E: these are the main notes, and D and A are embellishments. But what kind of embellishments? It might be that D is an IN to the E. But what about A? And doesn't D have the same kind of relation to F that A has to E? In both cases, the embellishing note is reached by a skip from a main note. It is a decorative skip referred to as S.

TRIAD   Another elaboration of a main note involves two embellishing notes. In simplest form, it

16

is seen in the first measure of $\boxed{4}$. The E♭ upbeat is a prefix. Then we hear A♭–C–E♭. This line includes the major 3rd A♭–C and the minor 3rd C–E♭. The three-note group is bounded by the perfect 5th, A♭–E♭. This unit is a *triad*. Observe that after the melody rises through the triad it returns to the main note, A♭. In the descending part of the arch, the upper of the two 3rds is filled in with a PT, D♭. One of the reasons that we perceive the first two measures as a small melodic unit, which we have described as an arch, is that it is built on a single triad.

Triads in a melody may be heard with one or another of the three notes transposed up or down an octave. The first three notes of $\boxed{1}$ form such a triad. In simplest form, the F would be a 3rd above the D and a 5th above the B♭; here it is a _____ below the D and a _____ below the B♭.

Two types of triad which may be defined now are

1. the major triad—reading from the lowest note, a major 3rd plus a minor 3rd; and
2. the minor triad—reading from the lowest note, a minor 3rd plus a major 3rd.

Identify as major or minor: the triad in $\boxed{2}$, third phrase (see phrase markings) is _____. The triad that begins $\boxed{11}$ is _____. The triad in the second measure of $\boxed{13}$ is _____. The triad that occupies $\underline{11}$ and $\underline{12}$ in $\boxed{21}$ is _____. The triad that begins $\boxed{24}$ is _____. The first three notes of $\boxed{34}$ make up a _____ triad.

Perhaps you already know something about the triad as a chord. Indeed, the triad is the normative simultaneous sound in tonal music. But the triad also plays an important role in melody, and this discussion serves to introduce the triad as an ingredient of the line.

PT $\boxed{13}$ begins with an upbeat-downbeat pattern that we have heard before: 5–1, the strong beat emphasizing the tonic note. The dominant is then elaborated with a major triad, and the line returns to A in $\underline{4}$. The return from E down to A is much like the rise from A to E, but one note is added. D fills in between E and C. The 3rd is elaborated with a note that passes from one to the other. This type of embellishment is called a *passing tone*, PT. A single PT always fills in the interval of a 3rd. Two PTs in succession fill in a 4th.

SP AND PS In the third measure of $\boxed{4}$ we may sense that B♭ is the main note. The A♭ at the end

of the measure is a PT, leading to the G in the next measure. What is the function of D♭ and C? How are they related to the B♭? The move to D♭ is a S. Rather than return directly to the B♭, the tune fills in the space of a 3rd with a PT, C. We hear the four-note group B♭–D♭–C–B♭ as a unit. It combines the skip and passing tone and is called SP.

Less often, the passing motion precedes the skip. In $\boxed{2}$, $\underline{5-6}$, the main note is F♯. The skip is between _____ and _____. The connecting PT is _____. We refer to this group as PS, passing tone and skip.

The interval covered by SP or PS is usually a 3rd. But not always. In the _____ that opens $\boxed{5}$, the interval covered is a _____.

GROUPING THE GROUPS Several of the embellishing units are variants of one principle: motion from the main note to a note farther away than a step and return to the main note. The distance from the main note is usually a 3rd, but it may be any other interval as well. The sketch shows the similarity. The main note is shown as a whole note, embellishing notes as black noteheads.

MORE ELABORATIONS The short melodic units introduced here do not always appear in their simplest form and are not always complete. A few possibilities of elaborating them are given below, but you should be aware that there is no limit to the ways of varying the basic patterns.

$\boxed{1}$, after the upbeat, moves through a large SP, B♭–D–C–B♭. Within that, the C is itself embellished with a NT, the sixteenth note D.

$\boxed{2}$ begins with a triad, D–F♯–A, with the D transposed up an octave. The 4th between A and D is partially filled in with an incomplete PT, B.

In $\boxed{3}$, an opening triad is elaborated with a PT, filling in the melodic 3rd.

The interval of a 4th is filled in completely, coming and going, in $\boxed{6}$, $\underline{5-6}$. B is the main note, E the top of the short arch; all the other notes are PTs. A shortened form of this embellishment follows immediately; it replaces the PT with a skip of a 4th, so that a SP is heard.

$\boxed{20}$ begins with a main note, D, and its NT, E♭. The E♭ itself has a NT, the grace note F.

$\boxed{13}$ begins with an ascent from 1 to 5. The dominant is then elaborated. In the returning descent, $\underline{4-5}$, G is embellished with B♭ and A. We might expect another G to follow, to complete a SP. But the tune has no **G,** and the SP is incomplete. The same is true of the elaboration of **F** that follows. The IN that decorates the **E** in the next measure seems like a shortened version of the incomplete elaborative patterns in 4–6.

Summary of embellishing tones

Complete the list below. One example of each type is given, with example number and measure numbers. Write the other examples, indicating measure numbers for each. Main notes are shown as whole notes.

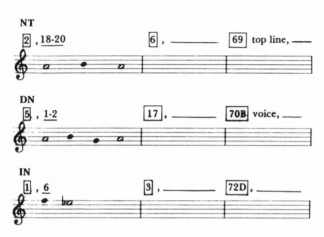

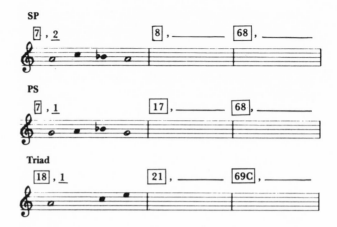

STRUCTURAL NOTES, EMBELLISHING NOTES Behind this introduction to melodic elaboration lies one of the basic concepts of tonal theory: certain notes serve as the backbone of a melody; others flesh out or embellish the skeleton. Each embellishment is built around one note, which we have called the main note. It may also be called the structural note, for all the main notes in a melody will be defined as the melodic structure. We take the position that there are at least two levels in tonal music, one being structural, the other being elaborative. The significance of these levels of meaning in tonal music emerges as we begin to study melodies in greater depth.

8

Melodic Structure 3: Tonal Structure

PITCH SUMMARY Students of music performance will be aware that a note-to-note kind of playing or singing is a rather unsatisfactory approach. A good teacher stresses larger units such as the phrase or groups of phrases. When we say that an instrumentalist or singer is musical we often mean that we are hardly aware of individual notes; we are made to hear the phrase as the basic unit. The same principle should be applied to the study of music, starting with melody. Can we group the notes of the tune into units, even larger ones than

the short patterns we have seen thus far? We have discovered that certain notes are dependent for their meaning on other notes, the main notes. Why not seek out all the main notes in a melody and see what kind of shape they have?

TONAL STRUCTURE OF 2 We begin by writing out all the pitches of the melody. Repeated notes are omitted, and rhythm is set aside for the purpose of this analysis. Pitches are indicated by noteheads only.

Now we group the notes within each phrase. We already know that the first five notes comprise a triad plus an embellishing PT. The last note of the first group is also the first note of the next group. This four-note unit is a PS. The move to D is an embellishing S. The E is unembellished, and is the goal of the first phrase; it is not stable, and asks for continuation. The second phrase has the same layout, but the line finds its way to the tonic, and there is a sense of completion.

The third phrase begins with a four-measure descent from 1 to 5. The downward motion is varied a bit by the A, which elaborates the C♯ with a S. The entire four measures are a filling in of the triad as stated in the first four measures of the piece. When F♯ returns in 21, it takes its place as the main note, whose elaboration has extended for seven measures and one beat. Then E is heard, again the temporary goal. The last phrase is the same as the second, and it reaches the tonic to end the song.

Extracting the main notes from the list of all pitches used, we indicate in whole notes the structure of the melody. This procedure is used in

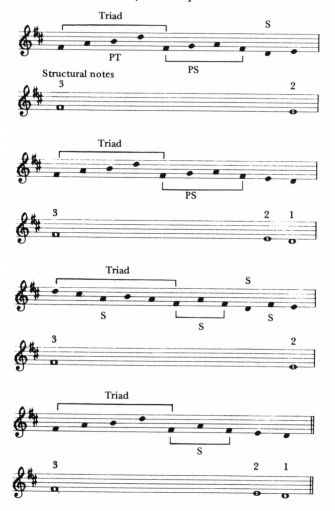

analytic sketches in this book: the pitch content is shown in black noteheads, the structural notes in open noteheads.

Studying the sketch, we realize that the duration of a note has nothing to do with the question of whether it is structural or elaborative. The main note for most of the piece is F♯, and it controls most of the measures. But E and D are just as much a part of the structure, even though they take up relatively little time.

We might observe that the note of tension and activity is 3, and the final goal is 1. The motion 3–2–1 is not completed in the first phrase, which makes us expect a second phrase. 2 plays the role that it so often has in tonal music—namely, a temporary goal. It, in turn, needs a destination, which is the concluding 1.

You also notice that we speak of the tonal structure not in terms of F♯s and Es but rather in terms of 3–2–1. The reason is that the tonal structure of this melody is the same as the tonal structure of a great many other melodies. Instead of thinking of such a structure in a particular key, think of it in more general terms, as scale degrees. This will help you to remember the pattern when you look for it in the course of analysis, and when you elaborate it into a melody of your own.

QUICK ASCENT While many melodies begin with a main note—that part of the tonal structure to which other notes relate—many others only reach the first main note after one or more preliminary notes. This means, among other things, that you cannot assume that the first note in the melody is the first structural note. Usually the prefix notes are in a rising line, leading to the first main note. The quick ascent characterizes many tunes. ⬜1 begins with two notes that carry the line to the structural D, which is then elaborated by a NT for a measure. The first two notes are preliminary, creating a rapid rise. The initial note of ⬜3 is also part of an ascent, as is the first note of ⬜4. We hear those notes as prefixes quite naturally because they are all on upbeats. Two elements, pitch and rhythm, cooperate to give the melody its initial impetus.

SAME PITCH CLASS, DIFFERENT FUNCTION In ⬜2, we may observe that a particular pitch class, such as D, may not always have the same function within a key. In a very general way, let us think of notes as having active or stable qualities. D is the tonic, and we might expect it to be stable every time we hear it. But the first D in the tune (see ⬜4) is part of the triadic elaboration of F♯, and its musical purpose is activity. Perhaps that is due to

19

its position in the range of the entire melody, for it is the highest note. However, the next D, in 7, is in the low position. Yet it, too, is a decorative note, arrived at through the embellishing S. Only in 16 do we hear a D that means stability, for it is the goal of the entire two-phrase group. The same D has meant both stability and activity. It is precisely this possibility of interpreting a note in more than one way that gives tonal music so much richness and variety.

STRUCTURAL LEVELS If you have ever seen a building under construction you must have realized that what holds up any building are not the bricks or sheathing that you see on the outside, but the internal framework of beams and girders. The stresses and tensions are built into the skeleton, not into the exterior. In a general way, we also speak of the musical framework, which we call the structure, and of the elaborations that make up what we might call the surface of the piece. The eyes of the layman see only the outside layer of the building, but the architect knows that beneath the surface is the structure that holds up the entire edifice. The musical architect, too, has to know what holds the notes together so that they form a coherent whole. The concept of structural levels can provide many of the insights we need in order to learn just what it is that gives a piece of music unity.

REDUCTION, ARCHETYPES The analytic process by which we summarize a melody and arrive at a tonal structure is known as *reduction,* or synopsis of the pitch content. Most reductions of tonal melodies show what we might call a musical law of gravity. With or without an opening ascent, the descent to the tonic characterizes these summaries. Now, at some point in your life you must have realized that although the number of jokes

that can be told seems to be infinite, there are only a few basic types of joke. The same is true of melody structures. These few basic types have the nature of archetypes; they recur again and again in different contexts and different styles, and lend themselves to manifold interpretations.

For study

Write the pitches of 6 below, using noteheads only and omitting repetitions. The phrases are two measures long. On the first staff write the pitches of the first and second phrases. On the third staff write the pitches of the third and fourth phrases. Indicate pitch groupings with brackets and explain each grouping. A group may start in one phrase and end in another. On the second staff write the structural notes of the first two phrases. On the fourth staff write the structural tones of the last two phrases. Mark the scale degree of each structural note.

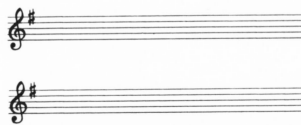

9

Rhythmic Aspects of Melody

RHYTHM IN FOLK SONG AND CHANT Under the heading of *rhythm* we include whatever

concerns the way music moves through time. We may start by observing that all the tunes in our collection have one characteristic in common: a steady beat. You can tap your foot or clap hands without speeding up or slowing down in the tune, which is another way of saying that the *tempo* is constant. When we try to group the beats, we find that in most cases in the folk songs there are groups of two, three, four, or six beats. Such groupings constitute the *meter,* which we indicate by such markings as $\frac{3}{4}$, $\frac{2}{4}$, and $\frac{6}{8}$. But no such markings are applicable to chant. The beats do group together, but in units that change constantly.

THE PHRASE, A MUSICAL SENTENCE As we sing a tune we must stop to breathe from time to time. Why stop in one place rather than another? For one thing, the fall of the line often suggests a breathing place. For another, the completion of a rhythmic unit acts as a punctuation mark. Together, these factors end a unit that we call the phrase. A phrase is a musical statement, punctuated at the end and roughly equivalent to a verbal sentence. Later we will see that harmonic forces are also very important in defining phrases.

RHYTHMIC MOTIVE A melody such as 9 is not just a series of eighth notes and quarter notes—specific patterns are heard. A short group—two eighth notes and a quarter—constitutes the first measure. The group is repeated at once, impressing it upon our memory. After two measures, we hear the group twice more. Altogether we hear it eight times. Clearly the repetition of the group is a major force in organizing and unifying the melody. Observe that although the pitches of the original three-note group are changed as the melody proceeds, the rhythm is not changed; and it is the rhythm that is the more important unifying element. What we have seen is a motive, consisting of three notes in a specific rhythmic pattern, which is used to give the entire melody rhythmic coherence. We will speak of a motive only when a pattern is repeated, not when it is stated once.

At times there may be differences of opinion about phrase lengths. If we look carefully for a strong sense of closure, we usually can identify the phrase ending. Thus, there is a small degree of punctuation in 4 at 4, but much more at 8. Here we may say that there is an eight-measure phrase lightly divided in the middle. But in 5, the clear descent to the tonic in 4 defines the phrase ending quite clearly. The phrases in 6 are ____ measures long; those in 10, ____ measures long. In 8, not all phrases are the same length. How long is each phrase?

VARYING THE MOTIVE An artful melody writer finds many ways in which to vary the motive, keeping the listener's interest while retaining something essential in the motive. In 11, the motive is four measures long; so is the phrase. The motive is heard four times, but each time it takes on a fresh aspect while keeping its main contour. The second phrase replaces the long last note of the first phrase with shorter notes, introducing the triplet. The third phrase elaborates an eighth note into two sixteenths, then slows down the activity with quarter notes. The final version has the same succession of pitches as the first, but the rhythms are varied and the triplet helps move the melody on toward its final goal.

RHYTHM IN CHANT Whereas folk tunes are associated with strongly metrical poetry and dance patterns, chant springs from the declamation of prose, without regularly recurring patterns. Consequently, no meter predominates in chant. There are short groups of notes, constantly shifting in length to accommodate the words and sometimes to point up their meaning. To notate the rhythmic values of chant is rather difficult, and all of the chants printed here are presented as approximations only. One interpretation of the rhythms of plainchant may be found in the introduction to the *Liber Usualis,* which you should read.

WORDS AND MUSIC IN CHANT Chant uses three distinct ways of setting words:

1. *syllabic*—one note to a syllable, as in 22;
2. *neumatic*—short groups of notes to one syllable, as in 23; and
3. *melismatic*—longer groups of notes to one syllable, as in 25.

The term *syllabic* is self-explanatory. A *neume* is a symbol used in medieval music notation to indicate a group of up to four notes sung to a single syllable. A melisma is a melodic turn consisting of several notes.

RHYTHM IN CANTILLATION Probably the oldest music in our collection is the Hebrew cantillation 36, whose origins go back to Biblical times. The original notation of this music is also in the form of neumes—that is, signs, each of which designates a short group of notes to be sung to one syllable. The reader connects these note groups to each other by making small adjustments at the ends of groups. The rhythm depends partly on the melodic shape of each neume and partly on the natural accent of the words. Again, what is notated in 36 is an approximation.

10

Phrase Groups

CONNECTING PHRASES Having looked at the pitch and rhythmic groupings within the phrase, we may now consider how phrases are organized into groups. How does one phrase lead into another? We observed in ☐2 that the first eight-measure phrase came to 2 as its destination; the punctuation is analogous to a semicolon. This sense of temporary halt with a promise of more to come leads us to say that the phrase is open-ended. By contrast, the second phrase ends 3–2–1, and is a closed ending, a punctuation mark we may liken to a period. The two phrases are a unit. The type of two-phrase group that opens ☐2, in which the first phrase sets up an expectation (return to the tonic) and the second fulfills it, is known as *antecedent* and *consequent*. Another folk song that begins with an antecedent and consequent phrase group is _____. But the first phrase may also have a closed ending, as in ☐4 (eight-measure phrase), ☐5 (four-measure phrase), ☐7 (two-measure phrase), and ☐8 (eight-measure phrase). Then a fresh start is made in the second phrase as it leads away from the tonic. ☐9 begins with a four-measure phrase that quickly descends from 5 to 1. The second phrase begins in a striking way by starting from the upper dominant. It arrives at the dominant and temporarily stabilizes it. The third phrase is a not-quite-literal repetition of the second, and the fourth phrase repeats the first.

Groupings of four phrases are quite common in Western music. One pattern, used not only in folk song but also in vocal works of many types, features an opening phrase, a second that is identical or similar, a third in which the same material continues, and a fourth much like the first or even the same as it. A clear example is ☐70B. This four-phrase grouping may have its origin in poetry; the quatrain is an old verse form in many lands. A melody with such a shape may be expanded simply by re-peating the last two phrases, as in ☐5, making a unit of five phrases.

CONTINUATION In ☐6, we notice that the third phrase, while using the same motive as the first two, has a slightly different contour. We refer to the third phrase as a *continuation,* meaning that the earlier material is used but given a different turn. The continued use of the opening rhythm holds the piece together, while the pitch variant offers a fresh view of the material.

A comparison of three melodies shows some of the possibilities in phrase grouping. The scale degree indicated at the end of each phrase implies open or closed ending; any ending other than 1 is an open ending.

☐2		☐4		☐15	
antecedent	2	phrase	1	phrase	1
consequent	1	repeated	1	transposed	5
continuation	2	continuation	5	continuation	3
consequent	1	phrase again	1	phrase again	1

An even larger grouping presents a miniature version of one of the most widely used forms in music.

Outline of ☐17

antecedent	2	first part	Ternary form
consequent	1		
another antecedent	5	second part	
another consequent	1		
first phrase again	2	third part	
second phrase again	1		

Describe the phrase structure of the melody of ☐70B and ☐77.

22

11

Comprehensive Analysis of *Tarantella*, ⑲

OVERVIEW The melody is in the key of E minor. The meter is ⁶⁄₈. This means that there are two beats to a measure, and each beat is subdivided into three. Since the tarantella is a dance, a lively tempo is suggested.

PHRASE GROUPINGS Phrases are each four measures long. Each phrase begins with an upbeat of half a measure. There are five phrases, which is unusual. The first phrase ends on 2. Perhaps we expect the second to end on 1; but it does not. Instead it moves to 3. The end of the second phrase sounds as if G is the tonic, at least for a moment. The third phrase emphasizes the dominant, and ends with it, leading into the fourth phrase. This

ends on 1, but is immediately repeated, now providing a stress on 1 to balance the 5 of the middle.

RHYTHM Both words and music are quite regular, following a consistent long-short pattern varied with a group of three short beats. The third phrase has more rhythmic activity than the previous ones, the quarter notes being replaced by two eighth notes. The rhythmic motive coincides with the four-measure phrase. But a pattern of quarter note–eighth note runs through much of the tune and is a strong unifying element. The half-measure upbeat provides a rhythmic impetus that carries through the entire melody.

Pitch summary

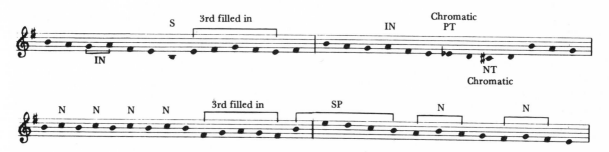

Tonal structure

23

12

Projects in Tonal Composition

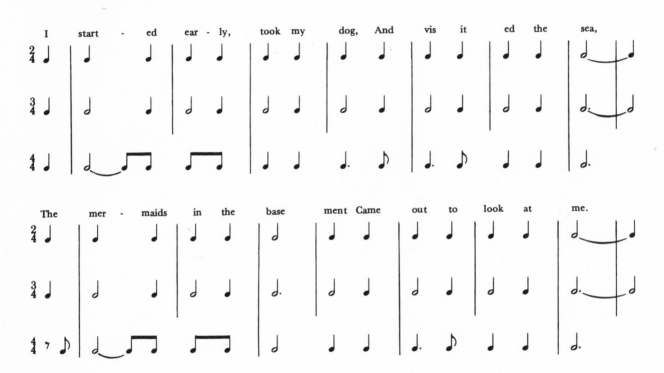

1. Preliminary exercises in rhythm

Examine the rhythm of the following quatrain. Strong and weak beats have been indicated by the signs customarily used in scanning poetry, — for strong and ⌣ for weak beats.

I start-ed ear-ly, took my dog,
And vis-it-ed the sea,
The mer-maids in the base-ment
Came out to look at me.
—Emily Dickinson

The strong beats in the poetry may readily be set to strong beats in the music, and weak beats may correspond in the same way. But how long are the beats to last? This is a musical decision, and there are different possibilities. Above are three rhythm settings of the four lines. In all three, strong beats are matched in words and music. In the first, strong and weak beats are equal in duration. In

the second, the accented syllable has twice the length of the unaccented one. Less mechanically, a variety of rhythms is used in the third.

Make three different rhythm settings, without pitches, of:

I never saw a moor,
I never saw the sea,
Yet know I how the heather looks,
And what a wave must be.
—Emily Dickinson

2. Elaboration of a tonal structure

Study this analysis of the melody of 69B.

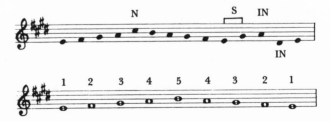

24

Using the same tonal structure, reverse the process and write a new melody. Elaborate the notes of the tonal structure in any way you think appropriate. The following is an illustration:

3. Write a melody to this text:

> Who has not found the heaven below
> Will fail of it above,
> God's residence is next to mine,
> His furniture is love.
>
> —Emily Dickinson

First scan the text, as in project 1. Then compose an antecedent phrase to the first two lines, a consequent phrase to the other two. Choose one of the three tonal structures given below as the basis of your melody.

	antecedent	consequent
(a)	3–2;	3–2–1
(b)	5–4–3–2;	5–4–3–2–1
(c)	1–2–3–2;	4–3–2–1

4. Write a longer melody in the style of a folk song or a chant. Use a language that you know well. Before setting the text, say the words aloud a number of times, experimenting with different durations. The rhythmic shape of the melody should be a musical version of the poem's rhythm.

5. Using these pitch classes—G, A, B, D, and E—write three short melodies, the first having G as the tonic, the second having E as the tonic, and the third having D as the tonic. How will you define the tonal center?

For further study

Find the entry "Folk songs" in the card catalogue of your music library. Browse through the collections of melodies without accompaniment and those with accompaniment. Examine those volumes of melodies that reflect the culture of any ethnic or religious group in which you are interested, and bring one of those melodies to class to perform. Listen to a selection from the Library of Congress recordings of American folk music.

The true musician ascends the ladder of counterpoint toward the angelic concert. Tones are brought up from the foundation to make a golden fire. On the surface, enemies gather tritones and ninths. They shoot arrows against the artist who is writing. The arrows break upon the shield of Minerva, goddess of wisdom and the arts. (A seventeenth-century German woodcut.)

Title page of *Regola Rubertina*, a manual of instruction in playing the viol, by Sylvestro di Ganassi dal Fontego, published in Venice, 1542.

PART TWO
NOTE-AGAINST-NOTE CONSONANCE

13

Some Practical Considerations

The basic medium of music making is the human voice. Much early music (to the end of the Renaissance at least) is vocal music. The most direct way to start studying the art of combining sounds is to write for voices. Much of what is learned in vocal writing is applicable to instrumental writing—the reverse is not true. Also, the voice is the medium that most clearly brings out the intervallic relations between sounds, whether those sounds are heard successively or simultaneously.

VOICE RANGES Human voices are usually divided into four groups, although more divisions are possible. The higher female voice is the soprano, the lower is the alto. The higher male voice is the tenor, the lower is the bass. The average range of each is:

THE CLEFS Until fairly recent times, each of these voices was notated in its own clef. To make this possible, clef signs were used in more than one position, especially the C clef. Today the C clef on the middle line is used only for viola parts, and on the second line for middle-register instruments such as cello, bassoon, and trombone. When a clef's position on the staff is changed, its name is changed as well, even though it is the same sign. Here is an illustration of G, C, and F clefs that you may find, especially in older editions, showing how middle C looks in each clef:

In this book only treble, alto, and bass clefs are used.

In choral music the soprano part is written in the treble clef. The alto part is written sometimes in treble, sometimes in alto clef. The tenor uses the treble clef, the written pitch sounding an octave lower (hence the small number 8 occasionally hanging from the treble sign). The bass uses the bass clef only.

THE SCORE Choral music is printed in open score—that is, with each part on a separate line.

The ability to read such a score is a basic skill. Therefore, you should practice playing 38 through 49 at the piano from the score.

If you lack fluency in reading the alto clef, you can only remedy this by using it. In every set of counterpoint exercises you write, at least one should use the alto clef. To speed up the learning process, play the viola parts of orchestral scores or string quartets at the piano.

14

Consonance and Dissonance

POLYPHONY By *polyphony* we mean "the simultaneous unfolding of two or more melodic lines in a specific relationship to each other." The blend of the lines adds up to something greater than the lines themselves. This something else, sometimes called *harmony*, gives polyphonic music an added dimension. By exploiting this dimension to the utmost composers have been able to increase the expressive power of music far beyond what could be achieved by purely melodic means. The development of polyphonic music is one of the supreme achievements of Western civilization.

Counterpoint and *polyphony* are two different terms. *Counterpoint* is a specific technical term for the art of combining melodies. It consists of a body of techniques and procedures. *Polyphony* is a more general term that is applied to music in more than one voice—that is, in two or more parts heard together. *Harmony* is an even more general term, describing the dimension added when we hear the combination of lines as chords. In this sense it has been applied so vaguely as to have almost outlived its usefulness.

Polyphonic music—that is, virtually all of Western music—is two-dimensional. One dimension is melody, and the study of melody was our point of departure. The other dimension concerns the way in which the melodies work together. Two tunes that sound well separately may make no sense when heard together. What kind of sense do we want

them to make? How have composers combined melodic lines into a whole that is greater than the sum of its parts?

INTERVALS MEASURE RELATIONSHIPS We find some of the answers to our questions in a piece of music, the rather simple *bicinium* (two-part piece), 38. The alto line is the melody of a well-known *chorale*—that is, a congregational hymn originally associated with the Lutheran forms of worship. The soprano was composed to make a duet with the alto by a little-known musician of the sixteenth century. In order to discover the way in which one voice is coordinated with the other, we measure the distance between them and identify the intervals. The figures between the voices in the first phrase denote the intervals between the voices. Now we can look for some kind of consistent usage of those intervals.

FUNCTIONS OF THE INTERVALS The first interval heard is a unison. The identity of the two sounds is so complete that they are actually heard as one. This sound expresses the most stable relationship possible between two voices.

The second simultaneous sound is a major 3rd. It, too, is at rest, requiring no particular follow-up, although it is not as stable as the first sound.

Next we hear a perfect 5th. Compared with the

28

previous two, this sound is not quite as stable as the unison, but more so than the 3rd:

Skipping over the quarter note for a moment, the next simultaneity is a minor 6th, which seems less stable than the major 3rd but not an active sound either. Returning to the quarter note, its role is to connect the 5th and 6th, which makes it a PT. The interval is a major 6th, also relatively stable.

The next two sounds are a major 3rd and a minor 6th. But then the quarter note G, an IN, rubs against the F and creates a different kind of relationship between the voices. The interval is a major 2nd.

After the next sound, the minor 6th, the C in the soprano is held while the alto moves from E to D, making the interval of a minor 7th. Where the 2nd was tucked away on the weak part of a beat and was thus largely hidden, this 7th is emphasized and in a longer note value; it generates a different kind of activity from that of the stable sounds heard up to this point. The 7th expresses tension and demands resolution. The downward step of the soprano, which creates a relatively stable 6th, is in response to the demand of the 7th. After this tension-release activity, the octave's stability comes as a satisfying close to the phrase.

DISSONANCE AND CONSONANCE Although a number of different intervals are heard in the phrase, there are only two functions they can perform. Either they agree or they disagree with each other. Agreement brings stability, under which heading most of the sounds fall. Disagreement brings tension, which impels the music forward to another stable point. Stable intervals are defined as *consonant;* unstable intervals are defined as *dissonant.* With a single exception, each interval is used consistently either as a consonance or a dissonance. Only the 4th is so mild a dissonance that it can sometimes be made to function as a consonance, as we shall see.

Scanning the figures that appear in the first phrase, you will notice that those denoting dissonant intervals have been circled. Use this procedure in showing intervals, both in pieces and exercises. Write in the intervals between the voices in the rest of the *bicinium.* The second phrase does include a 4th. It is a quarter-note PT that connects a 3rd and a 6th. The dissonance is not very striking, but passing dissonances rarely are. Observe that a PT may be in either a consonant or dissonant relationship with the other voice.

RELATIVE DEGREES OF CONSONANCE AND DISSONANCE Since there are various degrees of tension and stability, a summary of the intervals in those categories should be expressed as a continuum, not simply as a twofold division. Adding an octave to a consonance does not change the fact that it is consonant. Dissonance expressed in compound intervals is still dissonant, but not quite as active as in simple intervals. (See table below.)

DISSONANCE IN TONAL MUSIC By now you may have realized that the term *dissonant* does not mean discordant or unpleasant. On the contrary, the most interesting and beautiful sounds in music are usually the dissonant ones. Dissonance is the lifeblood of tonal music. Music without dissonance would be like a conversation in which everybody agrees with everybody else—utterly boring. More important, the interplay of consonance and dissonance is one of the most expressive resources in tonal music. It gives the composer limitless possibilities in working with both the melodic and simultaneous dimensions of polyphony.

How to study the dissonant-consonant relationship is a prime concern of music pedagogy—or should be. As a starting point we have taken melody. Now we proceed to the combination of melodies. We will soon reach chords, a by-product of the simultaneous unfolding of lines. This learning method approximately parallels the historical development of polyphony. But more to our point, this method provides a systematic way in which to learn how notes work together in tonal music.

consonant intervals						*dissonant intervals*	
S	unison				perfect 4th		A
T		major 3rd	minor 6th			major 7th	C
A	octave				minor 7th		T
B		minor 3rd	major 6th			minor 2nd	I
I	perfect 5th				major 2nd		V
L							I
I					tritone		T
T	(the perfect consonances)		(the imperfect consonances)				Y
Y							

29

HARMONY AND COUNTERPOINT The opinion has already been expressed that the term *harmony* is virtually useless. Supposedly, harmony deals with the study of chords, counterpoint with lines. But such a statement overlooks the basic fact that lines flow together to make chords, and the only reason that chords follow in a certain order is that the lines lead them there. If harmony books make any sense it is because they deal with musical motion—that is, counterpoint. The linear approach of the present text does away with the artificial distinction between harmony and counterpoint. Of course, you must learn all about chords. And there is much more to learning about chords than writing Roman numerals under them. But the way to learn about chords is through learning about the lines that generate the chords.

THE STUDY OF COUNTERPOINT Dissonant intervals depend for their meaning on consonant intervals which more or less surround them. We saw this in 38, and it holds true in tonal music generally. For this reason we start the study of counterpoint with consonant relationships and proceed systematically to dissonant ones. But since pitch relationships exist side by side with rhythmic relationships, we must devise exercises that move from the simple to the complex in both domains at the same time. For this reason, the first melodies we start combining have the simplest rhythm possible—namely, even notes. Then we progress toward more complexity of pitch and rhythm. Step by step we add the elaborative aspects of music, until we study the most sophisticated structures of the tonal era.

The Musician's Progress

from	*to*
consonance	dissonance
diatonic	chromatic
simple rhythms	complex rhythms
single timbre	many timbres
one-line texture	dense textures
regular phrases clearly set off	irregular phrases blended together

15

Two Parts with *Cantus Firmus*

OVERVIEW Counterpoint is the art of combining melodies. The way in which they are combined involves the interaction of consonance and dissonance. First studies in counterpoint deal with lines in consonant relationships only. We start with two lines, then proceed to three and to four. The combination of lines generates simultaneous sounds, chords, first in two-note sounds, then in three, then in four. The chords grow out of the combination of the lines, just as in most tonal music.

THE COUNTERPOINT EXERCISE The traditional counterpoint exercise starts with a given melody, the *cantus firmus*. Against that melody you add one and later two and three lines. The added voice is called the counterpoint (Latin: *punctus contra punctum*, "note against note"). The exercises are arranged in order of increasing complexity, as regards both pitch and rhythm. The classic formulation of the counterpoint exercise in five "species" was made by Johann Joseph Fux, whose *Gradus ad Parnassum*, first printed in 1725, is the basic treatise on the subject (see page 116). It is available in a fine English translation and well worth reading. The present text adapts the principles of species counterpoint in a somewhat modified form.

LINE AND CHORD Two powerful tendencies, pulling in what seems to be opposing directions, are held in balance in tonal music. On the one hand, each line should have as much life of its own as possible. On the other hand, the combined sounds should be as beautiful as possible. Each note has to be chosen so as to make for the greatest independence of line, yet each note is dependent on others for part of its meaning. The most skillful composers are able to reconcile the two impulses so that both line and chord have the utmost freedom of play.

TYPES OF MOTION   To make the most of the existence of more than one part, each should assert itself and be as independent as it can. Both rhythm and pitch factors can contribute to such independence. But since the first exercises will include only notes of identical rhythm, these lines can be differentiated only by pitch factors. How do the lines move directionally in relation to each other? What types of motion are there?

1. *direct motion:* two lines move in the same direction
    a. *similar motion:* two lines move in the same direction but not the same distance
    b. *parallel motion:* two lines move in the same direction and the same distance
2. *contrary motion:* two lines move in opposite directions
3. *oblique motion:* one lines holds a note while the other moves

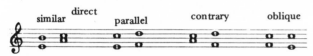

All these types of motion are used in music, but they serve different purposes. As an example, play a scale on the piano, right and left hands playing the same notes an octave apart. Then play the same scale in contrary motion, starting from a unison and moving in opposite directions. In which playing did you hear the two lines more distinctly?

While contrary motion is highly desirable, it is not available all the time, nor would you want to hear any one kind of motion all the time. Variety in types of motion keeps the exercise (and the piece) interesting. Parallel 3rds and 6ths sound euphonious, but if continued beyond three or four sounds they can become tiresome. Oblique motion is not often heard, but it can be quite useful.

PARALLEL 5THS AND OCTAVES   The most stable sounds, namely unisons, 5ths, and octaves, are not used in succession. Parallel unisons clearly make no sense in a texture that has independence of lines as one of its desired features. When you played a scale in parallel octaves, you heard that the two lines almost sounded as one, which means that parallel octaves do not serve our purpose. Parallel 5ths, too, destroy the independence of the lines, almost as completely as parallel octaves do. For this reason, they have been shunned in tonal music so consistently that they should be avoided

completely at this point. It remains to be added that it is important for the ear to be trained to hear parallel 5ths and octaves, not the eye to see them on the page.

For study

Analyze the first two phrases of 38 for types of motion. Indicate whether each motion is similar, parallel, contrary, or oblique. What types predominate? What type is used at phrase endings?

NOTE-AGAINST-NOTE CONSONANCE   In the first type of counterpoint—or, as Fux called it, the first species—the melody moves in whole notes. No time signature is used. Think of the half note as the unit. Against each note in the *cantus firmus* write one note in the counterpoint. All the consonant intervals are available, including unisons, 3rds, perfect 5ths, 6ths, octaves, and their compounds. Since unisons and octaves do not sound as full as 3rds and 6ths, they should be used sparingly. A unison in the middle of an exercise produces the kind of stability that is more useful at the end. Octaves and 5ths may be used if approached and left in contrary motion; otherwise their sound is disappointing.

TONALITY IN THE EXERCISE   The first simultaneous sound in the exercise must define the tonic. Unison and octave serve this purpose. When a 5th is heard, your ear tells you that the lower note of that interval is the tonic. Since all *cantus firmi* begin with the tonic, the counterpoint above the cantus may begin with 5. But if you add a 5th below the given note, you define the lower note as tonic, thus changing what should be the tonic note to the dominant.

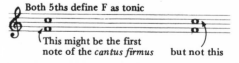

3rds are consonant but ambiguous; if you hear C and E, you are not quite sure whether they represent 1 and 3 in C major or 3 and 5 in A minor. To start your exercise with a clear statement of the key, only use the perfect consonances: unison, 5th, and octave.

Unisons, 5ths, and octaves are also useful in ending the exercise. But since the key has long since been defined, 3rds are also possible as the last sound. To achieve a sense of completeness, the last sound should not only confirm the key, but should also have the tonic in the bass. This precludes the possibility of ending with a 6th. Why?

SHAPE OF THE LINE Most of the melodies we studied began at a fairly low pitch level, climbed to a high point, and descended to their starting level. In these exercises, too, the melody should be directed toward a goal. Every note must do its part in shaping the motion. If the counterpoint is in the lower voice, the line may gravitate toward a low point. The exercise is more interesting if the focal point of the counterpoint and that of the cantus do not coincide. Of course, a melody that simply goes straight up to a high point and then straight back will be quite dull. The small changes of direction that break the essential course of the line are precisely what gives the line character.

SKIPS AND STEPS We seek a line that has a rather simple kind of unity, the kind that results from conjunct motion. But some disjunct motion is needed to make the line interesting. The balance of skips and steps that make a good counterpoint is much like that found in chant. A skip in one direction should be prepared and answered by motion in the opposite direction. A skip may also be used to launch an upward motion that is continued in steps. In reverse, falling motion in steps may accelerate and end with a skip. Skips of a 3rd or a 4th are used frequently, larger skips less often, skips of a 7th never. In these exercises, stepwise motion is diatonic; chromatic semitones are avoided, as are augmented and diminished intervals. The melodies of the *cantus* may be taken as models.

PROCEDURE Sing *cantus firmus* 1 (the *cantus fermi* may be found on page 33) and memorize it. Decide on a general shape for the counterpoint. In the early stages of study it may be useful to sketch the shape of the counterpoint as a wavy line, with specific notes at the beginning, end, and high point. This is shown in example (a), below.

Then sing the notes of a counterpoint (or imagine them), trying to hear them in relation to the *cantus firmus*. Write in the notes lightly. Example (b), below, represents one possible counterpoint to *cantus firmus* 1.

However, upon checking example (b) we hear at once that there are parallel 5ths in the beginning. The first D must be replaced. The repeated F in the counterpoint, while involving no parallels, holds up the melody in its rise to the high point. Replacing the first F with E creates contrary motion and gives the melody a more interesting shape, as well as makes the approach to the high note a

small skip. The revised and improved version is shown in example (c), below.

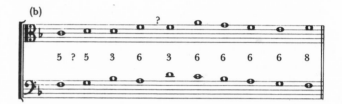

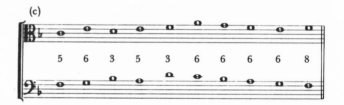

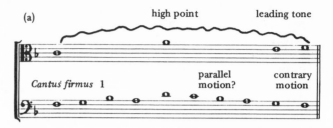

With more experience you will be able to imagine a general shape without necessarily sketching it in and will be able to do the exercise directly. But never start with the first note and go on, note after note, without some sense of the direction the line will take.

The setting of the Phrygian *cantus firmus* 9 illustrates the mixture of contrary and parallel motion that is desired. Observe that when one voice skips, the other does not. This puts the skips in relief, making the most of their effect. The Phrygian mode does not have the leading tone, nor is there any way to borrow it from another mode. In a sense, the F–E that closes the cantus is a leading tone, perhaps an upside-down leading tone.

The minor-mode *cantus firmus* 4 shows a way to use two skips at the same time. As the tenor moves from E to G, the bass goes from G to E—they exchange notes. This voice exchange creates a sense of activity although the pitches are not changed. Also notice the A♯. It is a leading tone, taken from the parallel major. Exercises in the minor as well as those in the Dorian and Mixolydian modes always use a leading tone before the tonic in the counterpoint.

☞ Worksheet 3

☞ Worksheet 4

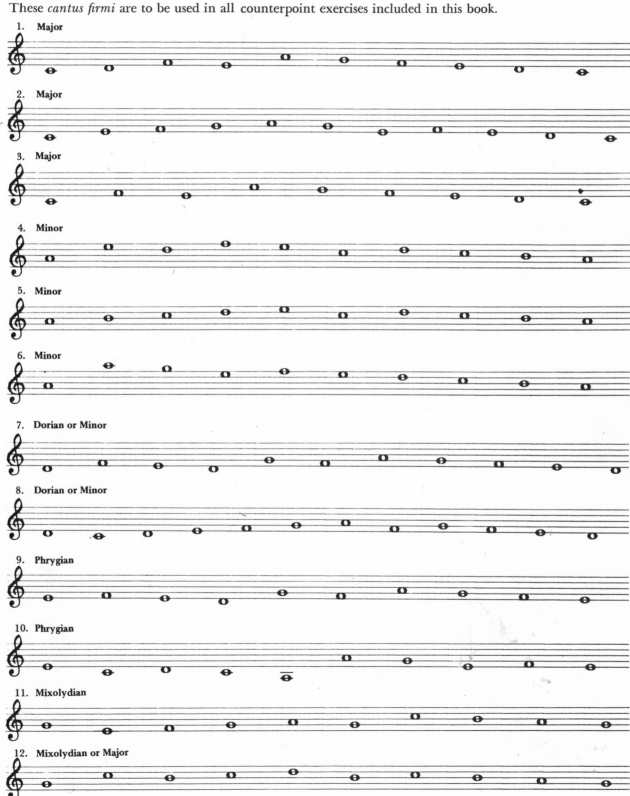

CANTUS FERMI

These *cantus firmi* are to be used in all counterpoint exercises included in this book.

16

Two Parts without *Cantus Firmus*

Going beyond the traditional counterpoint exercise, write two lines without *cantus firmus*. At first you may find it difficult to hear both melodies at once. It is important to approximate that goal as best you can and try to come closer with each exercise. Do not write one line first and then add the other since this defeats the purpose of the exercise.

Procedure for defining tonality is the same as in the previous exercise. To achieve the best sense of completion, one line should end 3–2–1.

17

Three Parts with *Cantus Firmus*

After writing two parts simultaneously you are ready to add two parts to a *cantus firmus*.

THE TRIAD AS SIMULTANEITY What interval combinations are possible in three parts that were not available in two? If two parts create a unison or an octave, the third part may add one interval, which does not go much beyond what we heard in two parts. This is what happens in the opening of 40. But the very next sound in the piece has three different pitch classes. We have seen the triad as a melodic configuration. Now we find it as a simultaneity—indeed, the basic simultaneity in tonal music.

ANOTHER FORM OF THE TRIAD Examining 40 further, we find that the sounds are of the same type as the first two for eight measures. The triad is heard literally as two 3rds superimposed. But in 10 the same three notes that were heard in the first measure, C, E, and G, are heard in a dif- ferent form. The lowest note is E, the next is **G**, the highest **C**.

Comparing this form of the triad to the first form, we see that since the **C** is an octave higher, its relation to the other two notes is inverted. The 3rd with the E becomes a ___6___, and the 5th with the G becomes a ___4___. In two-part writing we heard the 4th as a dissonance. Listening to it in its context, in 40, the chord that contains a 4th between the two sopranos seems just a bit less consonant than the triads that surround it, but far from dissonant. Why does the 4th now function as at least a semiconsonant interval? Because it is not heard in relation to the bass (lowest sound). The perfect 4th, the mildest dissonance of all, loses its power to disagree with other sounds if the bass is consonant with all the voices. Thus we have available two forms of the triad: the first (root position) is more stable; the other (first inversion) less stable but still consonant. We say that the 4th is "covered by the bass" if the 4th involves voices other than the bass. Tritones, too, may be covered by the bass to produce chords that are slightly more consonant than dissonant.

C-major triad

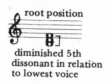

Diminished triad

root position

diminished 5th
dissonant in relation
to lowest voice

first inversion

or

first inversion
another way

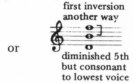

augmented 4th
but consonant
to lowest voice

diminished 5th
but consonant
to lowest voice

MODE MIXTURE In these exercises mode mixture may be used in two ways. The Dorian, Mixolydian, and minor modes lack a leading tone, and it must be borrowed from the parallel major in the next-to-the-last sound. The final triad in these modes, as well as in the Phrygian, may also include a note from the parallel major to make the last triad major. Remember that there is no leading tone in the Phrygian mode; perhaps the 2–1 move in that mode sounds like an upside-down leading-tone–tonic.

For study

Analyze 40 completely for consonant and dissonant relationships between all voices. Identify all triads as root position or first inversion. Identify all PTs and NTs. To what consonance does each relate?

Between which voices does contrary motion predominate? What type of motion is heard between the two upper voices in the first phrase? What type of motion predominates in the latter part of the piece?

Exercise

Write two melodies against a *cantus firmus*. The two counterpoints should be conceived simultaneously. The *cantus firmus* may appear as the upper, middle, or lowest line. Each position changes the problem, and you should work with all the possibilities.

Illustrations: S.A.B.

(a)

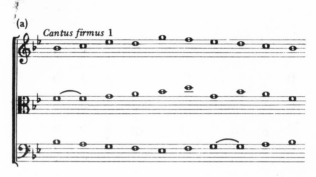

Cantus firmus 1

(b)

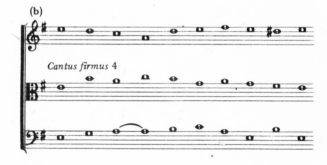

Cantus firmus 4

(c)

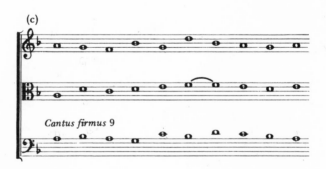

Cantus firmus 9

☞ Worksheet 5

35

18

Three Parts without *Cantus Firmus*

Write three parts in note-against-note consonance, without *cantus firmus*. Try to keep the three parts in your mind at the same time. The lowest voice must begin and end on the tonic. One line must end 3–2–1.

19

More about Triads

Early in our study we heard a melody from which we drew a list of the different pitch classes used. This was the scale. It enabled us to see at a glance the pitch vocabulary of any simple piece. Now we have combined lines, with consonance as our guide. The combined lines have generated triads, which we saw in two forms. Before going into the various positions of the triad, let us examine the possibilities for constructing them.

inside intervals	outside intervals	in root position
1. major 3rd + minor 3rd = major triad	perfect 5th	consonant triads
2. minor 3rd + major 3rd = minor triad	perfect 5th	
3. minor 3rd + minor 3rd = diminished triad	diminished 5th	dissonant triads
4. major 3rd + major 3rd = augmented triad	augmented 5th	

Types of triads

The triad is built on the ROOT

A 3rd higher is the THIRD ⟨ major or minor 3rd

Another 3rd higher is the FIFTH ⟨ major or minor 3rd

outside interval = 5th

Depending on the mix of major and minor 3rds, four types of triads can be built:

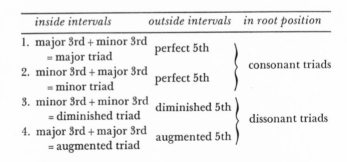

36

POSITIONS OF THE TRIAD The note that serves as root is not necessarily the bass (lowest voice). Any of the three notes that comprise the triad may be heard in the bass.

When the root is in the bass, the triad is in root position or $\frac{5}{3}$ position (consonant).

When the third is in the bass, the triad is in first inversion or $\frac{6}{3}$ position (consonant).

When the fifth is in the bass, the triad is in second inversion or $\frac{6}{4}$ position (dissonant).

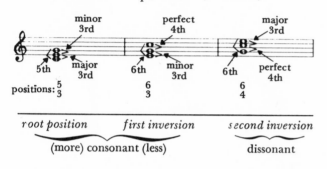

LIST OF TRIADS In a given key, the triads are numbered in the same way that the scale degrees are. To distinguish between the two sets of numbers, Arabic numerals are used for scale degrees and Roman numerals for the triads. The list below shows the Roman numerals without figures, then the Roman numerals with the figure ^{6}. This tells you that the first list contains only root-position triads, the second list only first-inversion triads.

Diatonic chord vocabulary

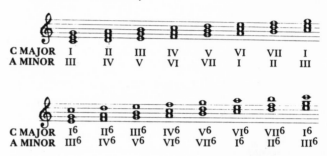

Over each chord in the list write either M (major), m (minor), dim. (diminished), or aug. (augmented).

☞ Worksheet 6

20

Four Parts with *Cantus Firmus*

FOUR PARTS THE NORM In tonal music four parts are the norm. Of course, there are many pieces with fewer or with more parts, but four seems to be the ideal number for allowing each part freedom to move and yet producing a satisfying sonority. This is true whether the medium is vocal or instrumental. Even piano and orchestral music, throughout the tonal era, rely on the four-part "weave."

DOUBLING If the typical three-note sound dominates tonal music, how are those three notes distributed among four voices? For some answers to that question, listen to [41]. The very first C-major triad has two Cs; we say that C is doubled, which simply means that it appears in two different voices. In the next chord, VI, the root is doubled again. The II chord has a doubled third. Then the I chord returns, with a doubled root. While this short example is not conclusive, it does tell us that although any note of the triad may be doubled, the root is the one most likely to be.

Doubling can mean different things. Because it results in an emphasis on the doubled note, the root is most often doubled. But sometimes doubling is a way of improving the voice leading. In the first phrase of [41], doubling the third in the II chord makes it possible for the alto and tenor to move down while the soprano and bass move up, thus avoiding parallel 5ths and octaves and gaining a denser texture. In the beginning of 11 , the melody (derived from the chant 29) has 7 in the soprano which goes on to 5 in the final sound. But Josquin seems to have wanted a 7–8 motion at the same time, with the sense of closure that the leading tone–tonic move imparts. For that reason he doubled 7 in the tenor, resolving it to 8 in the last chord; this doubles the third in the V chord. Some would have it that doubling the third of a triad is "against the rules." Perhaps Josquin never read the rules. Let us say that no member of a triad should be doubled without a reason. Please observe that if doubling the third means doubling the leading tone and both leading tones move on to the tonic, parallel octaves are guaranteed.

If there is no hard and fast rule against doubling the third, what guideline is there for doubling any member of the chord? What is the musical effect of doubling? To double is to emphasize. Doubling the root of a chord emphasizes its function, so that a particularly conspicuous chord, such as the tonic at the beginning or end of a piece, will almost always have a doubled root. Beyond that, voice leading influences doubling, as in 41 .

SPACING The list of chords on page 37 shows their pitch content, not their actual disposition in a piece of music. Any of the pitches may appear in any voice, and the simple intervals of the listed chords may actually be heard as compound intervals. Yet the pitch classes are the same, and we would say that the chord was the same as long as inversion is not affected. A triad may be spaced in a great number of ways—by changing simple intervals to compound ones and by inverting those intervals not in relation to the bass—without changing its identity.

VOICE CROSSING The notion that the soprano is the highest voice, the alto the next highest, the tenor next, and the bass the lowest need not always be taken literally. In 45 , the tenor moves in a lovely line that goes up, leaving no room for the alto. But the alto does find room, in a slightly lower register. The voices cross. This gives each line more space in which to maneuver and also creates a subtle change in the color of the ensemble.

48 is written in five parts, and two of the parts, canto and quinto, are equal voices. This means that they occupy the same register. As a result, those two voices cross frequently. Examine the entire ballata to learn how the two equal voices weave in and out to make a varying texture.

CHORD AND LINE, AGAIN Voice crossing may remind us of one of the ongoing preoccupations of tonal music—that each note has to play a role in a line and in a chord. In four parts, at first, there seems to be little freedom for the lines, and the chords become the center of attention. No doubt some of the lines will always be more interesting than others, but it still is true that the more the lines can say, the more they will contribute to the overall sound.

Exercise

Write three parts against a *cantus firmus*. Begin by laying out the first chord, spacing it so that the distance between voices is approximately equal. The largest spaces can be between the lower voices, as a rule. In the exercise, the first and last notes in the bass must be the tonic.

Illustration

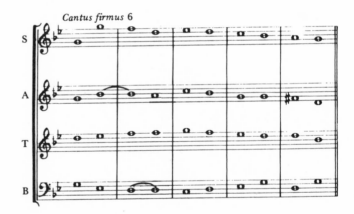

☞ Worksheet 7

38

21

Four Parts without *Cantus Firmus*

Exercise

The goal of writing all four parts simultaneously should be approximated as closely as possible, and attained as quickly as possible. Start the exercise with a well-spaced four-part chord; then sketch a possible concluding chord. One line must end 3–2–1. Remember, one of the learning goals in these exercises is to hear and organize the sounds in your mind.

☞ Worksheet 8

Title page of a collection of motets and songs by Orlando di Lasso, published in Munich, 1573. The central scene at the bottom of the page shows the court chapel of the dukes of Bavaria; it is possible that the conductor, depicted here leading the ensemble from the keyboard, is Lasso.

PART THREE
DIATONIC DISSONANCE 1

22

Passing Tones

DISSONANT FUNCTIONS Following the study of note-against-note consonance we begin the study of dissonance. At this stage, dissonant notes are literally dependent on the consonances that precede and follow them. A dissonant note can have two functions:

1. it can embellish a consonant note;
2. it can connect two consonant notes.

The types of dissonant usage studied in Part Three of this book include only those notes that are in the scale of the key. Thus they are diatonic dissonances. There are three main types: passing dissonance, neighbor dissonance, and suspension dissonance.

Each of these involves a somewhat different procedure or operation. For each we must ask how the dissonances and consonances are connected, what musical purpose is served by each kind of dissonance, and which kinds of treatment emphasize more or less the dissonant element. In this way we begin to study the interplay of dissonance and consonance, which, as we observed, is one of the most interesting and vital aspects of tonal music.

PT The musical value of the PT is that it makes possible stepwise melodic motion. Thus it links one note to another in a smooth and flowing way. All the folk songs and chants studied use PTs as details of the line. Polyphonic music, that is, music in more than one voice, also relies on PTs to build melodic continuity. These PTs may be either consonant or dissonant.

CONSONANT PT The most unobtrusive use of the PT is as a sound that is consonant with the other sounds heard at the same moment. Such a consonant PT is heard in 49B , 2 . The 4th heard between the moving A of the top line and the next line is covered by the C in the bass, thus treated as a consonance. The A connects the G and the C, and makes possible conjunct motion.

DISSONANT PT In 49B , 3 , the quarter note G connects the consonant notes A and F. The G is a 2nd from the F in the second line and a 9th from the F in the bass; both are dissonant intervals. Thus the G is a dissonant PT. Since it is on the weak half

of the beat, it receives little notice. It links two consonances in stepwise motion.

At the same time, the third voice has another dissonant PT, B♭. This moves in the same way as the G in the top line. That is, it connects two consonances, fills the space of a 3rd, and is rhythmically in a weak position. The two PTs move together in parallel 6ths, which sound well and make the dissonant element even less apparent than it might otherwise be.

For study

Examine the top voice in 50A , 1–12 . Find all PTs and determine whether they are consonant or dissonant with the lower parts. Indicate all dissonant intervals involved, relating the PT to one, two, or three other parts.

Exercise

Write one line in half notes against a *cantus firmus* in whole notes. Observe that this guarantees rhythmic independence of the voices in a rather mechanical way. The mix of types of motion should still favor the contrary. You will hear that the moving part is the more prominent, as are its strengths and weaknesses. Balance of skips and steps is essential.

Since strong and weak halves of the beat alternate, there is more than a suggestion of duple meter in this exercise. The half note on the strong beat

is always consonant. On the weak beat the half note may:

1. connect two consonances with a consonant PT;
2. connect two consonances with a dissonant PT;
3. skip from a consonance to a consonance (the only skip possible).

An illustration from Fux's *Gradus ad Parnassum* is instructive (see above).

No doubt this exercise is quite "correct," but it is also quite dull. It has unity; but does it have variety? The first six notes are repeated almost exactly in the next six. The skip of a perfect 4th occurs no less than six times in the counterpoint. The skips are all between consonances, so no rules of the game have been broken, but there are too many of them to hold our interest. The most serious problem concerns the overall melodic shape. There is no clear rise, no focus on a high point, no descent to wind down the momentum. The melody changes direction twelve times, losing any sense of purposeful motion toward a goal. Compare this exercise with another from Fux's book (see below).

Now there is a clear ascent to a high point, not in a straight line but in a series of small curves that move toward the goal. Although this cantus is longer than that of the previous exercise, there are fewer directional changes. The steady stepwise descent sets off the high point and prepares the end. There is time to balance the few skips to make them effective.

The exercise begins with a rest in the counterpoint, helping the ear to identify the two levels of melody. But rests are not used during the course of the melody. Repeated notes are also not used.

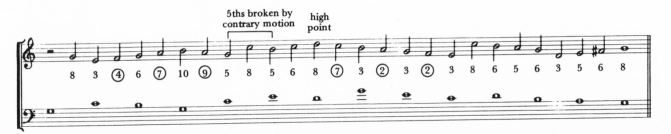

As a device to slow down the momentum in preparation for the last note, the next to the last note in the counterpoint may be a whole note.

Parallel 5ths and octaves are no better in this type of exercise than in previous ones. If 5ths are heard against successive notes of the cantus, contrary motion should separate them, as in the second Fux example.

☞ Worksheet 9

23

Neighbor Tones

CONSONANT NT Praetorius's cheerful *Gaillarde,* 50A , begins with three notes in the bass line: a main note, a NT, and the first note again. The NT, C♯, is consonant with all the other voices. This simple relationship, which we can transplant to our present exercises, involves the bass and the middle line. The intervals 5–6–5 show a typical consonant NT in two parts. The first and third intervals may be any consonance, not only 5.

DISSONANT NT In the chanson, 40 , 7 , the second soprano's four quarter notes are a reply to the four quarter notes the alto has just sung. Of the four notes, D, the second, is dissonant with both the other voices. Melodically it embellishes the consonant E, departing from and returning to it in stepwise motion. The dissonance is on the weak half of the beat. In effect, the dissonant NT hides its unstable quality as well as the dissonant PT (such as the F on the last quarter) and for the same reason: placement of the dissonance on the weak half of the beat draws attention away from it, and its chief value is melodic.

Exercise

Write one line in half notes against a *cantus firmus* in whole notes. The second half-note may be a consonant or dissonant NT as well as a PT or consonant skip.

☞ Worksheet 10

24

Suspensions

Our first example of two-part polyphony, the *bicinium,* 38 , began with intervals that were almost entirely consonant. But one strong dissonance came near the end of the first phrase. After the 6th, in which the soprano sang C and the alto E, the alto moved on to D, making a 7th with the soprano. In

43

answer to the dissonance the soprano moved down a step, turning the sound into a (consonant) 6th. The downward pull of the dissonance led into the leading tone of the dominant, which, although a chromatic tone, was made to seem quite natural as a result of the tension-release activity. This type of dissonant usage is the SUS (*suspension*). The operation may be summarized:

preparation	suspension	resolution
on weak beat	on strong beat	on weak beat
consonant	dissonant	consonant

The normal resolution of a SUS dissonance is down a step to an imperfect consonance. But there are occasions in which a resolution up is just as good, particularly if a leading tone has been suspended and then resolves to the tonic.

The figures you wrote in the second phrase suggest that another SUS ends that thought too. Again we hear the intervals 6–7–6, followed by the octave that ends the line. Another such configuration is heard in the next line, with the voices reversing what they did in the first phrase. The inversion of 6–7–6 appears, as we now have 3–2–3, with the leading tone again being heard as the resolution of the SUS. Identify the SUSs in the remainder of the piece.

What is the musical effect of the SUS? In the *bicinium*, it brings the moment of greatest tension in the phrase, drawing the activity toward it, then releasing the tension toward the goal of motion. This is only one of the purposes of the SUS, but it is an important one, and it is characteristic of much Renaissance choral music.

Where both PT and NT were on the weaker beat, the SUS is on the stronger beat. This makes the dissonance more conspicuous, reminding us how important rhythmic placement is in emphasizing dissonance or in de-emphasizing it.

Like PTs and NTs, the SUS is an elaborative device, two sounds extended into three. Another way of looking at the example we just studied is to hear

as a richer version of

While a tied note is often the sign of a SUS, the same musical result can be achieved without a tie. In 42, 17, the parallel 3rds between the soprano and bass are ornamented with a SUS. But the bass has four syllables to sing in the measure. A tied note would not do here, simply for reasons of text setting. The repetition of the D in the bass serves the same purpose as a tied D would—the pitch is continued from weak beat to strong, and the operation is a SUS.

Exercise

Write a counterpoint in half notes against a cantus in whole notes. Where possible use a SUS. It must be tied over from a consonance and resolve stepwise to a consonance, preferably downward. The 3–2–1 close of the cantus should be counterpointed in such a way as to create a SUS whose resolution is the leading tone.

☞ Worksheet 11

25

Application to Three-Part Counterpoint

DISSONANCE USAGE IN THREE PARTS
When used in three-voice writing, PT, NT, and

SUS may involve all three or only two of the voices. The three-part chanson 40 affords a good opportunity to observe dissonance techniques in a piece. Analyze the work for dissonances, and try to evaluate their musical strength. Which dissonances involve two of the voices and which involve all three? Which ones are important to the flow of the piece and which are incidental?

Exercise

Write one line in half notes and one in whole notes against a *cantus firmus*. Use all the diatonic dissonant techniques studied in Part Three.

☞ Worksheet 12

26

Application to Four-Part Counterpoint

DISSONANCE USAGE IN FOUR PARTS With four voices to manipulate, the many shadings between very active and very stable sounds afford the composer a marvelous resource, to which this section is but an introduction. Any sound may be in a dissonant relationship with one, two, or three other sounds. A few examples can show just some of the possibilities in four voices.

We have previously observed the two passing tones in 46, 3, and we now simply note that the PTs are consonant with each other while they are dissonant with the other two voices. The dissonant tones make a sonorous connection between IV and IV⁶, and their dissonant quality is subservient to the overall consonance of the measure.

The poignant ending to 45, 17, is an unusual instance of two PTs moving in parallel 4ths. This motion, in quarter notes, begins with two PTs that are dissonant with the two other voices. Perhaps the special sound of the 4ths makes these PTs seem just a bit more dissonant than most. The second pair of quarter notes is consonant. The F, which is the soprano's last quarter, is a consonant NT, while the alto's NT is dissonant. Those two notes meet the tenor's A, a PT that is consonant with the upper voices at the same time that it is dissonant with the bass. In the next measure, the tenor moves in two quarter notes, the second of which is consonant with the alto but dissonant with soprano and bass; it is a dissonant PT. The tied note in the soprano marks a SUS. In sum, there is a marvelously intricate interplay of consonance and dissonance in these measures, con-

tributing to the musical expression, leading into the SUS whose resolution brings the leading tone and the V that melts into the concluding tonic chord.

THE "CONSONANT 4TH" A special use of the chameleonlike 4th occurs in the final cadence of 44. The alto-bass relationship is 3–4–3, but if E♮ is a NT it should be a quarter note. Why does it take an extra half beat to resolve? The answer lies in the other voices. The E♮ is soon met by the F, creating a dissonance of a 2nd. This is so much stronger than the 4th that, by comparison, the 4th sounds relatively stable. The ear hears the 2nd as the dissonance that makes the E♮ resolve to D, not the 4th with the bass which, like all perfect intervals, is easily overshadowed by another kind of sound. Theorists have called this operation the "consonant 4th," which is not as cumbersome as the "less-dissonant 4th." Another instance is in 48, 6.

Exercise

Write one line in half notes and two in whole notes against a *cantus firmus* in whole notes. Use all the diatonic dissonant techniques studied in Part Three.

☞ Worksheet 13
☞ Worksheet 14

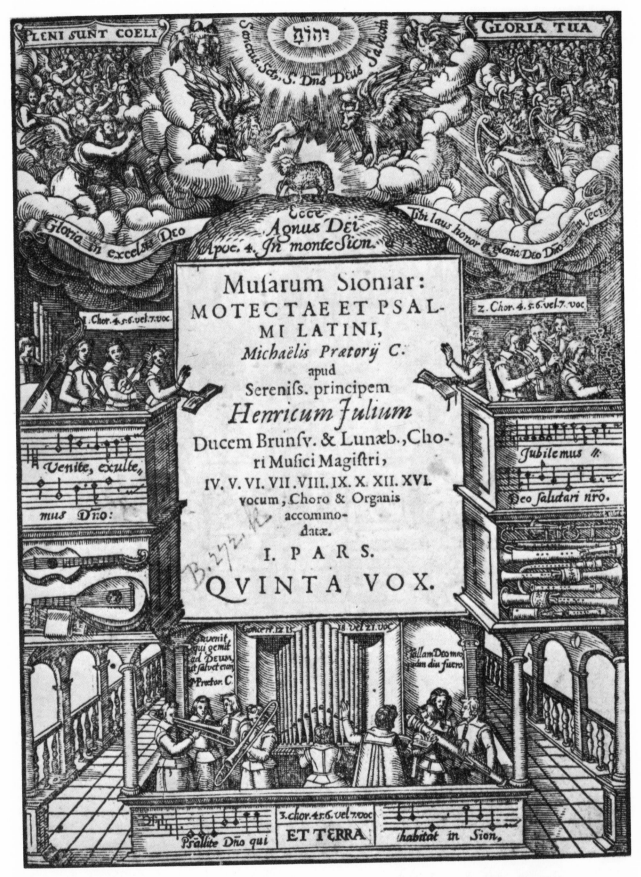

Title page of a collection of psalms and motets by Michael Praetorius, published in Nuremburg in 1607.

PART FOUR
TONAL MOVEMENT

מידע

27

The Harmonic Progression V–I

Tonal movement is of major concern throughout this study. This is because music is shaped by motion from the tonic through various secondary goals and back to the tonic. The same kinds of motion that take place in the small details also occur in the largest dimensions of a piece. The basic question in music theory is not "What chord is that?" but rather "Where is the music going and how does it get there?" In Part Four, aspects of tonal movement that have been introduced earlier are brought together to focus upon the whole piece from the point of view of both analysis and synthesis or tonal composition.

CONTRAPUNTAL PROGRESSIONS In your counterpoint exercises you have generated chords—grown them, as it were—by combining lines. After you created the chords you learned what to call them. This process approximately parallels the historical development of tonal music, as a tour through the first part of any good historical anthology of music will show. Without knowing anything about the classification of chords it is still possible to use them musically by putting the principles of counterpoint into practice. Indeed, most

of the chords in a piece of tonal music do grow out of melodic combination, usually guided by the controlling voices, the soprano and bass, with the triad as the norm for simultaneous sounds. Those chords may be called contrapuntal, or linear, chords since they grow out of lines combined according to the principles of consonance and dissonance. A series of such chords is a *contrapuntal progression*.

THE HARMONIC PROGRESSION Although every triad does have a root, the importance of that fact has been overestimated, for its bearing on musical motion of any kind is rather limited. In exercise and composition alike, motion is directed by soprano and bass regardless of the roots involved. Most chord progressions are linear or contrapuntal in origin. But not all. At the end of every piece from ⬚38⬚ to ⬚49⬚ (with the possible exception of ⬚42⬚) and of almost all the tonal music, we hear two chords that say "the end" with absolute finality. In this particular case the controlling factor is not so much the lines as the connection of the roots, from dominant to tonic. V–I is a somewhat different kind of movement than contrapuntal progressions; it is the *harmonic progression*. In this

47

book the term *harmonic* is reserved for this use only. Its application is not limited to phrase endings, but it can play a decisive role at such places.

CADENCE In folk songs and in chant we heard that a natural way in which to end a melody was the descent 3–2–1, a musical version of the voice's fall at the end of a sentence. We put that observation to use in seeking a convincing way to end a line in a counterpoint exercise. The fall of the voice to a conclusive point is called the *cadence* (Latin: *cadere,* "to fall"). In referring to a melody, we speak of a melodic cadence. In referring to the V–I that ends a phrase, we speak simply of a cadence.

All cadences do not have the same degree of finality. Some are relatively open-ended, others closed. A detailed study of the strength of various cadences lies ahead of us. The melodic cadence and the harmonic cadence are not always combined; but when they are, the punctuation mark is of the strongest.

CHORD VOCABULARY You have written Roman numerals under each chord in 41. What has this shown? It has indicated what the chord vocabulary of the piece is. By writing the numeral I under the first chord, you show that its content is C–E–G, and that it shares with I chords in other keys the property of being based on 1, 3, and 5. This is important insofar as it gives a description of the chord. What does it tell you about how the chord functions in the piece? Very little. Only when we grasp the larger fact of the neighbor motion in the soprano, the same motion in the bass elaborated with one skip, the resulting parallel 10ths in the outer voices—in short, the directed linear motion prolonging the tonic—do we realize that the first and sixth chords form the base of a short arch; stability is the function of the I chord. To label chords with numbers has the value of making a list—no more, no less. It is not analysis; it is description.

DESCRIPTION VERSUS ANALYSIS The distinction between description and analysis is a useful one. Describing a musical event is an attempt to find words for it. The description tells what the surface of the music is. Analyzing is an attempt to show how the music works. A good description can be of great value, especially when one person is trying to communicate his reactions to music in words, always a difficult task. For a musician, however, description is not enough. Analysis, involving process, operation, motion, and change, is needed if we are to get beneath the surface of musical events and gain some insight into what links them together in a meaningful whole.

28

Directed Motion

What gives a piece of music a sense of purposeful motion? Part of the answer certainly has to do with rhythm, the repetition and development of motives within a metric framework. We also know how a line creates a shape by rising against the pull of gravity and then falling to its starting point, with endless variations on that basic theme, each playing with the forces that propel a line upward and that curve it downward. In counterpoint exercises, the high point serves to focus a line. Chord progressions also have goals. What these goals are depends on the function of the motion. There are two kinds of motion:

1. prolonging motions;
2. motions from one point to another.

These give purpose to the successions of contrapuntal chords, which do not wander aimlessly about, but have specific functions. We now consider both of these functions in turn. In doing so we aim to get to the essential of how sounds move through time—we study directed motion.

29

Prolonging Motions

In a melody, a note may be prolonged by the use of NTs, PTs, Ss, and extensions of those techniques. We may now apply the same procedure to chord movement, for the same kinds of motion are used to prolong chords.

NEIGHBOR CHORDS The first three measures of ⌐42⌐ are taken up with stepwise motion in both soprano and bass. In 3, the soprano's NT, A, is met with the bass's NT, F. The inner voices supply consonance to fill out a triad. The contrapuntal or linear chord that is the F-major triad may be called a neighbor chord. It elaborates the tonic and depends on it for its meaning. At the end of the piece the tonic note is prolonged, literally, in the tenor, while soprano and alto move through NT motions. The bass skips to provide consonant support. The resulting I–IV–I motion is a way of circling around the tonic so as to add to the finality of the end. This has commonly been called a "plagal cadence"; but since the tonal movement of the piece has reached its goal, I, in 27, I–IV–I cannot in fact be any kind of cadence.

A comparison of the openings of ⌐42⌐ and ⌐47⌐ shows how two composers, writing within a few years of each other, used similar methods. Both use neighbor chords to prolong the tonic. In each, the top line rises a step to a NT and returns to the main note. Senfl delays the bass's return to G by sending that line to C first, taking advantage of a NT in the alto to generate a neighboring IV chord. The progression is I–VII–IV–I, with the two inner chords acting as consonant neighbor chords. Lasso opens with the same bass notes. The chords that result are also I–VII–IV–I, and the only difference is that the NT, C, occupies more time than it did in the Senfl. Hearing the opening measures of both pieces also gives us another opportunity to listen to the qualities of the two modes, Dorian and Mixolydian.

A simpler neighbor chord is heard at the beginning of ⌐47⌐, 4, embellishing a IV which proceeds and follows it. The bass skips to support the NT, F,

but then fills the space of a 5th on its way back with PTs. The soprano's NT is met with the bass's SP.

In just a few examples we have heard II, IV, and VII as neighbor chords. Indeed, any triad may function as a neighbor chord. A Roman numeral does not tell us whether a chord is a structural chord or a neighbor chord. To find out we must look at the music itself.

PASSING CHORDS At times, a passing motion in an outer voice is so strong that it controls the chordal motion. The chord heard with that PT is a passing chord. It may have two functions, both illustrated in ⌐48⌐. In 1, the quinto (the top line here) moves from C to the E in 2. Those notes are connected with a consonant PT, D. The other voices furnish the consonant notes of the G-major triad, the passing chord that links the A-minor triad with the C-major triad.

In 2, the C-major triad controls the first three beats. As the top voices exchange notes they pass through D, and the lower voices fill out C's dominant. This sound is a consonant passing chord; it also has the characteristic of the harmonic progression V–I in terms of C major.

OTHER CONTRAPUNTAL (LINEAR) CHORDS Clear-cut neighbor or passing chords are the most obvious kinds of linear chords. Most contrapuntal chords result from some combination of passing and neighbor motion. Further classifications are not necessary, but the linear origin and function of the chords must be understood in each case. Keep in mind that NTs elaborate a main note, PTs connect main notes, and that chords generated by those notes probably have the same functions.

Most of the pieces under study here use linear chords to prolong the opening tonic, starting the composition with a short area of stability. The opening gesture of the moving Huguenot Psalm, ⌐43⌐, is one example, being made of two short moves.

We might think of example a (below) as a "primitive" version of Goudimel's setting (example b).

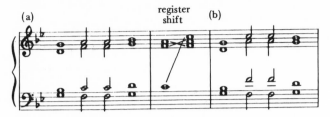

The shifts among the voices not only avoid parallel 5ths and octaves, they also give the three upper lines an opportunity to skip in a stepwise context. The NT in the bass directs the motion, and I is elaborated with VII. The NT motion in the bass is clear enough, but the PT in the upper part is disguised, being shared by soprano and alto. You can see, however, that VII is a linear chord whose function is to prolong I. This short prolonging motion is immediately followed with one directed by the SP in the soprano. The bass simply counterpoints the soprano, mostly in contrary motion, with consonances. VI and III are prolonging chords, within the orbit of I. The entire phrase is a tonic prolongation.

TONE PROLONGATION AND CHORD PROLONGATION From the above and other examples, you can see that prolongations of a single note and of a chord coexist in many cases. The simplest example might be a neighbor tone elaborated by a neighbor chord. An even more elaborated example is the opening of 40. As the sketch below shows, the melody is controlled by 3, and the chords by I. The tone prolongation is matched exactly by the chord prolongation.

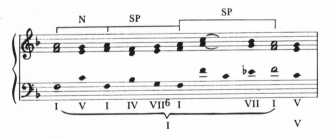

While a composer is always free to interpret melody notes in more than one way, the fact is that in Renaissance music there is usually clear congruence between melodic and chordal prolongations. Even in the seventeenth century this is the case. An exception that is more apparent than real is in 44. Schütz begins by prolonging E♭, both as a note and as a triad. But at the fifth sound he uses VI⁶. We may hear this chord as a substitute

for I. E♮ is still emphasized, but VI⁶ is not quite as stable as the tonic. The purpose of VI⁶ here is to open the end of the tonic prolongation just a bit, leading toward the V. This does not alter the fact of the tonic prolongation, but it does suggest that endings (and beginnings) of such prolongations may not be as tightly closed as might first seem to be the case.

SPECIAL FUNCTION OF THE BASS You may have observed that while most lines move stepwise most of the time, the bass usually has more skips. This is because the bass is doing things the other voices cannot do. Most obviously, the bass has to skip down a 5th or up a 4th in the harmonic progression. When a piece is made of only a few chords, they are likely to be I and V, as in the dance pieces 49. In such pieces the bass has more skips than steps.

The bass also skips to provide consonant support for NTs and PTs. This is seen in almost every piece, and needs no additional comment.

TONIC PROLONGATION The kinds of motion we have just studied circle around a particular chord, enlarge it, prolong it. Since the chord built on the center of gravity is emphasized most in a piece of tonal music, there will be more tonic prolongations than prolongations of other chords. Except for 43 or 48, each piece in this section begins with a tonic prolongation of one type or another, and you should analyze each opening, at least, to see how the prolongations work.

OTHER PROLONGATIONS In music that is short and relatively simple, prolongations of triads other than the tonic will be few. But any triad has the potential of becoming the center of attention for a short part of a piece—or even for a longer part. Aside from I, the triad that is most likely to be so emphasized is V. In the Arcadelt chanson, 40, 10–20, V becomes important enough to have its own dominant and its own leading tone. We saw the same tendency in some folk songs, and now that tendency is reinforced with polyphony. A prolongation of VI, without a leading tone, is heard in 45, starting with the last beat of 7. The NTs of the structural melodic note, F, are met with bass notes that lead to contrapuntal chords all under the sway of VI. The piece that is the most sophisticated from the viewpoint of tonal movement is 47, which prolongs V, VII, and II, moving back and forth from one to the other with a light and masterful touch.

PROLONGATIONS IN 44 Let us follow the course of all the prolongations in one piece to see how they work together. This kind of study builds on what was learned about different kinds of prolonging motions and leads away from a chord-by-chord approach and toward a grasp of larger gestures.

The first five notes in the soprano are the tonic and a NT. The bass has a skip that accompanies the NT with consonance, with the result that E♭ extends its domain for the five chords. But the fifth chord opens up the end of the prolongation thanks to the chain of SUSs in the tenor. VI⁶, which is the fifth chord, may be heard as a substitute for I; it also leads toward V, the goal of the phrase. The V is emphasized with its own harmonic progression, and we hear a cadence in B♭.

The next seven notes of the soprano outline the tonic triad, against which the bass has its own version of the same chord (as do the inner voices). But the first chord of this unit is VI, again substituting for I. The reason is not hard to hear. The second phrase begins with the same E♭ in the soprano as the first did, and to repeat bass and chord would not be as interesting as the version that Schütz chose. VI is doing the same job here that it did in the beginning of 45, where it varied the color of the soprano's repeated tonic note. But in the Isaac piece, this was done in two successive chords; here it is done at the beginning of two successive phrases. The opening of the prolongation is blurred as a result of the substitution of VI for I, and the result is a sense of continuing rather than of starting all over again.

The controlling voice in the third phrase is, again, the soprano. It has simply a tonic chord and two PTs. These are set with contrapuntal chords revolving around the tonic. Phrase and prolongation coincide.

The fourth phrase moves toward VI. The way is smoothed by a passing chord, V⁶. From the fourth chord, VI is the center of gravity, with its own leading tone and its own dominant, complete with cadence.

The prolongation of VI continues up to (but not including) the last chord in the fifth phrase. The powerful octave leap in the bass begins the drive toward the end of the piece. At the end of the phrase, V puts VI in its place and re-establishes the perspective in which E♭ is heard as tonic.

The strong return of the I at the beginning of the last phrase sets the course for the conclusion. The soprano prolongs 5 with a PS, inflected by a touch of Mixolydian. Its beautiful and unexpected D♭ is taken as the top of a neighbor chord that

settles back to I in the last tonic prolongation. Then the harmonic progression combines with a rapid descent in the soprano to make the final cadence a convincing one. Soprano and tenor exchange notes; but instead of skipping the 4th, each fills that interval with PTs which collide to provide the greatest dissonant tension of the piece, prolonging V for two very busy beats. The dissonant counterpoint is active at the same moment that the relatively mild suspension dissonance, creating a consonant 4th, occurs in the alto, all of which is resolved at once in the final chord.

By thinking in terms of prolonging motions we are able to find the tonal unity of each phrase, and to see how the same kinds of operations take place, phrase after phrase, but always in a different way. Perhaps, too, we can now better appreciate how, with a minimum of resources (three chromatic notes used quite sparingly), Schütz has composed music of great dignity and eloquence.

VOICE EXCHANGE In studying ways in which a chord may be prolonged, we find one technical detail that occurs in many pieces. When a chord is repeated, the repetition may be varied by having two of the voices exchange notes. In 44, second phrase, the fourth and fifth chords are both I. Soprano and tenor exchange notes, however, keeping the melody moving and giving the repetition some of the value of a chord change. A more complex exchange occurs in the next phrase, at the very beginning. The soprano's first note goes to the alto, the alto's to the tenor, and the tenor's to the soprano. Another voice exchange, involving soprano and tenor, is heard in the _____ measure.

The first sarabande of 50C carries the technique a step further. In 3 , the first and third instruments not only exchange notes, but fill in the space of a 3rd with PT, both dissonant with the bass.

ROOT, THIRD, FIFTH In voice exchange, the chord remains constant while voices move. The opposite happens quite frequently—a melody note is repeated while the chord under it changes. This is possible because any melody note (or any note, for that matter) may be thought of as the root, third, or fifth of a triad. Just as voice exchange makes chord repetition more interesting, chord change makes a repeated note change its coloration. The opening of 45 illustrates the point. F is heard first as the root of a (thirdless) triad, then as the third of a VI chord. In the opening of 47, the NT, C, is colored in two different ways—first as the fifth of a triad, then as the root.

51

30

Connecting Motions

In the music we are now studying, prolonging motions occupy most of the piece. At a few points, connecting links are heard between prolonging motions, and these we now examine. In more complex music, the connecting links take up more of the piece as the prolonging motions become less obvious.

The first two measures of 46 present the tonic, with one linear chord in the brief elaboration. In 4, the dominant is reached. Between the two is a connecting link, IV, which appears both in $\frac{5}{3}$ and $\frac{6}{3}$ positions. The pattern I–IV–V–I is one of the most common in music, but what does it mean? It is a short but complete tonal movement in which the first I is the point of departure, the IV represents motion, transition, connection, and V–I is the cadence. Even in this simple piece the opening I is prolonged, and the tonic in 5 is pushed on by the rhythm so that the cadential effect is swallowed up in the onrushing activity.

Triads serving as connections may themselves be prolonged. After the opening prolongation in 47, IV follows again as a link to the dominant in 5. But IV is elaborated in two short motions that blend into one gesture. First, the C–D–E of the soprano generates a passing chord, a G-major triad that functions more as a passing chord than as a tonic. Then E is prolonged with a NT. The bass first skips a 5th to support the soprano's F, then fills in that interval with passing quarter-note motion on the way back. Only then does IV move on to V, which unexpectedly becomes a momentary tonic in its own right.

More complex pieces will show more complex ways of getting from one point to another. But the principle does not change, no matter how long or how elaborate the transitional motion becomes.

☞ Worksheet 15

31

Rhythm, Meter, and Chord Change

STRONG AND WEAK BEATS One obvious difference between a counterpoint exercise and a piece of music is in the use of rhythm. In note-against-note consonance we minimized the rhythmic problem in order to concentrate on pitch relationships. In the first studies of diatonic dissonance we found the 2-to-1 rhythmic relationship useful. But in a piece of music, even a simple one, there are not only beats, but measures, phrases, and phrase groups, all having to do with duration.

We have talked about strong and weak beats. How does the basic rhythmic property relate to chord progression?

(a)

(b)

(c)

Play example (a), above. Where is the strong beat? How do you know? Certainly the melody conveys nothing about the rhythm. Nor does duration, ex-

cept for the final note. The only element that contributes to a sense of rhythm is the chord change, working together with the changes in the bass notes.

METER   Mark the strong beats by writing in bar lines. In the first measure you probably have four quarter notes. The 5–1 move in the bass and the V–I chord change that goes with it both define the strong beat. The very first beat proves to have been a strong beat, too, although this can be determined better after the first hearing. The recurrence of the strong beat defines the number of pulses that make a unit. That unit is the *measure;* the number of beats within it is the meter. In written music, the meter is indicated by the *time signature* or *meter sign*. The meter sign is written after the key signature in a piece. But whereas the key signature is repeated at the beginning of every line of music, the meter sign appears only once, at the beginning. Of course, if the meter changes during the course of a piece a new sign must appear. Write in the meter sign for example a.

Play example (b). Where is the downbeat? How many bar lines should there be? The pitches of the last chord are indicated. What duration must they have to complete the measure?

Example (c) has a rhythmic feature the previous two did not have. Complete the notation.

32

Words and Music

Following up on the connections between words and music, we turn from the single line of melody to polyphonic music. As in much of the folk poetry we saw, the lines are metrical. This simply means that the number of feet to a line and the pattern of strong and weak beats are fairly constant throughout the poem. These features have been reproduced in the translations, as has the natural accent of the words. In some pieces, such as those by Arcadelt, Senfl, and Donati, the regular rhythm of the poem finds expression in the regular

rhythm of the music. But in the Renaissance, the reign of strictly metered music had not yet begun, and the bar line did not enclose all rhythmic impulses. Side by side with pieces that are quite metrical we find pieces in which the rhythm follows the accent of poetry without fitting into any single meter. Although we are not back to the endlessly shifting, vaguely implied meter of chant, we are certainly not at the point where everything fits into a consistent double or triple meter.

Claude Le Jeune set to music a good deal of the

53

type of French poetry called *vers mesuré,* "measured verse." See 39. The music is called *musique mesurée,* "measured music." By this he meant that the long syllables were set to half notes or their equivalent and the short ones to quarter notes. Since the poems used varying groups of longs and shorts, the music did not fit any particular meter. Bar lines make no sense in music like this. If you say the words aloud, using the rhythmic values of the music, you see that Le Jeune has literally transcribed the accents of the poem into music. Rarely has the link between music and words been so straightforward.

The setting of the first verse of the Sixty-first Psalm, 43, follows the same principle, but in a less extreme manner. The natural accent of the first line, with modern time signatures applied, might be depicted as:

Hear - ken   to   me   Lord   I

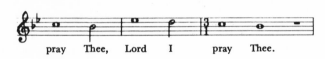

pray Thee, Lord   I   pray Thee.

Write bar lines, with meter signs, for the rest of the piece.

Even in pieces that are predominantly in one meter, rhythmic flexibility is introduced in various ways. Arcadelt, 40, approaches the cadence in 20 with the same rhythmic grouping of three-plus-three-plus-two beats that we heard at the end of Josquin, 41. The identical pattern occurs just before the final cadence in Isaac, 45, and we may expect it in other Renaissance music as well.

HEMIOLA   The lesson ·that music is for the ear and not for the eye is brought home, for example, in the fourth and fifth measures of 46. Something is wrong with the bar line between those measures. Both the chord changes and the text tell us that a strong beat comes on what appears to be the second (weak) beat of 5. Try hearing 4–5 as one long measure in $\frac{3}{1}$ time. Both words and music make much more sense. For that matter, try the same thing with the fourth and fifth measures of *My Country 'Tis of Thee.* The device we are describing is called a *hemiola,* and was often used well into the eighteenth century; that use persists even today. A famous example is from Handel's *Messiah,* where the line should be conducted and sung as if it were written:

And the   glo - ry, the   glo - ry of the

Lord   shall be   re - veal - ed.

Exercise

Set the first couplet of poetry from 40, 42, or 47 for speaking chorus (no pitch). Use triple meter.

Set in duple meter the first four lines of the poem of 46 for speaking chorus.

Set a short paragraph of prose for speaking chorus. Follow the changing accents of the words and use changing meter signs.

33

Other Aspects of 38 through 50

EDITION   The composers of the fifteenth and sixteenth centuries did not leave us scores of their works. Either they composed in their minds or virtually every score they wrote was destroyed, by accident or design. Music printing was well advanced by 1500, but what was printed were the individual parts. Modern scholars have reconstructed the pieces from the part books, and definitive editions of older music may be found in the complete-works editions which most music libraries now hold. These scholarly editions aim to present the music just as the composer wrote it but in score form. Many practical modern editions of older music are also available in which tempo, dynamic, and expressive markings based on the editor's judgments about the piece are usually added. Practical editions may also transpose the piece, reduce the time values, and add bar lines where none appeared in the original.

In this text, note values are the original ones, with the exception of 41 . The original key is always used unless there is an indication of transposition. Bar lines hardly existed in the originals, and when they did, they represented phrase or section endings. Bar lines have been added to some pieces here. The pieces that do not fit into a single meter are best left without bar lines.

PERFORMANCE It is essential that all of the pieces be performed often enough for you to know their sound and remember their important features. While all are printed here in S.A.T.B. format, it must be remembered that there were few female singers in the choruses of the Renaissance, and the choral concept as we know it today did not exist in 1500. As far as we are concerned, male or female voices may sing any part in which they are comfortable. Instruments may be used to double or even replace any part. The notion that all Renaissance music was sung *a cappella* (without instruments) is a myth that has been discredited. The instrumental pieces were written for any available group of the time and place, and may be played by any instruments that are fairly in balance with one another. Since the half note is the beat in most of the pieces, the music has to move more quickly than a first glance at the page might suggest. A light tone, clear articulation of the words, and a strong rhythmic impetus will bring out the qualities of the music. The secular pieces are lively, not deadly serious. The clue to the accent of the music is the accent of the words, which has been carefully preserved in the translations.

TEXTURE In your exercises, all voices were heard all the time, with the single exception of a rest that started a single line at times. In the pieces under study, most of the voices sing or play most of the time, presenting a rather homogeneous musical fabric or texture. However, the deviations from a solid texture are interesting to see, small though they are. The simplest is one we have used

in exercises, in which one voice moves twice as fast as another. This is to be seen in almost every piece. Another involves the SUS, in which one voice is held while others move.

But texture may be opened up in other ways. In 40 , the end of the third phrase moves to a V–I cadence in C, the dominant of F. The top two voices reach C, but the lower one first breathes, then rejoins the others to start the next phrase. Again, in 20 , the lower voice rests for a beat, then starts the next phrase with the middle voice. But the top voice now rests a beat, too, and has to catch up with the others in the ensuing measures. The rests ventilate the texture, reducing the activity and making the return of the missing voice a small event in itself.

The same kind of thing happens in the latter part of 42 , and the voices become more independent until near the end. Their drawing together into a tight texture is one of the signals that the music is coming to an end, and is thus a factor in the musical form.

IMITATION As the Senfl piece, 42 , moves into its middle section, in 16 ff. we hear a melodic fragment from the tenor which is echoed immediately by the soprano. Then the soprano introduces a rising line in 21 , answered closely by the bass. These are simple examples of imitation. Another instance comes near the end of 47 , where 24 has successive entrances of the closing phrase in the alto, tenor, and bass. While a thorough study of imitation will come much later, you should be aware of it in these pieces, for it is an important and widely used musical technique.

FIVE PARTS The richness of sound that five parts can offer made it a favorite in much late Renaissance and early Baroque music. There are two approaches to the five-part format. In one, the S.A.T.B. concept remains, and a fifth part is added in such a way as to be equal with one of the basic four. This fifth part is usually called quinto, no matter where it lies. Thus, in 48 , the fifth part is another soprano and has the same clef as the soprano, or canto. The two voices share the same range, and, as a result, they cross frequently. It was precisely this interplay of two voices in one area that was so appealing a feature of the five-part chorus.

Another possibility consists of simply dividing the available space into five more or less equal parts, each keeping to its own range. The *Courante* of Praetorius, 50B , uses this approach, with a minimum of voice crossing. There are no breaks in the fabric, and the sound is full and sonorous.

34

Comprehensive Analysis of *Innsbruck*, 45

BACKGROUND 45 is a setting of a folk melody by an important German musician of the late fifteenth and early sixteenth centuries. Ostensibly written when the composer left his home in the Alpine town he loved, the piece achieved wide popularity. The melody was soon attached to a hymn, and Bach made several settings under various titles. The continuing appeal of the melody is attested to by its appearance in what is probably the last work composed by Johannes Brahms, the final *Chorale Prelude for Organ* Op. 122, completed in 1897, 119 .

SOUND, TEXTURE The original clefs show two altos, tenor, and bass, presumably all male. This would result in the rather low sound and dark color favored by many composers of northern countries. The texture is largely note against note, broken in a few places by voices that move independently of the predominant rhythm. Rests separate the phrases.

TONAL STRUCTURE The key is F major, which means that all of the notes in the piece are related to F. The way in which they are related is shown in the sketch and discussion below.

Phrase one (1–4): prolongation of I
Phrase two (4–7): continued prolongation of I, motion to V;
Phrase three (7–9): prolongation of II, delaying the return to I
Phrase four (9–12): prolongation of II leads into the prolongation of I
Phrase five (12–15): same as phrase two;
Phrase six (15–20): return from V to I, then I–IV–V–I
Phrase seven (16–20 , with second ending): same as phrase six.

A factor that is not implied by the bass-soprano skeleton is the important role played by a single interval, the 3rd, in the top line. In the sketch, those 3rds are shown by dotted lines. Almost all of the melodic motions fill the space of a 3rd in one way or another.

A comparison of the chord progression that opens the piece with the first four chords of 41 is instruc-

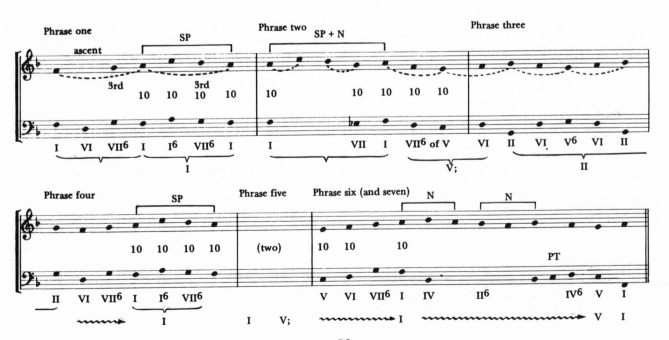

tive. The two are quite similar. In the Josquin, after the initial tonic, the color of the melody note is changed by the VI that is an extension of the tonic. But where Isaac moves directly to VII⁶, Josquin adds a II, then changes one note at the last moment, just touching the VII⁶.

In addition, we can't help hearing in the Isaac that VI–VII⁶–I accompanies the soprano's 1–2–3 three times, creating a short but effective unifying element. Bass and soprano come together on F only at the beginning and the end, which helps keep the continuity going between those points. Finally, the bass touches the low F only to signal the end of the piece.

RHYTHM Although obviously led by the words, the rhythm does not follow the prosody literally. Each phrase ends with a long note, the last phrase with the longest. The eight beats preceding the final chords in 20 (first and second endings) show a change of meter. Rather than consisting of alternate strong and weak beats (equaling two measures each with four beats), they group into three plus three plus two. This is indicated by the bar lines in 17–19 .

CONSONANCE AND DISSONANCE Note-against-note consonance is the rule, with dissonance moving the piece forward at crucial points. The SUS in 3 , alto, is a lovely detail. A dissonant IN, 5 , in the soprano, is softened by the consonant PT in the tenor. The emphasis on the dominant that strengthens the end of the second phrase is heightened by the leading tone of the dominant, introduced by a SUS in the tenor. Maximum dissonance combines with maximum rhythmic activity in 17 and 18 to provide the tension the release of which is the final tonic.

CONTINUITY The only phrase with a strong cadence is the last, which alone uses the 3–2–1 descent over the V–I progression. All other phrase endings are open in one way or another. In phrase 1 the melody ends on 3; in phrase 2 the goal is V, which leads on; in phrase 3 the end leaves us on II; phrase 4 again leaves the melody on 3; phrase 5 ends on the dominant; only in the sixth phrase do we hear bass and soprano agree on the tonic, the kind of punctuation that says "the end," confirmed by the repetition.

35

Projects in Tonal Composition

While the compositions we just studied are the models for the following projects, they are to be used more as guidelines for techniques and processes than for style. The purpose of writing such pieces is to continue the development of writing skills. Whether or not the pieces sound just like Renaissance music is not as important as whether they have a clear overall shape, whether the motion arrives at its goals, and whether the results sound musical.

1. Set couplets of metrical poetry for S.A.T.B., creating antecedent and consequent phrases. Suggested structural notes for the soprano:

a. 3–2; 3–2–1
b. 5–4–3–2; 5–4–3–2–1
c. 1–2–3–2; 3–2–1

In a key or mode of your choice, sketch out structural notes as whole notes. Add a consonant bass note to each soprano note and determine the structural chords. When you are thoroughly familiar with the rhythm of the poem, develop the contrapuntal chords to fit the words.

Illustration:

> The robin is a Gabriel
> In humble circumstances,
> His dress denotes him socially
> Of transport's working classes.
>
> —Emily Dickinson

Main melody notes

Ideas for elaboration

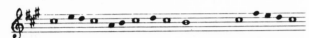

Setting

2. Set a complete poem, approximately eight lines long. Use the same procedure as in project 1. 40 through 48 may serve as models.

3. Set a short paragraph of prose or several lines of free verse. Change meter signs as the rhythm of the words requires it.

4. Using the same guidelines as in project 1, write a short instrumental piece for an available combination. The dance pieces of 49 and 50 may serve as models.

For further study

A selection of Renaissance pieces is included in each of the following: *Historical Anthology of Music,* I; *Masterpieces of Music before 1750;* and *Music Literature,* I and II, by Hardy and Fish. A good deal of French music of the period was edited by Henri Expert, under whose name it can probably be found in your school library. German and Austrian music is included in two large sets of publications, *Denkmäler der Tonkunst in Österreich* and *Das Erbe deutsche Musik.*

A far-ranging discussion of Renaissance music that locates it in a general historical context occupies chapter 9 of Paul Henry Lang's *Music in Western Civilization.* Donald Grout writes about the musical developments of the period in *A History of Western Music,* chapters 6 through 8. Original writings by contemporary musicians and theorists are in Chapters 5 through 7 of Oliver Strunk's *Source Readings in Music History.*

INTERLUDE ONE
A LOOK AHEAD

In folk song and chant we saw a type of tonal music that relied on 5th relationships, on linear motions gravitating around the tonic, and on rather little use of leading tones. Renaissance polyphony showed much the same tendencies, the added chordal dimension flourishing within a largely diatonic context. In the succeeding periods the importance of the dominant grew, aided by the increasingly complex prolongations that were first developed in Baroque keyboard music; the leading-tone tendency combined with greater use of mode mixture to increase chromaticism; and by the latter part of the nineteenth century the sense of key itself began to weaken. Early in the twentieth century some composers pushed those tendencies to the point where all the resources of the chromatic scale became equally available, without reference to a tonic, writing music that is called atonal. At the same time, other composers sought out new possibilities within tonality. Turning away from chromaticism, they found various ways of using a tonal center without relying too heavily on the dominant, the leading tone, or highly dissonant chords. This trend may be described as the extension of traditional tonality. By surveying a few applications of extended tonality in twentieth-century pieces, we will put to good use much of what has been learned about older music and gain insights into some of the music of the recent past.

We ask different questions of different pieces, but our chief concerns are: How is tonality established? What are the norms of consonance and dissonance? How does the approach to rhythm, phrase structure, and phrase groupings differ from Ren-aissance music to the present? Is the S.A.T.B. concept still applicable? What part does texture play?

Five pieces from Béla Bartók's collection of piano pieces, 51, illustrate one approach to extended tonality. Written as piano studies, *Mikrokosmos* is also a set of studies in compositional techniques. The same procedures that Bartók uses in his large-scale works are found in miniature in these short pieces.

In 51A tonality is established by circling motions around the tonic, much like folk music and chant. The lower voice centers around the tonic, D, while the upper voice gravitates around the dominant, A. All other notes embellish those two or connect them. The scale that uses white notes of the piano only and is based on D is Dorian. The only chromatic note is the F♯ which makes the last sound major. Listening to the simultaneous sounds, 3rds, 5ths, 6ths, and octaves predominate, but the occasional 2nds, 4ths, and 9ths seem to have no special function. The distinction between consonance and dissonance is no longer an important factor here, and any note of the scale may be combined with any other note. Tonality is maintained partly by melodic means and partly by the emphasis on the 5th, D–A, as the basic simultaneity. The piece is continuous, there being only one slight pause at the end of 7. That punctuation is felt more because of the two half notes closing off the quarter-note motion than because of anything the pitches do. The same rhythmic slowdown leads to the final chord, which brings together tonic and dominant plus the major 3rd.

The Phrygian of 51B has B as dominant, unlike

A preliminary version of the decor by M. F. Larionov for Bronislava Nijinska's ballet, *Le Renard*, premiered in Paris on May 18, 1922. (Courtesy Dance Collection, The New York Public Library at Lincoln Center, Astor, Lennox and Tilden Foundations).

its medieval counterpart. The pitches maintain the same level of tension throughout, there being no sound that functions as a strong dissonance. Tension is increased by means of dynamics. The crescendo builds to a climax, working together with a rhythmic contraction in the upper voice that has a three-beat rhythm disagreeing with the four-beat pattern. This reaches its apex at the beginning of the fourth line, and the level is kept up for four measures of quarter-note activity. Then dynamics and texture taper off to define the end.

Two different scales are used in 51C. The first eight measures are built on a pentatonic scale. The 5ths are arranged so as to suggest A♭ as tonic, with one 5th above and one below. In 9 the introduction of two new notes, C and F, brings F into the position of tonal center. F predominates through 16. In the third part, we hear the return of the pentatonic A♭, but F makes a surprising comeback at 26. After a moment of silence, F is put in its place by the last two measures, which confirm A♭ as tonic. The move from one key center to another that is heard in older music, but in terms of tonic and dominant, here takes the form of two alternating modes with overlapping pitch content. The modes are readily distinguished from each other by the emphasis on the 5th in each. The changes of mode determine the form of the piece. To make the differentiation of sections even clearer, the sections in F have less rhythmic activity and quieter dynamics than the pentatonic sections.

You have probably observed that the left hand plays whatever the right hand plays, half a measure later and a 12th lower. We call this technique of answering one line with the same music at a different level *imitation*. It was widely used in Renaissance and Baroque music, becoming gradually rarer until the twentieth century. When imitation is carried out literally for the entire piece, with the possible exception of phrase endings, as it is here, the technique is called *canon*. Canon is not a form, but a way of combining two or more lines, and it may be used in different forms. When, in the last two measures, the canon stops and the two voices play the inversion of each other's lines, it is a closing gesture, a cadence.

Although 51D has the word "Oriental" in its title, the scale of the first seven measures is identical with that of many Hungarian and Romanian folk songs. The interval of an augmented 2nd is characteristic of much Balkan and Near Eastern music. The addition of E and F gives us a seven-note scale sometimes called the "Hungarian minor," a variant of which is exemplified in 20. G and D are the poles between which the lines move, so that

the ending on D–A sounds like a close on the dominant, similar to the end of many Russian folk songs.

Canon, as used in this work, is a natural technique for developing both of the young pianist's hands to play in a singing style. Imitation is at the octave. The time distance between the parts grows shorter as the piece goes on—three measures, one measure, finally half a measure. The intensification continues to the end, though quietly.

Mode mixture provides much of the interest in 51E. Each part goes its own way melodically, there being only the faintest suggestion of imitation. The phrases overlap, coming together for one punctuation point in 6 and another at the end. Both resting places are on a stable unison C, the dominant. While modality is mixed, tonality is not, and F is clearly the center of gravity throughout.

The S.A.T.B. concept, each voice important but soprano and bass guiding the tonal direction, flourishes in 52. A serene invocation to the Alpine countryside, the poem is set to music of calm beauty. There are four spacious gestures of which the first three are prolongations of triads and the fourth is motion to a cadence. The first phrase is built on I, the top three voices flowing in parallel motion over a bass that is stationary except for one NT, a 3rd away from the principal note but still functioning as a NT. Motion within the tonic is pushed farther in the next phrase, but C major is still in control. The third phrase begins unexpectedly with A major, the E of the C-major triad being used as a link. The whole phrase flows around the A-major triad, coming to rest on a clear statement of the chord. The fourth phrase moves from A through D and G to C, and the piece ends with a form of V–I that de-emphasizes the leading tone.

In each phrase, almost the only triad to be heard without simultaneous embellishing notes is the one on which the phrase is built. That acts as the basic consonance, and all other diatonic and even some chromatic notes may be combined in a way that produces a mild flavor of dissonance that keeps the music flowing toward the next consonance. All the simultaneities, then, are triads with added notes, which add to the richness of sound without exercising any strong tonal function.

At first glance, 53 seems to have as many as eight parts. But doubling reduces that to six. Listening closely, we realize that there are two streams of sound, two lines. But they are unlike any two parts we have studied before. Each part is thickened out into a triad. The upper strings play a line expressed as a root-position triad; the lower line is in the form of triads in second inversion. Compared with the strong dissonance generated by the two conflicting lines, the 4th loses its dissonant power completely, even in relation to the bass. Contrary motion between the two contending lines helps generate the sense of tension that characterizes this music. F♯ is the magnet that draws the lines, and the melodic motion in the upper line, F♯ to C♯, sketches out the 4th that contributes to the definition of the tonality. The triads are all major or minor, but their combination yields some very chromatic dissonant sounds. Observe that, yes, parallel 5ths do eliminate the individuality of the lines involved. Here, those lines are meant to be heard as a single unit, together with the thirds that complete the triads—which explains why there are two real parts in the music. And they struggle against each other in contrary motion.

The technique of expressing a line as a triad is used to advantage in ⬜54⬜. The upper triad is arpeggiated and made into a motive the rhythm of which is heard in every measure of the piece. The top line prolongs the tonic G-major triad with its neighbor A-major triad for eight measures. In counterpoint, the bass begins with the color-changing triad (G as fifth, G as root), then begins to fill the space between C and F that it has staked out, using B♭. F now appears as a lower neighbor. Then E is heard, and D, which then moves on to C but transferred up an octave. The two lines of triads are carefully combined to produce mild clashes, separated by more consonant notes.

We know that a new thought—or rather a new continuation of an old thought—comes next be- cause we hear a change in texture, tempo, and dynamics. The melody moves between descending chords in the lower part and moving eighth notes in the upper part. A line in the form of first-inversion triads starts from G in ⬜9⬜, interrupts itself and starts again in ⬜11⬜, and fills the octave to G, starting the next phrase as it does so. Again, tonal movement defines phrase structure, helped by textural and dynamic differentiation. The third phrase is much like the first in chordal content but with the melody of the second phrase superimposed. The remainder of the piece involves a series of descents through the octave, all centering around G, mixing contrary and oblique motion. When the two lines come together in ⬜29⬜, it is a signal that the end is near. The short motive, the diatonic melody, the occasional lengthening of the phrase, all help create the nostalgic atmosphere of this evocative piece.

If the Copland piece has some of the flavor of an American small town, the Hindemith chanson, ⬜55⬜, brings us back to the world of Renaissance musical tradition. Perhaps the main point here is the similarity between the kind of tonal structure we expect to find in a sixteenth-century piece and the tonal structure of this chanson. The same technique of reduction used in earlier music results in the example below.

Phrase one: The opening sound suggests E as tonic (5th above, also 4th above, 4th below), but without the tonic in the bass the sound is not stable. Consequently, the piece seems to be in motion from the very start. The long opening gesture is spun out by oblique motion, the soprano centering around one note while the bass fills the octave.

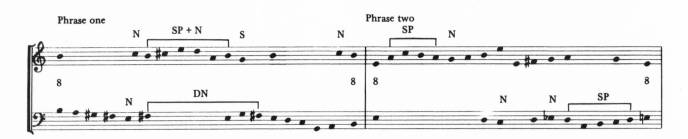

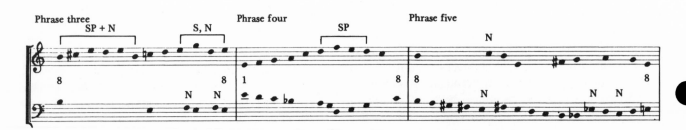

The top line uses neighbor motions and skips, plus an extension of the same kinds of operations. The second group may be thought of as

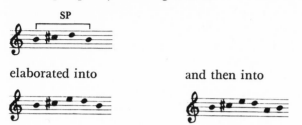

elaborated into   and then into

The bass does not move in a straight line, but pauses to dwell on both F♯ and E, with NT motion, side-stepping the lower B to touch G before reaching the goal. The major sound at the end of the phrase is a clear punctuation mark.

Phrase two: Without moving from B as tonal center, the ·tenor contradicts the mode with the minor sound as the phrase opens, bringing a texture change as well. Contrary motion leads the piece to a particularly lovely moment, the soprano's descent from A to G being made by a transitional motion whose chief feature is the pair of skips, 4th up and octave down. The G in the top line is colored by an unexpected E♭ in the bass, a NT to the structural D. In contrary motion, the outside voices find their way to the tonic in a cadence that seems quite Phrygian in the sense ·that if the 3rd in the soprano were to be filled in, F is a more likely choice than F♯.

A detail in the soprano part shows how Hindemith builds on traditional techniques in his own way. The descent from 5 to 1 is, in itself, as familiar as can be. Not being interested in V–I relationships, Hindemith omits the 2 that is normally heard over V, and arrives at the tonic by melodic means—which is to say that both soprano and bass close in on E and reach it together at the last sound. The motion from 5 to 4, however, is elaborated into an expressive melodic gesture, as suggested here:

Phrase three: The. men sing what the sopranos sang at the opening, then shift down toward E in this short phrase. The soprano's first group is a variant of the similar group in the first phrase and is followed by an upward gesture to the E that leads to the climactic fourth phrase.

Phrase four: Contrary motion and the octave are exploited to build tension in this phrase. In barest terms, both soprano and bass are built on E–D–C. But octave displacement throws open the large spaces in which the contrary motion can flourish. The second sound of the phrase, a minor 3rd, is reflected at the height of the curve by the same pitch classes two octaves apart, after which the voices change direction and move toward the C that will, in turn, lead to the B of the tonic chord.

Phrase five: This retrospective gesture sums up the content of the first two phrases. Calm is restored by the oblique motion, G is again colored by E♭, and the same cadence that ended the second phrase leads to the E, now made final by the major triad.

Much of the musical imagery stems from the poem. The vision of the slow-moving swan is suggested by the soprano line that centers around one note. Key words receive special emphasis by being set with major triads, both with doubled thirds. "Migrating space" has many empty 4ths and 5ths. When the image is "redoubled," the reflection of the soprano's melody is heard in the lower voices. The emotional climax of the poem finds expression in the contrary motion and the contrapuntal expansion within a large amount of musical space. The picture of the swan and its reflection, seen together, is set to music that grows quieter as the scene disappears. The poem has shaped not only the line-by-line setting of the music, but also texture and sonorities throughout the piece.

COMPREHENSIVE ANALYSIS OF 56 This march serves as the introduction to *Renard*, a stage piece that is sung and acted. The tale of the sly fox and his attempts to outwit his fellow creatures is common to many lands. In this version a few amusing situations are loosely strung together to make a show whose informality belies its sophistication. During the march, the four characters enter the stage. The little orchestra consists of piccolo, soprano clarinet, oboe, bassoon, two horns, trumpet, cymbal, bass drum, tambourine, and cimbalom, a Hungarian instrument much like a dulcimer. The ensemble is calculated to produce with just a few instruments a great variety of tone colors that do not necessarily blend. In this reduced score, all transposing instruments have been notated at concert pitch, except for the piccolo, which sounds an octave higher.

FORM The piece is in three sections, the third of which is identical to the first. Thus it may be said to be in *ternary* or *three-part form*. The sections are differentiated by key, mode, timbre, texture, register, and meter. The pulse is constant throughout the piece and the dynamic level is loud and without nuance.

TONALITY The first interval that might define a key is a 4th, from A down to E, and after the skip up from A to D we sense that A is indeed the tonic, surrounded by the two 4ths. The F♯ gives a Dorian flavor. The second degree of the scale has two forms, B and B♭, and C♯ is heard as a chromatic embellishment. The cadential gesture consists of a descending A-minor scale, mixed with F♯ and B♭.

The center of gravity in the second section is a 5th, E♭–B♭. It is prefixed by a neighboring 5th, F–C. The tonic is prolonged with NTs and skips, the leap to A♭ being rather unexpected. At 35 the C changes its function, moving from the domination of E♭ back to the realm of A and starting the transition back to the first part.

TIMBRE The melody in the first part is played by the bassoon, with various and changing doublings by the brass. Thus the color of the line changes constantly. Cymbal and bass drum play on every beat, unchanging. The instrumentation changes almost completely for the middle section; only the two horns continue.

TEXTURE, REGISTER The first part has only one line until the cadential scale passage. There it moves out into two parts. In the second part the piccolo plays the melody as relentlessly as the bassoon did in the first part. The other instruments play accompanying chords, whose parallel 5ths

and octaves bring us very close to "one-part counterpoint." So-called wrong notes plus the clarinet's seeming inability to match the piccolo's rhythm suggest a country band with more zest than accuracy. Observe how each section has its own register. The highest note in the first section is middle D; the lowest note in the second section is middle E♭. Within each section texture and register are fixed. When the bassoon descends a full octave in 18, 19 and 20, it is a signal that the first section is over. When the second horn comes down to middle C in 35, it is a signal that the transition back to the first section is under way.

CONCLUSION From this brief excursion into the twentieth century we may learn that many of the principles of tonality apply in more than one era, possibly in all. The operations of structure and prolongation, the methods by which melodic elaboration works, directed motion, all have their counterpart in the extended tonality of Bartók, Hindemith, Copland, Milhaud, and Stravinsky. The music of these composers, and many others who wrote in a similar language, is not as mysterious as it may seem to a person whose knowledge of twentieth-century music is somewhat limited. Among other things, this study should encourage you to listen extensively to the music of the five composers introduced here. The extension of traditional tonality is discussed again and in greater detail near the end of Book Two. By the time that study is reached, you would do well to be familiar with the sounds of twentieth-century music. Analysis and synthesis will then come naturally.

Chamber music in the conservatory, engraving by Daniel Nikolaus Chodowiecki (1769). The woman at the harpsichord is accompanying the singer standing to her left; the instrumentalist doubling the bass line reads directly from the continuo part.

PART FIVE EXPANSIONS OF HARMONY AND COUNTERPOINT

36

Diatonic Dissonance 2

A MUSICAL EXAMPLE In order to study additional usages of dissonance, let us look at [88], a movement from a sonata for violin and *continuo* by Corelli. At first glance there seem to be three parts, but in fact, there are only two. The lower two parts show what Corelli wrote; the upper part represents what the English publisher called "Corelli's Graces." This is the music as it might actually have been played, in one of many possible versions. Playing exactly what is on the printed page was not always the custom in Baroque music, and to play such a piece as this literally would be to falsify it. The melody was a skeleton around which the performer improvised. Since Corelli was a violinist as well as a composer, we may assume that his improvisation was appropriate to the occasion. Just what notes did the composer-performer add in order to "grace" the melody?

CONSONANCE AND DISSONANCE The first note to be added is C in 2. It embellishes the consonant octave by adding a dissonant 9th. The *continuo* (keyboard) player would also play D in the second chord, to which the C would also be dissonant. We hear a leap into a dissonant sound. The dissonant 9th resolves to the consonant octave; we might say that the octave explains the dissonance. Thus the C acts as a neighbor to the B♭. But it is an incomplete neighbor, the group consisting of only two notes. Since the dissonant note is in a stronger rhythmic location than the consonant note, we describe the C as an $\overset{>}{\text{IN}}$. The rhythmic placement calls attention to the dissonance, so that it strikes the ear more forcefully than a NT or IN (on weak beat) would. An $\overset{>}{\text{IN}}$, approached by skip, is sometimes called an appoggiatura. In order to use as few terms as possible in this book that word is replaced by $\overset{>}{\text{IN}}$.

In $\underline{3}$ the space of a 3rd (G to E♭) is filled in with a PT. The E♭ is then prolonged with a DN, whose second and third notes are dissonant. Again a skip is involved with a dissonance, but under the guidance of the surrounding consonances. $\underline{4-5}$ repeat the music of $\underline{2-3}$, but are centered around C minor rather than E♭ major. The dissonances are of the same kind as in the previous two measures, but the leap to the $\overset{>}{\text{IN}}$ is more striking since it is now a skip of a tritone (D to A♭).

The melodic figure SP is a way of gracing the E♭ in $\underline{7}$. The passing note itself is different from the ones we saw earlier. We must realize that the strong-weak relationship operates on many levels. Within a measure there may be not only strong and weak beats, but also strong and weak parts of a beat. The third beat in $\underline{7}$ is subdivided into eighth notes, the second of which is divided in turn into sixteenth notes. Comparing the last two sixteenth notes in the bar, the first is stronger than the second. Thus we hear a (relatively) accented PT, abbreviated $\overset{>}{\text{PT}}$.

Among many points of interest in this piece, $\underline{9}$ has particular relevance. The skip of a 6th in the original is embellished, after the opening G has its own NT, with a florid passage that fills in that large interval with PTs and NTs. The original had a D at the end of the measure, a dissonant AN (anticipation) of the consonant D that is to come. In the elaborated version, the D shrinks to a sixteenth note, but its role is the same, an AN.

In $\underline{25}$, the C on the second half of the second beat in the original, itself a dissonant PT, is elaborated by a NT that is relatively accented, a $\overset{>}{\text{NT}}$.

This completes the repertory of simple dissonant techniques. However, the resolution of SUS dissonances is elaborated in a new way. Simple examples of such resolutions are to be found even in the original melody. In $\underline{16}$, the suspended F steps up to G before resolving to E♭, and the same embellishment is heard in the next measure. The elaborated version of $\underline{17}$ shows how a decorative note may itself be enlarged. The F, in fact, is replaced by G and C, outlining a triad, and followed by the AN D. $\underline{18-19}$ show a S embellishing the resolution of a SUS in a melodic formula familiar to anyone who has heard Baroque music.

For study

Compare the *Sarabande,* $\boxed{81}$, with its *Double* (variation). Specifically, what notes are added as elaboration, and what is the function of each?

37

Four Notes against One; Two Parts

SUMMARY OF DISSONANT TECHNIQUES
Available dissonances include all the procedures of tonal music in diatonic form, namely:

passing tones, both PT and $\overset{>}{\text{PT}}$;
neighbor tones, both NT, $\overset{>}{\text{NT}}$, IN, and $\overset{>}{\text{IN}}$;
DN, the four-note group;
SUS, which may be embellished by step or skip;
AN, on a weak beat preceding the same note as consonance.

Exercise

In order to see clearly the relationship between the embellishing notes and those being embellished, your first exercises in four notes against one are themselves based on exercises in note-against-note consonance. The four notes either elaborate one whole note or connect two whole notes of the original counterpoint. All dissonant techniques may be used, although SUSs are not very effective in small note values. ANs should be saved for the end of the exercise. Because of the large number of notes in a line the counterpoint will have to change direction several times. The more these changes can be made at such significant places as high and low points, the better the melodic shape will be.

☞ Worksheet 16

Exercise

Throw away the crutch. Write four notes against a *cantus firmus* of your choice.

38

Suspensions against a Moving Bass

One texture that is typical of Baroque and early Classic music consists of two upper voices, sometimes equal in range and sometimes merely close together, accompanied by a *continuo*. The inner voices are implied by the figured bass, which is explained on page 82. Two examples are the Purcell duet, 58, and the Corelli movement, 89. In both, the quarter note is the beat. The particular charm of the latter work lies in large part in the way the upper voices move in and out of SUS dissonances with four attacks to the measure, while the bass moves in eighth notes. Other pieces that use the same technique include another Purcell duet, *Lost Is My Quiet*, the opening of Pergolesi's *Stabat Mater*, and, in a keyboard translation, the *Prelude No. 24* from Bach's *Well-Tempered Clavier*, I.

of the upper voices may move through dissonant relationships with the bass. Before doing this exercise study 89 and show the intervallic relationships between the top two voices by writing the numbers that indicate their relationships. Mark all SUS usages.

Illustration

Exercise

Write three parts simultaneously, without *cantus firmus*. The two upper lines are equal voices or soprano and alto. Both move in half notes, but one starts with a quarter rest and remains one beat behind the other. The bass moves in eighth notes. Use as many SUSs as possible between the two upper lines, which may cross freely. Any or both

68

39

The Expansion of Lines in Musical Space

WHAT IS MUSICAL SPACE? We use the term as an analogy, comparing the distance from the highest to the lowest notes of a piece with, for instance, the space available to a painter using a canvas. Although the space is continuous, we may divide it approximately into segments, which we call registers. In some music, the way in which the notes are deployed in the various registers is of great importance. In the Renaissance choral pieces studied earlier, musical space was filled in a rather consistent and homogeneous way. Register change, for example, played little part in the compositional process. Starting with the development of instrumental idioms in the seventeenth century, it became possible for composers to use musical space more freely.

THE S.A.T.B. CONCEPT The simplest use of musical space may be found by following the ranges of the human voice. Through the sixteenth century, each line kept pretty much within its own territory, with a certain amount of voice crossing. The limitations of the human voice literally were the spatial limitations of the music. Nor did this state of affairs change quickly or die out entirely during the tonal period.

As long as the S.A.T.B. format is used, it is difficult for a single line to get from one register to another. In this we find one of the reasons that skips were not very useful in music based on the human voice and its natural registers. Skips are indeed useful in changing the register of a melody, but that function can also be performed by a long stepwise motion.

BEYOND THE S.A.T.B. CONCEPT Now examine the melody of 80. It is for keyboard; thus it is not limited by vocal ranges. Within the first four measures it covers two full octaves. This spread comprises both soprano and alto registers. The left-hand part does not have as wide a range, but it does cover a 9th in the first four measures. In some way, all four voices have been represented, even though we hear only two notes at any one time. Because of that, when we hear three notes at once in the second half of the piece, we find it a logical continuation of the music of the first half.

The sketch of the tonal structure (below) shows the soprano and bass. Unlike previous sketches, this one shows all structural notes in the main

(a) Sketch: first 8 measures of 80

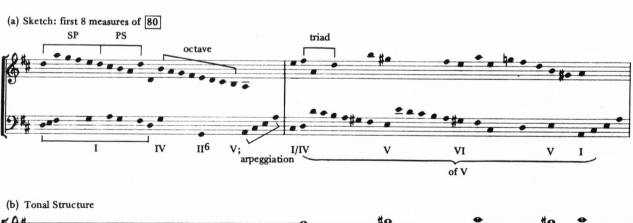

(b) Tonal Structure

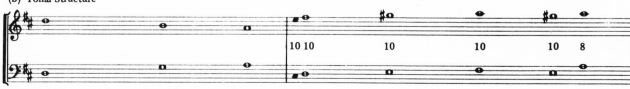

registers, and movement out of those registers is taken as an aspect of elaboration. Comparison of the sketch with the music shows that the melody moved down to the alto register in 3 and 4. How did it get there? By means of the scale passage in eighth notes. How was the soprano register regained? Simply by a large skip, as large as an octave and a half. The right-hand part seems to be keeping both the top voices going at almost the same time. This impression is confirmed at the cadence. After the soprano has finished the tune in 7, the alto reiterates the last 7–8 move. The two registers are connected this time by arpeggiation, involving more skips.

MELODY AND TOP LINE It is necessary to distinguish between the melody and the top line or soprano line. The melody is the tune, which may be in any register or may move through any number of registers. The top line is the group of structural notes that controls the upper dimension of the polyphony. It is not necessarily the highest note heard, first, because its notes may descend momentarily into an inner voice and, second, because notes from an inner voice may be transposed up an octave and sound higher than the top line.

POLYPHONIC MELODY How many voices are heard in 84? Only one note is heard at any given moment. The ear, however, connects not only the successive notes but also others, separated in time but linked by belonging to a particular register. The outer voices are the easiest to follow. The SUS between top and bottom lines in 7 and 8 are unmistakable, as are the parallel 10ths in 9 and 10. In every measure, in fact, you hear the implication of two or more voices, whose notes are heard successively rather than simultaneously. The melody of this and many similar pieces is a polyphonic melody. The same triad that binds the notes together when they are heard simultaneously also acts as a unifying force when the notes are heard one after the other, or even when separated by other notes.

POLYPHONIC MELODY IN A FOUR-PART TEXTURE The Handel concerto movement 91 is written for four-part string orchestra. Compare the use of musical space with that of a four-part Renaissance choral piece. In the earlier piece the melody and the top line would have been identical. But there is quite a difference between a soprano part and Handel's first-violin part. Let us accept the first sound as defining the center of each instrument's register. The second note in the melody moves immediately into the second violin's range,

and that instrument is constrained to double the viola's note to make room for the melody. Thereafter the first-violin part traces two lines of thought. One is A, prolonged by reiteration until it moves to G$\sharp$ at the open-ended cadence. The other involves notes from both the second violin and the viola parts, some heard an octave higher.

At the start of the second phrase the first violin climbs an octave and a 6th simply by starting with the note the second violin has just left and moving up a triad that at first seems like A minor but turns into C major. The type of motion seen in the opening measures continues throughout the piece. The melody uses many skips to delineate more than one strand of thought, sometimes dipping into the second-violin area, sometimes, as in 7, keeping two levels going at once by moving back and forth between them.

COMPARISON OF CHORUS AND KEYBOARD How differently musical space was used in choral style as compared to keyboard style may be seen in comparing the chanson by Lasso, 47, with a keyboard transcription made only a few years later by Peter Philips, 78. Such transcriptions were fairly common in the sixteenth and seventeenth centuries. They made it possible for the amateur who could play a keyboard instrument passably to enjoy a wide range of madrigals and chansons, playing them at home for his own pleasure.

The most obvious feature of the keyboard version is that the sustained notes of the original have been turned into figuration in much the same manner that we turned the whole notes of note-against-note counterpoint into four against one. NT, PT, SP, and arpeggiation are used abundantly. But that does not tell the whole story. A new dimension is added when, as in 13, the melody moves through the range of both soprano and alto, accompanied in 10ths by another voice that moves through the ranges of tenor and bass.

Another new device is *inversion*. The step F–G in the bass, 7, becomes a 7th when the G is displaced down an octave. The flow of sixteenth notes that moves up to balance the downward skip carries through bass, tenor, and alto ranges and binds them together. The sixteenth notes persist in one voice or another for many measures, and when they stop they are replaced by continuous eighth notes, then triplets, then more sixteenths. All these move freely from one register to another, creating the kind of texture we associate with keyboard instruments and making a fascinating "translation" of the choral piece into instrumental terms. In this translation, the expansion of lines in musical space is a crucial element.

ARPEGGIATION In studying melody we learned that one way to elaborate a main melody note is to build a triad on that note. Later we saw the triad used as a simultaneity, also extending the control of a central note, the root. When the notes of a chord are heard in succession rather than simultaneously we speak of *arpeggiation*. It probably originated at the keyboard and in lute music. Arpeggiation is one of the common techniques of instrumental music.

The scale as elaboration

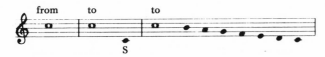

COMPOSITIONAL USAGE OF REGISTER
The variations on a gavotte by Rameau, 60, show the expansion of lines in space in a larger composition. While this piece has many fascinating aspects, we will concentrate on texture and register —that is, how the space is filled. These, plus rhythmic changes, are the significant differences between variations since the tonal structure of all is identical.

The first phrase of the theme sets forth the middle register in three and four parts. The second phrase expands the range only slightly. We might expect the third to be similar to the first; instead, it moves up a surprising octave, thus opening a new register and leading the theme to an ending that is higher than its beginning. We should be alert to the possibility that variations may or may not conclude with the higher A in the melody.

In the first variation (called *double*) the bass and soprano, originally an octave apart, are compressed into a 3rd. Rameau takes C as the first structural note of the soprano and omits the ascending A–B. Notes that were in the inner voice form the basis of the sixteenth-note melody, which ranges over an octave in the first four measures. The bass picks up the lower A and elaborates it into an arpeggiation that adds another octave. The moving part travels down to middle C at the second ending, and again the bass takes the concluding note of the upper part and spreads it into an arpeggiation, this time starting an accompaniment figure that will occupy the lower register for the middle of the variation. At the end of the second phrase, the sixteenth-note motion descends to its lowest point. This, in turn, sets up the possibility of the third phrase starting on high C, but in four measures it is back below middle C once more. Here is a line that truly covers all registers. Interestingly enough, it finally comes

to rest in what one might call the tonic register, abandoning the high A of the theme.

Compare, in 60, the first measure of the piece with the first measure of the second variation (*double*).

In the second variation the sixteenth-note motion is heard in the bass throughout. In the first four measures, each of the original bass notes is elaborated into a scale. We saw that a scale may be used to prolong a structural note, just as a triad may. The scale carries the central note from one register to another, extending its control much as octaves in the left hand might have done. But not all the sixteenth notes make up scales. One measure, 5, varies the texture by expressing two lines, and another, next to the last, uses NTs to prolong the structural notes.

The third variation begins with a different texture. The moving part is now in the middle voice, with the melody, almost like a *cantus firmus,* in the upper register and the bass in arpeggiated octaves. In the first phrase, the moving part is based on the moving part of the first variation. From then on it goes its own way. By the third phrase the sixteenth-note motion has affected the upper part, and the duet between soprano and alto gains momentum toward the end of the variation.

Alternating notes and arpeggiation characterize the fourth and quietest variation. For the first time, the third phrase does not reach out for the high register. The way in which the entire variation is limited to the middle register contributes to its intimate character. The use of musical space here is an important factor in making this section seem like the calm center of the entire piece.

By contrast, an arpeggiated figure that runs through all registers permeates the fifth variation. The top line is partly hidden by inner-voice notes flung up an octave on the third sixteenth note of the first three measures, a procedure that is used again in later measures. The low register is also heard in several measures, and in two places low C and high C are heard together. Indeed, all registers are in play in this variation.

The sixth variation makes a pair with the fifth. The figuration previously heard in the right hand now is played by the left. The texture of the right hand part is thickened into three notes to make this final variation the most powerful one.

Despite similarities between pairs of variations, no two are alike. The differences are in the domain of texture, involving octave shifts, changing densities, and the expression of intervals on more than one level. These observations bear out what we saw in the comparison of a choral chanson with its keyboard transcription. Voice leading is as essential a part of one style as the other, but the means by which it is expressed are quite different, which spells out the distinction between the S.A.T.B. concept and instrumental idiom.

SPECIAL FUNCTION OF THE TRITONE As long as each line stayed in one register, the melodic tritone, either as an augmented 4th or a diminished 5th, was avoided. The reason may be clear now. The tritone splits a line into two components, giving it polyphonic implications. We now can see how those implications were put to use in a polyphonic melody.

At the beginning of ⟦85⟧ we hear G♯ and E as part of the I chord. In ⟦4⟧ we hear the same two pitches in the same chord, but the major 3rd of the opening has changed into a minor 6th. What happened in the melody to carry the ear through the inversion? Was it the scale passage in ⟦3⟧? But that scale is incomplete, for it has in it the leap of an augmented 4th—which is precisely the point at which the inversion takes place. The D♯ moves through the octave and takes the upper position, E, while the A of the tritone pulls down to the G♯. Any large skip may suggest the twofold nature of a melodic line, but the tritone is particularly strong in that role.

☞ Worksheet 17

40

Pieces Built on Bass Patterns

CHACONNE AND PASSACAGLIA An immediate application of the techniques just studied in the preceding section may be seen in a number of pieces that are built on repeated patterns. Such pieces may be considered to be continuous variations. There are two types: those in which a bass line is reiterated, and those in which a chord progression is the repeated element. The term *passacaglia* has been applied to the first type of variation, the term *chaconne* to the second. But composers did not use those terms consistently. Since a repeated chord pattern is also likely to involve a repeated bass pattern the distinction is not always clear. The English term *ground bass* for a repeated bass pattern is useful, and its application to such pieces as ⟦57⟧ and ⟦58⟧ is clear.

The possibilities of constructing a piece on a repeated bass pattern are explored in a fairly straightforward way in ⟦57⟧, which includes the first six of the piece's twenty-two variations. One way to study this piece is to make a reduction (see right), which exposes the basic counterpoint. Then we may examine the way in which each variation extends the structural notes into the available musical space.

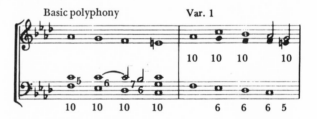

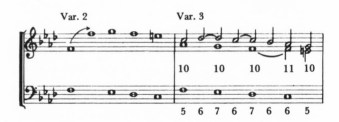

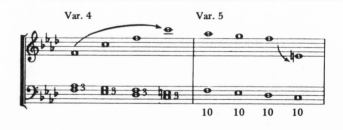

Var. 6

10   10   10   10   10   10

Since almost all of the eight-measure variations consist of four measures played twice, a feature that does little to enhance the variety of the piece, the sketch of each variation shows only the first half of each, with the exception of the sixth variation.

Studying the sketch, we note that parallel motion between the outer voices predominates. Returning to the piece, observe how that framework of parallel motion is elaborated. In 2 , the expressive octave leap followed by two downward skips is the way in which the melody wraps itself around the structural G, then gets across the bar line with contrary motion. The second variation begins by opening up the higher octave. The move expands the range of the piece and is itself interesting, bringing with it a change of texture as we hear imitation in the upper voices. The same 10ths that were the basis of the theme are heard in the third variation between the inner voice and the bass, while top line and bass alternate 6ths and 7ths. The 10ths are then reduced to 3rds in the fourth variation. The top line fills a large space, two octaves, moving up as the lower parts move down.

Having found its way to the higher register, the melody in variation five becomes a polyphonic one, taking over both soprano and alto at the same time. The inner voice here is little but a filler. The rhythmic intensification that began in the fifth variation continues into the sixth, whose second half, for once, is not a carbon copy of the first half. While the SUSs of the third variation are transferred to the inner voice, the upper voice begins the parallel 10ths with the bass in its lower octave, then switches at the third note to the higher register. In the second half of the variation, the sixteenth-note activity generates an inner voice. The two levels of the polyphonic melody are separated explicitly at the end by the tritone. To resolve the tritone, heard melodically, two simultaneous sounds are needed. The cadence ends not only the sixth variation but also the first large section of the *Chaconne*.

An example of a ground bass in a trio texture is 58 The bass is not as simple as the piece previously studied, being an elaborated version of

Literal repetition of the pattern fills the first half of the piece with alternations of tonic and dominant chords, a way of emphasizing the tonic that we refer to as a *harmonic prolongation* (see page 77). The top voices are disposed in varying ways, now imitating each other, now singing together. The second ending has a four-note transition to A major, whose regime begins in the middle of 15 (second ending). The pattern is heard twice in A, after which another transition brings the tonal focus to VI. After a brief sojourn in that area, half a measure is all Purcell needs to regain the tonic. The melodic material is all rather similar, and the return of the tonic does not bring any repetition of the opening tune. An interesting point about this piece is the way in which the composer avoids the monotonous regularity which is the pitfall of continuous variation forms. The bass pattern ends every two measures, but the upper voices overlap and maintain the continuity without a break; the single exception is the large punctuation mark at the end of the first half of the piece.

For further study

Listen to two pieces built on a chromatic descent from tonic to dominant—Purcell's *When I Am Laid in Earth* from *Dido and Aeneas,* and the *Crucifixus* from Bach's *Mass in B Minor.* A different, more elaborate bass pattern may be heard in Bach's *Passacaglia in C Minor* for organ.

Exercise

Continue the elaborative studies begun on Worksheet 17. Now only a bass pattern is given. Use each bass pattern as the ground bass of a short set of variations.

For each bass pattern

1. write a soprano line in note-against-note consonance;
2. write an inner voice, so that the basic polyphony is in three parts;
3. expand the basic polyphony into variations, using the techniques of Worksheet 17.

(b) basic polyphony in three parts

Illustrations

(a) soprano line with ground bass

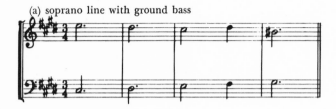

(c) sample variation

41

Pieces Built on Chord Patterns

Continuous variations based on chord patterns are similar in many ways to those built on bass patterns. A comparison of a piece that Handel called *Passacaille*, 59, with ground-bass pieces shows that the structural notes of the bass are found in every variation. In Handel's piece these notes are connected with PTs, elaborated with NTs and Ss, displaced in register, and even replaced when other inversions of certain chords replace the original chord positions. Nevertheless, these notes remain the pillars of the bass part. The following reduction shows the basic pitch material of the piece:

The entire piece should be analyzed for techniques of elaboration, using the reduction as a guide. The following observations are limited to a few salient points:

The second note in the bass is alternately E♭ or C. The chord over the bass note is either IV⁶ or IV. Both serve the same purpose.

The approach to the dominant, in the theme, uses II⁶, breaking the progression of 5ths in the bass. Handel probably wanted to avoid the tritone simultaneity between E♭ and A that would have resulted from the use of II. In those variations where E♭ is not heard at this point, the bass descends to A.

An overview of the piece shows that within the fifteen variations there are various groupings.

Outline of [59]

variation	description
1	Theme, whose basic elements are the chords and bass line, while the melody is simply elaborative.
2–4	A line made of the outlined triad followed by the same triad filled in with PTs appears in the top, the bottom, then the top again, now with each eighth note set with a counterpoint.
5–6	A pair; triplet figuration in the top, then the bottom.
7	The dotted rhythm of the opening is heard in a scale.
8–9	A pair; the scale is now in sixteenth notes, making the by-now customary move from the upper to the lower register.
10	The sixteenth notes move in a polyphonic line reminiscent of violin or organ music.
11–12	The same kind of figuration in both variations of this pair, in the same register.
13–15	The final group. This time, the characteristic figuration is introduced in the lower part, then moves to the upper, and then fills both registers.

The intervals expressed as simultaneities in the theme are soon broken into polyphonic melodies, one of the chief techniques of variation used in this piece. Inversion is called into action at once, the opening 3rd of the piece appearing in the second variation as a (filled-in) 6th.

Unexpectedly, chromatic voice leading appears in the eleventh and twelfth variations. The top replaces the INs of the original with chromatic PTs. The bass accompanies this with parallel 6ths and one diminished 7th, abandoning the motion in 5ths. The three upper notes of the right-hand part in variation 11 are recombined to make the continuation into the next variation, the chromatic line moving to an inner voice as a result.

The brilliant ending is made by combining the two preceding variations to achieve maximum activity. This was foreshadowed in the other group of three variations, 2, 3, and 4.

For further study

The epitome of Baroque variation technique is Bach's *Goldberg Variations*. Like the Handel *Pas-*

sacaille, these pieces are built on a bass pattern. While they sound remarkably good on the piano, the original harpsichord version does present the piece as the composer heard it. Another good follow-up to the Handel *Passacaille* is the *Thirty-two Variations in C Minor* for piano by Beethoven. The last movement of Brahms's *Fourth Symphony* is built on a line that is heard by turns in upper and lower parts. A useful discussion of continuous variations, including both types introduced here, is in chapter 7 of Douglass Green's *Form in Tonal Music*.

Exercise

Three progressions are given below. Each may serve as the basis for a short set of variations. Study the bass-soprano framework before starting to work out the elaborations. The progressions may be put in a more melodious form to serve as themes or they may be used as they stand.

(a)

(b)

(c)

75

42

Pieces Built on Repetition of Short Sections

The *Fitzwilliam Virginal Book,* our largest single source of Elizabethan keyboard music, includes many pieces made up of sections, each of which contains one phrase and its varied repetition. Such a piece is the *Pavana* by William Byrd, 61. Each of the three phrases is four measures long in its initial version; the second and third phrases are somewhat longer in the repeated form. Examination of the two statements of each phrase in detail shows the repertory of elaborative devices that Byrd put into play in this piece, combining ornate brilliance with expressivity. The composer, like many of his English contemporaries, makes striking use of mode mixture. F and F♯ contradict each other frequently; the same is true of B and B♭. Points of imitation enrich the texture in the repeated phrases. An interesting detail: the line that runs in sixteenth notes from the upper into the middle register in the conclusion of the first section returns at the very end of the piece, tying together the two sections in the listener's mind. Many aspects of the S.A.T.B. format remain in this music, yet the new possibilities of the keyboard make their presence felt unmistakably.

43

The Expansion of Chords in Musical Time

RENAISSANCE AND BAROQUE One of the great watersheds of music history is the beginning of the seventeenth century. While the human voice never lost its important position, the center of musical thought shifted from voices to instruments, the keyboard in particular. One of the new resources consisted of longer and more varied chord prolongation. In earlier music, it was more or less assumed that the chords in a piece would change regularly on every beat. Those chords were grouped together in contrapuntal prolongations or in contrapuntal motions from one point to another, always allowing for the harmonic motion that gave the cadence its meaning. But keyboard composers began to find new ways of spreading out one chord over a longer period of time, thus creating a method of contrasting slow and fast rates of chord change. In time, this proved to be an effective way of giving expression to varying moods and also of building larger musical forms. Composers began to understand that more rapid chord changes were effective in the middle of a piece, while fewer chord changes made for the stability they were seeking at the beginning and at the end. It might be observed that at the very time that Champlain and Hudson were exploring the New World, and while Newton, Galileo, and Kepler were exploring an uncharted universe of knowledge, composers such as Monteverdi, Frescobaldi, and Schütz were exploring new ways in which to embody human emotions and communicate them in sounds.

Pachelbel's *Toccata,* [63], opens with a gesture that could only have originated at the keyboard, and must have been improvised many times before being written down. Indeed, if the term *toccata* means anything in seventeenth-century music, it means "a written-out improvisation, often with changing tempos and a continuous phrase structure in each section." The opening measure takes us from the highest to the lowest registers, sketching out the musical space in which the entire composition is to move. The sustained E in the pedal of the organ is an example of a *pedal point,* the word *point* meaning "note," just as it does in *counterpoint.* The tonic is prolonged, in all, for six and one-half measures. Over the pedal point, soprano and tenor descend in parallel 10ths, while the middle voice prolongs E with NTs. Each of the four voices uses a different durational value. The initial prolongation of the tonic gives a sense of stability, after which the music is ready to move more actively. Beginning with 7, the rate of chord change speeds up, being mostly two to the measure. And when the bass arrives at the dominant in 20 and stays there for two and one-half measures, the musical meaning is unmistakable: this is the dominant that points to the final tonic. The dominant pedal point, although shorter than the tonic pedal point that started the piece, answers it even while it sets up the concluding tonic. That, in turn, is prolonged for the last three measures of the toccata. While the rate of chord change is largely in terms of half notes, the figuration moves much more rapidly, and the note values, as a result, range from tied whole notes to thirty-second notes.

Quite different in mood is the toccata by Frescobaldi, [64], in the Phrygian mode. While the prolongations are less obvious than in the Pachelbel, the music takes advantage of the possibilities of varying the rate of chord change. Thus the opening E lasts one full measure; the D triad, major and minor, half a measure; a D-major triad persists through 4 and 5. Presently we hear more motion within chords, but no great change in the chord rhythm. The final E occupies the last two measures, embellished with a NT that generates a particularly lovely SUS. We realize only gradually that this is the end, just as with many Phrygian cadences. The leading tone from above, F–E, replaces the 7–8 that we expect in all other modes. The piece as a whole is a marvelous example of the sense of adventure that abounds in early seventeenth-century music. What it may lack in tonal unity is more than made up for in sheer imagination.

Contrapuntal prolongations of various lengths, using musical space in a number of ways, open many Baroque pieces. Compare the initial gestures of [61], [80], [84], [85], and [92]. What techniques are used to elaborate the tonic triad? How long does each prolongation last? How does each prolongation move through musical space?

HARMONIC PROLONGATION [87] begins with four and one-half measures of rapidly moving figuration in which tonic and dominant alternate. The effect is to emphasize D as tonic. The motion circles around the D, and thus prolongs it. This movement from V to I is not a cadence, for a cadence ends a phrase. Since it is a prolongation of the tonic, and since the V–I move is what we have called the harmonic progression, this motion is known as a harmonic prolongation.

[88] begins with the same prolongation, spread over three measures. [90A] also begins with a harmonic prolongation, seven measures long, elaborated with arpeggiation in the bass, but still clearly I–V–I. [92] has a particularly interesting beginning, combining harmonic movement with a series of short contrapuntal elaborations to make one large statement of the tonic that takes five very busy measures. When this music recurs during the course of the piece it serves as a refrain or ritornello; against its relative stability, other parts of the piece offer their contrasting activity.

The fact that these examples of harmonic prolongation come from the late Baroque is a clue to the pace at which prolongation techniques developed. The possibilities in harmonic prolongation for dramatic effect and for building stable areas that would be needed in large-scale musical forms were not fully realized until the latter part of the eighteenth century. Then Haydn developed ways to make the harmonic prolongation work for him in longer pieces, a lesson that was quickly learned by Mozart and later by Beethoven.

44

Long-Range Melodic Connections

The increased ability to project one sound through time, developed in the Baroque, has many implications. One of the most interesting is the way in which Bach (and very few others) was able to spin out long melodic lines that make a unified impression in spite of their length and complexity. Since each is a case in itself, we will make only one general statement about them: the connections are not only between successive notes in the melody, but also between notes farther away, almost always a step apart.

Rather than start with a finished melody, we will synthesize a melody as the projection of a single note, using the elaborative processes we have studied. The third degree of the scale is probably the favorite melodic note in the major mode. It is represented by example (a), right. Example (b) is the first elaboration, the familiar SP. Example (c) opens up new space with an octave leap, making room in which the melody can now maneuver. In example (d), the downward motion is balanced by a skip up to B, and the 9th from B down to A is divided into two 5ths. The low A suggests a second voice, possibly part of a polyphonic melody. This is followed up in example (e) with the A's NT, B, and the 5ths are divided into 3rds. Finally, in example (f), NTs, PTs, and ANs are used to flesh out the melody—that of the Bach *Air,* 86 .

This is not to imply that Bach synthesized the melody in the manner outlined. He almost certainly composed it together with all the other parts, conceiving of the piece as a whole in which the melody played the decisive, but not the only, part. Bach had used the basic motions of tonal polyphony many times over, and had the resources with which to express them in what seems to us to be an infinite number of ways. Although Bach

would not have discussed what he was doing in twentieth-century terms, of course, he had inherited not only a repertory of melodic and chordal usages, but also the framework in which those usages were deployed, the archetypes of tonal music.

The understanding of long-range melodic connections depends on our being able to see specific ways in which one note can be projected through time. This is true even in folk songs and popular tunes. Bach carried this idea further than most, but the principles he used are, still, neighboring motion, passing motion, and skips that open up large areas of musical space.

45

A Small Repertory of Polyphonic Motions

Certain bass-soprano motions occur so frequently in music that they may easily be learned. These specifics can be memorized, which will make it easier to recognize them in a piece and to use them in tonal composition. The best way to express such notions is not in terms of chord vocabulary, but rather as interval successions.

BASS MOTION IN 5THS The pattern of descending 5ths (ascending 4ths) is a stand-by of Baroque and early Classic music. If the motion starts with the tonic chord, the soprano often starts with the fifth of that triad. The interval between the bass and soprano is alternately 5th–10th, 5th–10th, resulting in contrary motion.

An example is the opening phrase of 81A. Observe, in 3, that the bass balks at skipping the diminished 5th from 6 to 2, replacing 2 with 4. Thus it skips a 3rd rather than a tritone. The third chord from the end of the phrase, as a result, is not in root position, but in first inversion. Review the analysis of 59 on page 75, in which the same motions are found. The Vivaldi piece, 92, adds an element of dissonance to the motion in 5ths. Instead of placing triads squarely over each bass note, the composer sets up a chain of SUSs, as implied by the figure 7 under the bass part. The familiar progression now functions at a noticeably higher level of activity.

PARALLEL 10THS The framework of parallel 10ths between outer voices offers many possibilities, some of which we saw in the Pachelbel *Chaconne*, 57. A particularly imaginative realization is in the sarabande by Couperin, 82. Parallel 10ths between the outer voices are in the first phrase, 2–5; but the parallel lines may be concealed. A comparison of the sketch below with 9–16 reveals how the framework is elaborated in both time and space. The regularity of the progression is broken by octave displacement in the soprano's descent. The notes of the top line disappear into the inner register at the start of the phrase, but emerge clearly after the octave leap. The bass seems headed for an octave skip, too, but finally remains in one register.

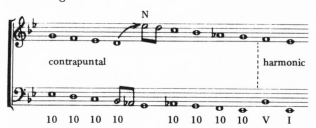

PARALLEL 6THS Parallel 6ths, usually implying parallel first-inversion triads, may be used to prolong a structural chord or to connect structural chords. An example is in the Handel aria, 93. Starting on the last beat of 19 the line rises steadily, supported by a series of rising $\frac{6}{3}$ triads. The melody spells out the triads as it goes. The top line of the melody moves in parallel 10ths with the bass. An interesting detail: the expected high G♯ in 21 is not heard, but the lower G♯ is. The effect is to turn the line around and prepare for the final cadence.

5THS AND 6THS The alternation of 5ths and 6ths may provide a polyphonic framework for musical motion. Let us imagine:

But instead of the repeated note in the bass, add a chromatic PT by writing a sharp before both the second G and the second A. Now compare with 86, 13–14.

6THS AND 7THS In studying SUSs we learned that parallel 6ths could be elaborated by alternating them with 7ths as SUS dissonances. Such a motion can be expanded in time and space. A good example is in [57]. In the first variation, bass and soprano move in parallel 6ths. While the second variation returns to the parallel 10ths of the theme, the third builds on the 6ths of variation 2. But the D♭, which creates a 6th with the bass's F in 25, is carried across the bar line. The resulting SUS adds variety to the sound, which has been largely consonant up to this point. Another short chain of SUSs appears in the sixth variation, 49–52.

10THS AND 5THS A progression that occurs in Baroque, Classic, and Romantic music originates as a descending move alternating 10ths and 5ths. The bass line moves down a 4th and up a step, alternately. The top line is a descending scale. In simplest form:

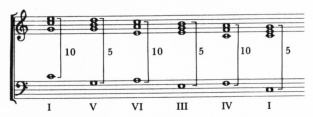

Comparing this with [81B], we see that Mattheson's melody moves in parallel 10ths with the bass. But this is possible only because that melody shares the alto's note at the end of each measure. The note the top line would have had in 1, if it had continued in stepwise motion, is D. The tenor takes that note, but delays it for half a beat in the hope of disguising the parallel 5ths with the bass.

The same succession, which also uses triads in root position, is found in a chaconne by Pachelbel (see below), in D major. The succession also begins *Prelude 21* in B♭ major in the first book of Bach's *Well-Tempered Clavier.*

If the second chord is heard in first inversion, the bass becomes a descending scale, and the original interval succession is lost. The chord progression, now using inversions, is I–V⁶–VI–II⁶–IV–I⁶ (or I). If the melody is made only of the top line, parallel 10ths result. But more often the melody is polyphonic. Examples include the gavotte from Bach's *French Suite No. 5,* the finale from the Mozart *Piano Quartet in G Minor* K. 478, the last movement of the *Piano Sonata* Op. 79 by Beethoven, and the *Étude* Op. 25 No. 9 by Chopin.

SEQUENCE When an interval succession is repeated on adjacent scale degrees, either higher or lower, there is a natural tendency to repeat the melodic material as well. Such repetition of a melodic motive is called a *sequence.* It is a rather simple kind of melodic activity, and is most useful when the composer wants to avoid complications in moving directly from one point to another. Conspicuous examples include [63], 14–16, and [92], 7–9. Some of the most interesting elaborations of archetypal polyphonic motions, however, are not sequential at all.

46

Some Free-Form Pieces

Unlike pieces with repeated patterns and clear phrase structures, certain works are relatively open in form. Phrase endings are deliberately blurred, and the continuity of the music is emphasized. Even the meter may not be too obvious, and tonal unity is not stressed.

TOCCATA Highly improvisational in spirit, the organ toccata eschews the dance and song prototypes so characteristic of much Baroque music. The Pachelbel toccata, 63, was discussed in terms of varying rates of chord change on page 77. As if to announce its character at the outset, the piece begins with the kind of gesture an organist might make as he sits down to improvise. It then settles down to a four-part texture not too far removed from the S.A.T.B. format. There is no statement of a tune, but rather a continuous unfolding of figuration. We might expect a cadence in 8, but it melts away as the expected D♯ becomes D. Although the bass moves 5–1, there is no sense of closure. Indeed, there is no strong punctuation mark in the piece until the end. 8–13 all begin with dissonances, maintaining the flow and allowing no pause. 14 arrives at V⁶, which proves to be a jumping-off point for a sequence built over a bass motion in 5ths. Imitation, using a motive sequentially, varies the texture but propels the piece on without any letup. The tonal movement avoids stability; the melody avoids periodicity; the texture changes frequently. The only point of repose is the final chord.

Given the fact that both are toccatas, the difference between the north German piece, 63, and the Italian, 64, is astonishing. Both works begin and end with tonic prolongations, and both maintain an unbroken continuity from beginning to end, but in character and mood they are quite unlike each other. The clearly directed tonal movement of the Pachelbel is nowhere in evidence in the earlier Italian piece. Instead there is an exploration of chromaticism in the literal sense, as color, together with a play of SUS dissonances that delights the ear at every turn. Wayward bits of imitation appear and disappear in no systematic way. The unexpected occurs time and again. All these factors make it difficult to believe that the piece is to be played in a steady tempo from beginning to end. Intensity of expression and subtlety of coloring mark this striking piece.

That there was a great tradition of organ playing and composing in France may come as a surprise to those who think of Baroque organ music as entirely German in origin. The *Plein Jeu* of de Grigny, 65, shows the solidity and imagination of the French school at a fairly advanced level. The work is not called a toccata, but it shares many of the characteristics of the two pieces discussed above. It is a continuous work, with an irregular phrase structure and an improvised quality. The title means "full organ" and the piece is meant to be played as the last movement of an organ Mass.

Plein Jeu is lightly divided into three phrases, but the emphasis, as in Frescobaldi's toccata, is on continuity rather than contrast. The first phrase goes to the middle of 8; the second, brief phrase continues to the middle of 12; the third phrase is the longest. Each is built on a descending line in the soprano. In the first phrase, the bass moves in elaborated parallel 10ths with the top line; in the other phrases the bass is in contrary motion to the top line for the most part. A good deal of the beauty of this music lies in the artful use of SUSs, which should be studied in detail.

RECITATIVE Baroque opera thrived on the format of recitative and aria. The closed form and clear phrase structure of the songlike air had as its foil the speechlike flow of the recitative, more like prose than poetry. Once again we see a kind of music that takes its shape from the way in which the words are spoken. Recitatives also serve to link two numbers tonally; they are apt to begin in a key close to the aria just concluded and move toward that of the piece to come.

The Handel recitative, 93, is a straightforward setting of a conversation, and it should move rather quickly. It begins on the V⁶ of A minor, and ends on a G♯-minor triad, which G♯ is taken as III of E major, the key of the aria. While the words of the agitated couple move swiftly, chord change proceeds much more slowly. The polarization of Baroque music in the outside voices is seen here in an extreme example; the inner voices, which would be realized by the *continuo* player, are entirely subordinate. The melody line is heightened speech, both in the rise and fall of pitch and in its rhythm. This recitative should not be sung in strict time. We would expect the singers to push forward or hold back according to the sense of the words. And a descending skip of a 3rd, as in the last measure, would be filled in with a PT, so that the last three notes of the vocal line would be B–A♯–G♯.

Operatic techniques found their way into cantata and oratorio, and Bach made much use of recitative and aria. 62 is a dialogue between a male and a female voice. There is no tempo marking, but the highly expressive nature of the music suggests a slow tempo. Bach did not limit himself to speechlike musical gestures, but varied those with more lyric sections on important words. Such a section is called an *arioso*. Again, a rhythmically free performance is needed to bring out the meaning of the words and to allow for the chromatic motions to be heard. It was the practice for the keyboard player to pause just before the cadence, as in 5 and 11, wait for the singer to finish the phrase, and then to play V–I.

47

Continuo Music

BACKGROUND In the seventeenth century, musical texture polarized at the extremes of the working range of sounds, emphasizing the soprano and bass and subordinating the inner parts. Composers came to favor a clearly etched melody supported by a more or less continuous bass. These two lines implied the choice of chords. To make the implication more specific, musicians gradually developed a way of writing figures under (sometimes over) the notes of the bass. This was a purely practical guide for the player, showing him at a glance what intervals were to be played over the bass. Since the intervals indicate pitch classes but not their placement, the player had to use his skill and imagination in making the added notes sound good together with the written notes. The keyboard performer whose job it was to realize—that is, "make real"—the figured or unfigured bass, would usually play the bass line with his left hand and improvise the chords according to the figures with his right hand.

Among other things, this means that we cannot always accept the score of a Baroque piece as the representation of the entire work. Many times there is no trace of the inner voices in the notes themselves but they are still very much a part of the music. Practice varies from one composer to another, and from one country to another. The score of the Telemann pieces, 90, is a mere skeleton, requiring an imaginative realization of the figured bass to sound as the composer intended. Works such as 88 and the recitative of 93 appear to be in two parts but actually are in three, four, or five, with the inner voices to be realized by the *continuo* player. The Vivaldi, 92, has but three written-out parts despite the many lines on the page, and realization of the bass is an essential part of the piece. Both the Handel concerto movement, 91, and the Bach air, 86, have four completely worked-out parts, and the *continuo* has few additional notes to add, simply enriching the sound with its doublings.

THE FIGURES Figures denote intervals from the bass. They do not indicate where the notes actually appear in terms of register, so that octaves will often be added to the figure. Nor do they tell the order in which the notes come in relation to the bass. The figure $\frac{6}{3}$, for example, may mean that the top voice has the 6th, or the 3rd, or even doubles the bass. The logic of the music comes not from any particular succession of chords, but from the voice leading.

Each symbol uses as few figures as are needed to distinguish one chord from another. Thus, all of the figures required to form the complete chord are not always seen. They must be known in advance. However, the abbreviations are used consistently.

symbol	meaning
no figure	$\frac{5}{3}$ position: the bass is the root of the chord
6	$\frac{6}{3}$ position: the bass is the third of the chord
$\frac{6}{4}$	$\frac{6}{4}$ position: the bass is the fifth of the chord
7 or $\frac{7}{5}$	complete seventh chord: the bass is the root of the chord
$\frac{6}{5}$	first inversion of a seventh chord: the bass is the third of the chord
$\frac{4}{3}$ or $\frac{6}{4}{3}$	second inversion of a seventh chord: the bass is the fifth of the chord
2 or $\frac{4}{2}$	third inversion of a seventh chord: the bass is the seventh of the chord
$\frac{5}{4}$	dissonance, usually a SUS: look ahead for the resolution
9	dissonance, usually a SUS: look ahead for the resolution

Use the notes of the diatonic scale, as indicated by the key signature, except where accidentals are marked in the figured bass. These appear as follows:

symbol	meaning
6̸ or 6♯ or 6+ (or any other interval)	sharpen—i.e., raise the 6th half a step
6♭ (or any other interval)	flatten—i.e., lower the 6th half a step
♯	sharpen the 3rd

If one or more notes following a figured-bass note is not figured, it probably is a PT or NT, and the chord in the right-hand part is held or repeated until the next figure. Sometimes the held chord is indicated by a horizontal line following the figure, but often it is not.

If there are no figures, the keyboard player must watch the melody part closely to decide what chords are implied, or at least suggested, by the two parts. An unfigured bass requires more imagination than a figured bass, and it also requires more knowledge of the style of the piece. At the same time, it offers more scope for improvisation.

Accompanists must fit their realizations to the nature of the melodies they are accompanying whether the bass is figured or not. Beginners probably will play block chords in three or four parts. With more experience they may learn to break up the chords into lines whose character matches that of the lines being accompanied.

For further study

If you play a keyboard instrument, more advanced work in realization can benefit both your study of harmony and counterpoint and your historical understanding—not to mention your skill as a performer. A valuable book from which to work is *Thoroughbass Method,* by Hermann Keller. It contains not only instructions and selections from the writings of Baroque musicians, but also many examples of *continuo* music in many styles.

Dance in the open air, oil painting by Nicolas Lancret (1690-1745). The famous ballerina, La Camargo, dances in a park surrounded by musicians and courtly admirers.

PART SIX
DISSONANT CHORDS

48

Diatonic Dissonance 3

BACKGROUND Throughout the Renaissance, composers explored the possibilities of dissonance by using dissonant notes to embellish or to connect consonant ones. The changes in musical thought that took place early in the seventeenth century, making the keyboard rather than the chorus the norm, resulted in greater attention paid to simultaneous sounds than to lines. Perhaps one reason is that it became possible for a single person to play many notes at once on an instrument, and to enjoy many-voiced music without requiring the help of other people. Composers became more conscious of chord vocabulary and sought ways to expand it. At the same time, the drive to gain increased expressivity in music that characterized the Baroque led musicians to seek chords with more color and tension. Consonant sounds serve such a purpose only in a limited way. Composers soon found that dissonant chords could be most effective in portraying the varied moods and feelings so essential in opera, in dramatizing the clash of solo and tutti in a concerto, or in expressing the religious feelings of the congregation in a chorale.

HOW DISSONANT CHORDS ARE DEVELOPED
The same techniques that were used to elaborate consonant chords are extended to "grow" dissonant chords. PTs and NTs are incorporated into the triad, which remains the normative sonority. The dissonant tones resolve as they did before. The example below shows three ways of elaborating a C-major triad. The first uses a PT, the second and third NTs. Combining the three, a dissonant contrapuntal chord is generated. The dissonances still have the same functions they always had. Just as each dissonance, used separately, may link two consonances, so does the dissonant chord link two consonant chords. The operations NT, PT, and SUS may be used not only with single notes, but also to generate dissonant chords.

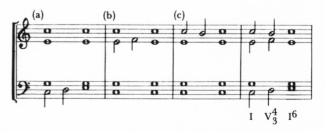

SUCCESSIVE DISSONANT CHORDS Most often, especially in Baroque and Classic music, a dissonant chord is surrounded by consonant chords which directly stabilize the active elements. But when composers want more continuous activity, they may string together a number of dissonant chords in succession. Perhaps the simplest way to do this is in a format that has two voices moving over a bass in such a way that as one voice resolves a SUS the other forms one. SUS and resolution are heard together, in different voices. The reduction (right) of 92, 6–9, shows the process in simplified form.

* from continuo part only

The same progression is found in 90A, 7–10, where the *continuo* player must realize the voices implied by the figured bass. Again, each dissonance resolves to a consonance, but as it does so a different voice brings in a new dissonance. The result is that a higher level of activity is maintained than would be possible using only consonant sounds.

49

The $\frac{6}{4}$ Position of the Triad

The $\frac{5}{3}$ and $\frac{6}{3}$ positions of the triad are stable, consonant sounds. The $\frac{6}{4}$ position is heard as unstable and dissonant due to the presence of a 4th between the bass and one of the other voices. We can understand its functions better if we see how the dissonant interval, the 4th, functions in each usage.

AS PT The opening phrase of 91 begins with a tonic chord prolonged through 1 to the middle of 2. In the course of its motion the bass proceeds from A down to D, passing through E on the fourth beat of 1. At that point we hear the notes of the A-minor triad—that is, after the suspended D in the first violins resolves to C. The intervals over the bass are a 6th and a 4th, and the chord is I_4^6. Here it is a passing chord, part of a contrapuntal prolongation. The dissonance of a 4th is heard in relation to the bass and is resolved at once. The I_4^6 has connected two consonant chords, IV⁶ and IV. When the same music is repeated, transposed to C major, in 4, the same PT in the bass generates the same passing $\frac{6}{4}$ chord. (We might observe that the Roman numeral I does describe the content of the chord—A–C–E—but not its function; it is hardly a tonic.)

The PT need not occur in the bass, and 63, 21, begins with a passing I_4^6 in which an inner voice comes from a 5th, passes through the 4th, and goes on to a 3rd. Here is a comparison of the two examples, showing only the basic voice leading:

A minor I_4^6

E minor $\begin{smallmatrix}5\\3\end{smallmatrix}$ $\begin{smallmatrix}6\\4\end{smallmatrix}$ $\begin{smallmatrix}5\\3\end{smallmatrix}$

V

AS NT Since a NT may involve a 4th, neighbor motion may generate the $\frac{6}{4}$ position of a triad. This is what occurs in 63, second half of 8 and first half of 9. The NT is in the top line, which embellishes the main notes D♯–E–D. The B-major sound in 8 leads to I_4^6. The 6th then goes on to a 5th while the 4th continues, extending the dissonance. The situation is much the same as the consonant 4th, for again it is the 7th between E and F♯ that seems stronger than the 4th between E and B. Interestingly enough, the melody does not go back to the D♯, as expected, but goes down to D, opening up what would have been a closed cadence and leading into the next part of the piece.

A DN, too, may play a role in generating a $^6_4$ chord. In 63 , starting from the last beat of 2 , we hear B–C–A–B in the melody. The familiar four-note group is over a pedal point which prolongs the tonic. That group is set with parallel 10ths in the tenor. The intervals over the bass are $^5_3$, $^6_4$, $^4_2$, $^5_3$. The two dissonant linear chords are part of the four-chord group prolonging the tonic, itself part of still larger tonic prolongation which runs from the beginning through 6 .

AS SUS   Where the first two phrases of 91 arrive at open-ended cadences on V (in I and in III), the third cadence is directed to V–I of III. In 9 , the bass reaches G, and above it we hear a 6th and a 4th in the violins. The 4th is prepared and subsequently resolved, functioning as a SUS dissonance in relation to the bass. This I$^6_4$, then, is part of the V–I cadence that ends the phrase. Again, the function is not accurately described by the Roman numeral since the chord is dominant and not tonic. Furthermore, the "root" is a dissonant tone that promptly resolves.

CADENTIAL I$^6_4$ The most frequent use of the I$^6_4$ is in the cadence. There it functions as a prolongation of the dominant. For this reason, the term *cadential I$^6_4$* is sometimes used. The term locates the chord but does not explain its origin as PT, NT, or SUS. While this usage was known as early as the Renaissance, it did not become a characteristic style trait until the Classic era. A clear example of the cadential I$^6_4$ may be found at the conclusion of 69A .

ANOTHER NOTATION OF THE I$^6_4$ Many theorists, dissatisfied with the notation I$^6_4$ for a chord whose function is dominant, use the Roman number V and show the intervals in the $^6_4$-position triad and whatever comes next within brackets. Thus, in 69A , 15 , the second and third beats would be described as V($^8_6{}^7_5$). In 79B , 9 , you can see how the figures of the bass part indicate the voice leading in the resolution of the $^6_4$-position triad. The same resolution is implied, though not written out, in the concluding cadence of 79C .

50

Seventh Chords in Root Position

HOW SEVENTH CHORDS ARE GENERATED By a seventh chord we mean a triad plus a 3rd, which results in the formation of a 7th from the bass. The same operations that gave us the $^6_4$ position of the triad generate all dissonant chords, including seventh chords. NTs and PTs are attached to the triad, retaining their functions as they create four-note chords. In Baroque music, the origin of seventh chords is fairly apparent. As later composers gained more mastery over all types of dissonant chords, those simultaneities took on more independent lives. In Classic and, even more, in Romantic music, dissonant chords rely less obviously on the consonances that surround them. But every dissonant chord in tonal music is an elaboration of a triad.

THE EVOLUTION OF A V⁷ The historical development of a seventh chord—in this case, the dominant seventh—is roughly paralleled by the successive cadences in 59 . The last measure of the theme shows a dominant triad, with C, a 7th from the bass, as a NT. That note is not mentioned in the top line of the first variation, but it is heard as a PT in the second, then echoed in the paired third variation. Again omitted in the fourth, it returns as a PT in the fifth and sixth variations. It is a PT in the seventh and eighth, and not heard in the next three variations. But in variation 13, in which the chords are expressed as arpeggiation, the top line sounds C against the D of the bass, making a clear statement of the V⁷. As the top line moves down into an inner voice in the fourteenth variation, the 7th is heard in the midst of the arpeggiation, but the chord is still very much V⁷. Having infiltrated the sound of the dominant seventh by linear means, Handel uses it directly in the last two variations, preceding it in the final variation by I$^6_4$, with the 4th as a SUS. Thus we observe the evolution of the seventh from a single decorative tone between consonant sounds to a component of a relatively independent dissonant chord.

TYPES OF SEVENTH CHORDS The term *seventh chord* includes major, minor, and diminished sevenths. In combining major and minor 3rds to make up four-note chords, we find many possibilities. Five common types are listed below. Reading up from the bass:

1. one M 3rd + two m 3rds = dominant seventh
2. three m 3rds = diminished seventh
3. two m 3rds + one M 3rd = half-diminished seventh
4. one m 3rd + one M 3rd + one m 3rd = minor seventh
5. one M 3rd + one m 3rd + one M 3rd = major seventh

RESOLUTION OF SEVENTH CHORDS The resolution of a seventh chord follows from the nature of its dissonant component. Since those notes originate and function as NT, PT, and SUS, their resolution will follow the natural pathways of those tendency tones. This holds true no matter what degree of the scale serves as root for the seventh chord. The same principles guide the resolution of I⁷, II⁷, III⁷, and the others.

The diatonic seventh chords in both major and minor are listed below. Under each write the Roman and Arabic numerals that describe them. Under the number write the type of chord, one of the five shown above. In the minor mode, mixture provides the leading tone in both V⁷ and VII⁷.

51

Seventh Chords in Inversion

Any of the four notes that comprise a seventh chord may be heard in the bass. Thus a seventh chord may appear in root position or in any of three inversions. Composers writing music do not actually spend their time inverting seventh chords (or triads either, for that matter). What happens in the flow of the music is that dissonant tones adhere to triads, resulting in a kind of contrapuntal chord which we call a seventh chord. Each inversion is described by figures that indicate the intervals from the bass. Under each chord position in the following list you find:

1. all the intervals that comprise the chord;
2. a shorter, abbreviated version.

	root position	first inversion	second inversion	third inversion
1.	7 5 3	6 5 3	6 4 3	6 4 2
2.	7	6 5	4 3	2

In writing about these chords and in figured-bass notation, we use the fewest numbers necessary to distinguish one position from any of the others. For example, since only the third inversion has a 2nd, the superscript figure ^{2} suffices to indicate that inversion.

SOME FUNCTIONS OF INVERSIONS A rich variety of dissonant chords becomes available when sevenths and their inversions are added to the chord vocabulary. Only a few are discussed here, but they illustrate the chief ways in which such chords may be used. The relationship between consonance and dissonance remains of paramount importance, and each dissonant chord is seen to be related to a consonant one.

The somberly expressive sarabande by Couperin, 82, begins with a I–V move that occupies four measures. IV is a stepping stone to the dominant. As the bass moves from C to F, it uses not E♭ but E, the leading tone of F. This chromatic note helps push the motion on to F. The chord over the E also drives toward IV, and we call that chord V$^6_5$ of IV. Such a chord is an applied dominant, discussed on page 103. The second four-measure group within the eight-measure phrase begins with V$^6_5$. Again, the leading tone in the bass is an active note, the chord above it active, dissonant.

Although the dissonant chords in the recitative 62 are quite chromatic, they are all clearly related to consonant chords. The understanding of this relationship is the first step toward learning how such sounds function. We should also be mindful of the expressive purpose of the music, as set forth by the words. Most of the dissonant chords accompany Fear's anguished plaint, while most of the consonances reinforce Hope's serene expression of faith. No sooner has the organ sounded the opening B-minor triad than the bass leaps a 4th to a dissonance and we hear the third inversion of V^7. The figure should include a sharp after the "4," as we learn from the voice part. Had the bass leaped a 5th to F♯, then passed stepwise down to the E, we would have seen the PT function of E quite readily. The sketch below shows how the explanatory consonance is bypassed, making a striking accompaniment to Fear's first outcry. The third chord is simply V^6 of IV (E); but then the figures show that the B of that chord moves to C. Figures can show voice leading, too. The chord D♯–F♯–A–C is a diminished-7th chord. All those notes are NTs to the upcoming E-minor triad. Since D♯, the root, is the leading tone to E, we speak of a leading-tone chord. As explained on page 83, 7♭ denotes not a flat, but a flattening of the 7th. In this case, C♯ is "flatted" to C♮. A move similar to that of 1 occurs in 4, where the bass again leaps to the seventh of a dominant-seventh chord in the last inversion, resolving, as usual, to a first-inversion triad as the seventh acts as a PT. The $^{7♭}_5{}_3$ of 6 is identical with the 7♭ of 3, but this time it precedes rather than follows the simpler form of E's dominant.

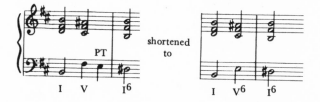

The main use of the inversions of V^7 is in tonic prolongations, of the kind used so frequently by Haydn, Mozart, and Beethoven. The discussion of those dissonant chords is continued as an aspect of phrase structure, in Book Two.

☞ Worksheet 18

89

The folk singer. Original drawing by E.A.D.

PART SEVEN
HARMONIZATION OF FOLK SONG AND CHANT

52

Settings for Chorus

HARMONIZATION OF MELODIES Much of what we have studied in the previous sections can now be applied to folk song and chant, enabling us to add another dimension to such melodies. True, addition is not always an improvement; some folk songs and chants are most convincing without any accompaniment. But the eloquence of folk song, particularly, has lured many a composer into trying to enrich a melody with a polyphonic setting. We can learn much about the relation between melody and polyphony if we examine some of these settings, and we can continue to develop writing skills by arranging melodies. This section is devoted to settings for chorus; the following section, to settings involving the use of instruments.

ANALYSIS OF THE MELODY One way to set a melody is to start with the first note, proceed to the second, and go through the entire tune on a note-by-note basis. It is barely possible that sheer intuition might triumph over such a worm's-eye view of the music and produce an admirable harmonization. A better approach might be to study the melody's structure, find its tonal organization and rhythmic shape, and work out an accompaniment to fit. Highly experienced musicians will perform some kind of analytic survey before harmonizing a melody, perhaps without even realizing what they are doing. Students would do well to think before they start writing.

In Quiet Night, 69A, has the four-phrase lay-

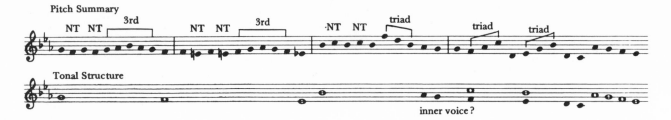

Tonal Structure

inner voice?

out of many Western European folk songs. The first and second phrases are antecedent and consequent, the third rises to the climax, and the fourth uses a melodic descent to arrive at the final tonic. The sketch above shows the tonal structure of the melody.

The melodic motions are the familiar ones, but some interesting details merit attention. After the two NTs, a 3rd is filled in ascending and descending. Repetition of the opening pattern a step lower is colored by the leading tone of 2, E♮, which makes the E♭ all the fresher when it arrives at the end of the second phrase. The third phrase begins with an inversion of the opening NT motion, and having twice reached up one step, it skips up to the highest note in the line. The descent is elaborated with triads that suggest a polyphonic melody. It reaches the tonic note twice, posing a small problem in setting. If the bass reaches the tonic together with the soprano's first E♭, the piece is over prematurely. But the bass meets the soprano's first E♭ with G, and only the second E♭ receives the confirmation of a tonic bass.

The rhythmic motive corresponds with the four-measure phrase, and thus is heard four times with only slight changes. Within that motive a four-note motive, one measure long, is an important element. Whether the tiny pauses in the last phrase are part of the original folk song or the work of Brahms, they add to the twilight character of the setting.

Tonal structure of the setting

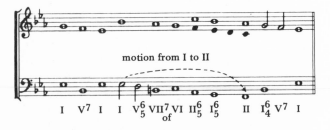

motion from I to II

I   V⁷ I   I   V⁶₅ VII⁷ VI II⁶₅ I⁶₅   II   I⁶₄ V⁷ I
                    of

Comparing sketch and music, we see that the structural chords are often on the second beat of the measure. Dissonant chords on the first beat give the piece a quiet but very definite sense of

motion. These are the most expressive chords in the piece, and they inflect and color the melodic line. The first underpins the NT, F, while the alto holds the tonic and the tenor matches the NT with one of its own, stolen from the parallel minor. The bass skips to a note that is consonant with all the upper ones to support them. The chord is II⁶₅. The tonic prolongation continues to the end of 3, on whose third beat a connecting II⁶ leads into the I⁶₄, derived from a PT, ushering in the dominant.

That dominant, in turn, is prolonged as the second phrase begins, so that the end of the first phrase and the beginning of the second blend smoothly. The neighbor chord in 5 moves over a repeated note in the bass, as the three upper voices sing NTs a half step below the chord tones. The sound is that of a diminished-seventh chord. At the corresponding place in the third phrase, 9, the NT of the melody finds NTs in all the other voices, creating a neighbor chord that sounds like a dominant seventh but does not function like one. In the interest of variety, the tonal direction is steered away from I to a substitute, VI, in 12. This is preceded by its own leading-tone chord, VII⁷ of VI. The disguised parallel 10ths lead to I⁶₄–V⁷–I, the cadence.

Looking back at 13 to the end, we see a more complex situation than is usual in simple melodic settings. If the polyphonic implications of the melody are to be realized fully, four voices are not sufficient, because the soprano cannot keep both melodic strands alive at the same time. Brahms's solution is to divide the altos. The first-alto part sustains the lower line of the polyphonic melody, which the sopranos also touch as they move through the triad. But then the melody descends into the inner voice for two notes. The D, an unresolved SUS in the second alto, is picked up by the soprano and resolved to C, reinforced by the alto. Then the soprano resumes the descent from 5, the alto returns to its normal place, and the tenor catches on to the C and carries it down to its destination in the final triad, in parallel 6ths with the soprano.

Although the setting does not stray from the

S.A.T.B. concept, the density and texture are varied several times. As early as 3 , the tenor takes over the role of the bass, and only three parts are heard for a measure. The dominant prolongation is built over an octave in the divided bass for two measures, then the echoing two measures bring the basses together again until the cadence. Only half the basses start the third phrase, and in the higher octave, lightening the color. As the crescendo reaches its peak all the basses join in. Divided altos provide the fifth voice in the concluding phrase, the sopranos moving to join and then separate from them, while the cadence gains weight from the basses' octave.

INTERPRETATION OF MELODY NOTES Is there only one possible interpretation of each melody note? Not at all. While the notes of highest structural importance are usually quite clear, the meaning of many others can be thought of in more than one way. Comparing the two settings of *O Maiden,* 69C and 70C , both agree that the first C is an inner-voice note (look at the inner voice that continues it), that F is part of the ascent, and that A is the first structural note. What about the G in 2 ? In the choral version it leads directly back to F and is a dissonant PT. But in the setting for voice and piano, G has a higher order of importance, with its own consonant bass, and the last F in the measure is a dissonant PT. By making the bass move to B♭ with the consonant G, Brahms turns the A into a SUS dissonance, where it had been a consonance in the choral setting. Within the large framework of the tonic and dominant, the composer still has many choices to make.

53

Settings with Instruments

In this section we consider both settings for keyboard instrument alone and for voice (or voices) and piano. We will be particularly interested in seeing how the lines and the chordal implications of the melodies are expanded into the additional dimensions that become available with the use of keyboard instruments.

Two seventeenth-century settings, 66 and 67 , may be considered together. The first uses a folk song, the second, a chant. The Sweelinck is the first variation of a set of six. No instrument is specified, and the piece may be played either on an organ or a harpsichord. The Frescobaldi is an organ piece meant to be played as part of a church service. Both treat the melody as a *cantus firmus,* although Sweelinck feels free to vary the tune slightly. Frescobaldi simply presents each note of the chant as a whole note, making the last one ten times as long as the others. Both melodies use B♭, but sound as much Dorian as minor. Sweelinck's setting colors the melody with mode mixture,

bringing in C♯, F♯, B, and B♭ as chromatic notes. Both vary the texture freely, but not much more than is usual in a late Renaissance madrigal or motet. Indeed, the S.A.T.B. concept is not far behind these pieces.

Both settings use imitation, but in different ways. Sweelinck anticipates upcoming phrases of the melody in the lower voices. In the upbeat to 6 the tenor begins and is imitated by the soprano two beats later. The figure of two sixteenth notes and an eighth, which starts in the soprano in 8 , is picked up by the alto and tenor. A new figure is heard in counterpoint to the melody in 10 , imitated at once a 5th above, later at the octave. In 15 , it is the bass that anticipates the melody, so that again the soprano seems to be imitating. Thus a number of different imitative devices have been used. But in Frescobaldi's setting, the figure characterized by three quarter notes as a large upbeat is heard in the first measure and permeates the entire piece. This adds a motivic interest to the chant setting. A subordinate motive, based on a dotted half note and two eighths, also makes its presence felt, and the two motives make for a highly unified work. In both settings, chord change proceeds at a fairly steady rate, much like in Renaissance music, but prolongations such as that of the A-minor triad in 66, 10–11, and that of the G-minor triad in 67, the last five measures (except for the final chord), testify to the developing potential of the new style.

Beethoven's arrangement of a Scottish tune 68 is quite elaborate, but the parts are easy to play, and it is intended chiefly for home performance by competent amateurs. The instrumental parts support and elaborate the voice parts and provide an introduction, connecting links, and a conclusion, thus placing the setting in a rather formal framework.

The sixteenth-note figurations in the instruments are worth studying in detail. They elaborate not only the melody, but also the voice parts. Some of these elaborations assume the status of motives and add to the textural interest as they develop.

DRONE BASS Sometimes the piano imitates the sounds of various folk instruments. Since the bag-

pipe is found in many musical cultures, it is not surprising that a drone bass, built on reiteration of the interval basic to the instrument, a 5th, should appear in many folk-song settings and folk-like pieces. Such a setting is 71. The interesting feature of the melody is that it is built in three-measure phrases rather than four. The variant of the opening that appears in 4 may be Rimsky's own. Here, D functions as an embellishing NT, even though it is a 3rd from the structural note rather than a 2nd. In the same way, an IN is added in 11. The entire setting is built over a pedal point, expressed as two notes.

Three-measure phrases also characterize 72A. The entire tune is set twice, and the two settings should be compared. Has the arranger changed the melody in the second setting? The tune ends on 5, as do many Russian folk songs. This does not alter the fact that the tonal center is F.

What can be done with a melody that is four measures long? One answer is to write an eight-measure counterpoint to two playings of the tune, which is what Tchaikovsky does in 72B. Then, by reversing the roles of the two players, he makes a sixteen-measure setting out of the four measures.

54

Settings Using Extended Tonality

While triadic tonality, with its emphasis on the dominant-tonic interaction, can be used in harmonization of folk songs to good advantage, some melodies seem to resist such treatment. Tunes in modes other than major or minor rarely sound well unless the accompaniment takes account of their modal character. And many melodies that can be harmonized with I–IV–V–I can also be set in different ways. The extension of tonality introduced in Interlude One includes many procedures that lend themselves to folk-song setting in a natural way.

The Hungarian folk song 73, in a setting for

voice and piano by Bartók, is in the Dorian mode, transposed to E. The tonic is disguised at the opening, the piano beginning with a 3rd, G–B. As we know, that sound might be part of either a G-major or an E-minor chord. Only when the voice enters is the implication of E made evident.

The melody moves within the octave E–E, while the bass starts from G and moves down through E, coming to rest on F♯ at the midpoint. Another descent brings the line to A♯, a tritone from the goal. In the short piano epilogue, the bass finds its way from A♯ to B via a chromatic motion that is both eloquent and conclusive. The upper part of the piano moves remarkably little, centering around D in the first half, working its way to G in the second half, then arriving at E before either the melody or the bass. The chord vocabulary includes major, minor, and diminished triads. But more dissonant chords are also heard. There are dominant-seventh chords used as passing chords, never resolving by a 5th motion. A SUS makes a strong effect at the beginning of 11, and a NT at the beginning of 17 colors the melody notes beautifully.

The melody of 74 is a fascinating one, its B major constantly in danger of being undermined by the E♯s. Prokofiev's setting follows the tonal drift of the melody and colors it in a natural way. Many of the melody notes—but by no means all—are reinforced in the piano. The technique of notes added to the triad that we observed in the Milhaud chorus, 52, is used. Many of the chords are partly dissolved in lines, and a mildly dissonant counterpoint is the result. A move typical of this composer is a chord shift based on a common tone, here used to provide an unexpected coloring for the last high D♯ of the melody in 23. Prokofiev interprets that note as E♭, the third of a C-minor triad. It is approached directly from the preceding B-major triad, the parallel octaves drawing attention to the B–C motion. The C-minor triad moves to an A♯-minor triad that descends through G♯ to F♯, from which arpeggiation leads down to B.

The serene melody of the Gregorian Kyrie 35 is the basis of the theme that opens the Dello Joio *Piano Sonata No. 3*, 75. The composer has invented a rhythm that works the pitches into a metrical framework. The phrase is five and one-half measures long, so that the first repetition begins in the middle of 5. The second repetition begins in a lower register and finishes in the bass.

The tonality of the chant is reinforced by the added voices, which move in a flowing counterpoint that is almost vocal. The bass gets to the tonic at such crucial points as 7 and 9, but then avoids emphasizing G until it becomes part of the melody in the last three measures.

Triads and seventh chords comprise most of the simultaneities. A chord built on 4ths starts 6, and one built on minor 7ths or alternating 4ths occurs on the third beat of 7. 7ths, major and minor, are heard in every measure and hardly seem more dissonant than 6ths. Even the 4th in relation to the bass no longer seems dissonant. The last chord shows the added-note technique again; it seems that the NTs and PTs that connected triads in Renaissance music are now grafted onto them.

The only chromatic note used is F♮, which becomes a way of avoiding the leading tone in the bass, in 9. It also provides a cross relation with the F♯ of the tenor in the previous measure, coloring the parallel 10ths as they move to the G-major goal at the end of the second phrase.

All the musical elements fit together with the chant to form a convincing whole. This would hardly be possible were it not for the many procedures and practices shared by all styles of tonal music.

76 is a contemporary arrangement of a Jewish melody, also used by the seventeenth-century Italian composer Benedetto Marcello as the basis of a Psalm setting. The vigorous rhythm of the tune strongly suggests its popular origin. At first glance the tonality seems to be B minor. But the melody gravitates toward F♯ insistently. Looking at the song as a whole, we see that it is in the Phrygian mode, with F♯ as tonic. The melody circles around that note, above and below, gradually coming to the Phrygian tonic via the "leading tone from above."

Weisgall's sonorous arrangement is in four parts throughout, the massive texture being varied once, in 13, for a point of imitation. The only chromatic note is A♯, which makes the tonic triad a major one at the end of a phrase. The chord vocabulary includes not only major and minor triads, but also chords built on 4ths and 5ths, many of which are very close to minor-seventh chords. Almost any simultaneous combination of diatonic notes can be used, just as in 52 and 75.

Tonal movement follows the direction of the Phrygian melody. After the opening B, the line moves down through F♯ to D, then back up to the F♯, reached at the cadence in 4. It is the contrapuntal prolongation of the F♯ triad that gives it weight and confirms its role as the goal of motion. The same four measures are heard again in the second strain of the tune. In the third phrase, the melody takes a fresh turn, starting with a D in 9 and rising to the high F♯, from which it falls through a 9th. Weisgall interprets this phrase as centering around D, already used as a momentary tonal axis in 3. The melodic 4th D–A in 14 and 15 suggests the continuation of D major, which gives way to the tonic F♯ only in the last measure. With relatively simple means the composer has made a strong and fluent setting in which melody and accompanying parts seem to have been created together.

Aaron Copland's setting of a Shaker melody, 77, seems quite simple, but the simplicity is artful. Chord changes, instead of following the tune's downbeat, are an eighth note behind or ahead of the beat. The overlapping that results is one of the key features of the arrangement. Each half of the melody is first introduced in the higher register of the piano. With the word "turn" the piano be-gins a rocking two-note figure, whose return in the coda ties the piece together. The final V–I (not V⁷–I) has a deliberately plain sound in keeping with the nature of the tune and the meaning of the words.

55

Techniques of Harmonization

Preliminary exercise

Since the tonal structures of many melodies fall into a few basic patterns, it is advantageous to set several of those prototypes before harmonizing an entire melody. Below are tonal structures similar to those found in Part One. The first is the structure of the first two phrases of ②; the second is based on ④. A realization of the first is given as a model. These exercises may be done in any key and in both major and minor modes.

3–2; 3–2–1
1–2–3–2; 1–2–3–2–1
1–2–1; 5–4–3–2–1
1–2–3–2; 5–4–3–2–1
5–4–3–2; 5–4–3–2–1

Illustration

Analysis of the melody

Thinking ahead before setting a melody may con-sist of locating the structural notes and finding appropriate chords for them. The prolonging and connecting tones of the melody then suggest pro-longing and connecting chords. The way in which one of these chords moves to another is, of course, one of the techniques you have studied in counterpoint exercises.

One procedure

The setting of a simple melody is illustrated with an American folk song, *Go Tell Aunt Rhody.*

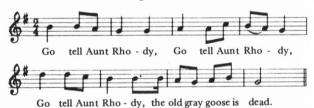

Go tell Aunt Rho - dy, Go tell Aunt Rho - dy,

Go tell Aunt Rho - dy, the old gray goose is dead.

Write the pitches only, eliminating repetitions.

Bracket pitch groupings, explaining each. Write the tonal structure.

The simplest choice of structural chords:

96

These chords may be varied in any number of ways, but they can serve as a guideline for the tonal direction. To this bare outline we now add the contrapuntal chords. Many choices are available since there is no one ideal harmonization. Keep in mind:

1. variety of chord vocabulary, including the use of inversions;
2. a bass line that has an interesting shape;
3. good counterpoint between bass and soprano;
4. dissonance that can add color and motion.

As just one example, we observe that I occurs three times in the chord sketch. The second I may bring the motion to a halt unless, in the final version, a rhythmic accompaniment carries the action forward. Another way of dealing with the fact that the melody sinks to 1 so early in the tune is

to replace the I with another chord that is consonant with the G, which means VI or IV.

Among the considerations involved in choosing the remaining (contrapuntal) chords, two are particularly important:

1. Control the rate of chord change. More rapid rate means more sense of activity; less rapid rate means less activity, repose. In the melody under consideration, one chord to a measure, two chords to a measure, even three chords to a measure, but also one chord to two measures are all possible.
2. Any melody note may function as the root, third, or fifth of a triad. A repeated note in the tune will sound more interesting if its function is not the same twice.

Here is one complete version of *Go Tell Aunt Rhody* (bass and soprano only), with chord indications, plus a suggestion of other possibilities:

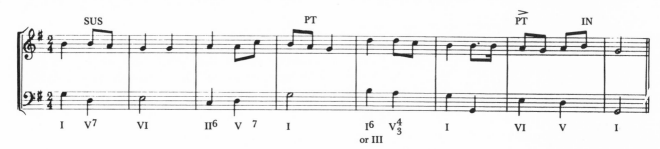

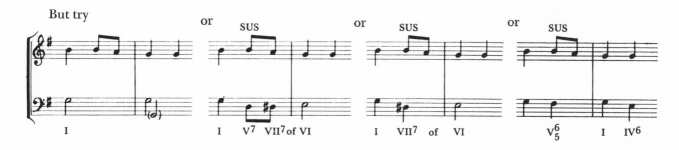

Realization for S.A.T.B.

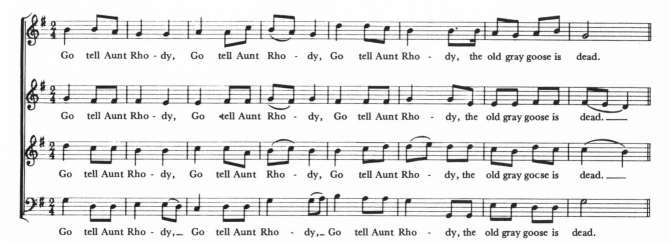

Realization for voice and piano

Go tell Aunt Rho - dy,   Go tell Aunt   Rho - dy,   Go tell Aunt Rho - dy, the old gray goose is   dead.

General procedures in harmonizing melodies

Once you understand the way in which the structural chords underpin the structural notes of a melody, your analysis need not always be written out. With experience you learn to identify the notes on which the others depend and to use them to guide the direction of the polyphonic setting. When problems arise, of course, reduction can clarify them and often lead to a solution.

☞ Worksheet 19

Guidelines:

1. Check off important notes in the tonal structure and locate the cadences.
2. Sketch a bass note under each structural note of the melody.
3. Sketch chords for each of those bass notes.
4. Complete the bass part, modifying previously sketched notes as needed.
5. Fill in the inner voices.

PART EIGHT
TONAL MOVEMENT
AND FORM

56

A Shaping Force in Musical Form

Among the forces that give any piece the shape it has, one requires more study at this point. It is the way a composer directs the tonal movement away from and eventually back to the tonic. Virtually every tonal piece begins with a statement of the centrality of a particular note, then departs from that toward other areas. The departure leaves the listener awaiting the return, creating tension and thus interest. The composer plays on the listener's expectation in any number of ways. In a general way and also in detailed ways, tonal movement defines form.

A very short musical statement, such as that of the Handel *Passacaille*, [59], requires no motion away from its tonal center precisely because of its brevity. In each variation, musical interest is brought about by changes of texture and register as well as by the figuration of the melodic line. But if those procedures were the only ones available, it would be difficult to maintain the interest over a longer span of time.

As simple as Kirnberger's *Bourée,* [80], is, it illustrates an important point about tonal movement and form. The first eight measures proceed from D to a cadence in V. What is the effect of that move? It arouses an expectation of a return to **D**. The repetition of the first section satisfies that expectation by beginning again in D. But, once again, the move to A makes the listener want more. The tension is maintained for four more measures by the prolongation of the dominant, which puts off the return to the tonic. Then the tonic is re-affirmed. First it is touched on by I⁶, then connecting chord IV brings V, which is not resolved at once but is prolonged for a moment before reaching the final I. The tonic in both bass and soprano has been reserved for the very end. Tonal movement has helped shape the piece.

The Mattheson *Sarabande,* [81A], also moves to the dominant, C, at the end of the first section, 8. But then it appears to go back to F, only to move through that to the subdominant. A cadence lends weight to the B♭, making it a momentary tonic. We see here another way of maintaining interest—by not returning directly from the dominant to the tonic, but rather by moving to a third point. Only after the cadence in IV is there a clear move to I. Both top line and bass help reduce momentum by mentioning the tonic note, but they are not together on the tonic until the last sound.

The noble sarabande by Couperin, 82 (still one flat short in the key signature), begins on C and moves to a cadence on G in 8. But an ending on V is an open end; anything may follow. Whereas in the previous two pieces the second section began with the same sound that ended the first section, Couperin imaginatively starts afresh on E♭, which is III of C minor. III is prolonged for eight measures, using parallel 10ths, as we saw on page 79. The return to the tonic is done rather subtly, with inversions and a smooth bass line rather than with root-position triads and a 5th leap. And the tonic keeps turning into the dominant of IV. The repetitions of the last phrase are spun out to give weight to the close. The unexpected turns in tonal direction give the music its interesting shape.

The three pieces we have just examined show only a few of the possible shapes tonal works may have; the only limit is the resourcefulness of the composer. We see that in describing the overall format of these or other pieces, tonal movement is a prime consideration. For the way in which the phrases work, the manner in which phrases are grouped into sections, and the connections between sections making the whole piece are all governed more by motion from one tonal point to another than by any other single factor.

For study

The Bach *Air*, 86, begins with I, which is prolonged into _____. The first goal of motion is in _____. In 16, the next goal, _____, is reached. Before the end of the piece, the bass touches on the tonic in _____.

57

Modulation to a Cadence

What do we mean when we say that a piece of music changes key? Can a piece have more than one tonic? In the large view, no. But any scale degree may be emphasized, as we saw even in folk songs that stressed the dominant by using its leading tone. Any scale degree that can support a major or minor triad may be prolonged, becoming thereby a temporary tonic. At the same time we must keep in mind the long-range connection between any temporary tonic and the tonic of the piece as a whole. When the temporary change becomes important enough to shape the direction of a phrase or phrase group, we speak of a *modulation*. When the temporary change is a detail that

does not influence the shape of the phrase, we speak of *tonicization*.

Modulation leads to a goal that is usually defined by a cadence. Such a cadence, like all cadences, ends a phrase. This is what is meant by the modulation shaping the tonal direction of a phrase. Once the cadence is concluded, the music may prolong the new tonal center, or move to a different goal, or return to the central tonic.

Some modulations are quite abrupt. There is little, if any, link to the previous sound, and the music gives the impression of simply starting off in a new key. The Purcell duet, 58, after prolonging I for the first half of the piece, goes on with the ground bass transposed to the dominant, starting in the second half of 17 . The two notes, C♯ and B, that precede the A-major sound are the only clue to the modulation. In the Couperin sarabande, 82 , there is no transition after the first phrase, but a surprising start on III after the cadence in V. The return to I, eight measures later, is different. The III, which has acted as tonic, resumes its place as mediant, and the outside voices lead back to I with stepwise motion in 17–19 . Another modulation that is simply a fresh start in a new key is found in 87 . The opening five-measure phrase comes to a cadence on V. But in the next measure, that A-major sound is heard as I and proceeds from there.

PIVOT CHORD Many modulations are effected more smoothly because they use transitional chords to lead from one key to another. A chord that has a certain function in the departing key but is interpreted as having a different function in the upcoming key is called a *pivot chord*. A simple example is heard in 80 , 5 . On the third beat VI of D major is interpreted as II of A. The flowing eighth notes in the bass carry the music in the most unobtrusive fashion through the G♯, the note that spells the difference between D and A major. The abbreviation VI/II is read "VI becomes II," and describes the operation.

A chord which has been heard as having one function very clearly may suddenly be heard as having a different function, thereby creating that sense of tonal motion associated with modulation. The A-minor triad that dominates the opening of 84 changes its meaning in 11 , and the listener is made aware of a tonal shift—I/IV. The same pivot chord is used in 86 , 5 .

A more leisurely modulation may be heard in 90A . Again I/IV, in 7 , but the progression of the bass in 5ths does not arrive at its goal, the dominant of C♯, until 10 . The modulation back is also spun out over a number of measures, and might well be considered a group of modulations. These lead from V to IV, in 31–35 ; then to III, in 36–38 ; after which I/III.

CADENCE AS THE GOAL Almost all phrases move toward a cadence, which serves as their goal.

There are two kinds of cadences. When we hear a strong close, it has usually been accomplished by V–I or V⁷–I. Such a close is often described as an *authentic cadence*. If the close is less conclusive, promising more to come, we may call it open-ended; this is sometimes called a *half cadence*. Modulation means that the phrase does not cadence in the same tonal center in which it began.

FIVE SEMICOLON When V is the goal at the cadence, it completes a motion from the chord that began the phrase, I or another chord. This V has the force of a semicolon—that is, an idea is finished but there is more to come. We use the term V; (five semicolon) to indicate that the motion is completed, but that since it is on the dominant, there is more to follow. After V any chord may be heard, and after V; some of the most interesting surprises in tonal music occur.

CADENCE ON VERSUS CADENCE IN In 80 there are cadences at the end of the first four-measure phrase and at the end of the second. In each goal is an A-major triad. The same triad means two different things, however. The first triad ends a cadence on V; (of D major), an open cadence that leads to a resumption of motion in the tonic. But the second follows a modulation and is a cadence in V. To describe the cadence in the last half of 7 we should say $\underset{\text{in V}}{\overset{V–I}{\frown\frown}}$. The cadence *on* V; is simply a motion to the dominant; the cadence *in* V follows a modulation.

The same principle may be observed in longer pieces. 83 and 84 both move to the dominant at mid-point. Yet the tonal structure is different. The *Allemande* is in D minor, and the A-major triad at the double bar is the goal of motion for the first half of the piece. It is simply V; embellished with its own leading tone, G♯. The tonicity of D is not shaken, for there is no modulation. But there is a modulation in the solo sonata. We saw that the A-minor triad of 11 is the pivot chord, I/IV, and the rest of the first half of the piece is in E minor. The cadence is in V.

☞ Worksheet 20

Frontispiece of the volume of Scarlatti sonatas from which ⏐87⏐ is taken.

58

Tonicization 1: Applied Dominants

Modulation is a large-scale tonal motion, an important part of the overall tonal movement of a piece, and thus one of the forces that shapes musical form. On a smaller scale, short contrapuntal or harmonic motions may center around scale degrees other than I, applying the dominant or leading-tone principle to any major or minor triad. Any of those stable chords may be preceded by its own dominant or leading-tone chord. We say that such a triad is tonicized, meaning that it acts as tonic in relation to at least one other chord.

Couperin's sarabande, 82, begins with a tonic chord, which will move to the dominant by way of the connecting chord IV. To propel the motion toward the IV, the composer follows the stable tonic with the dissonant V_5^6 of IV. The most active tone, the leading tone of 4, comes to our attention because it is a chromatic tone and is in the bass. In 21 the dominant of IV becomes so much a part of the musical idea that, in the form of V^2 of IV, it actually replaces the tonic. It is also used to launch the two phrases that round off the entire piece. The applied dominant does not direct the form in the way that the modulation to V does. Rather, it is an expressive detail.

A further study of 86, 13–14, shows us more about the meaning of the chromatic PT in the bass, which was discussed on page 79 as an elaboration of the 5th–6th alternation. These chromatic notes function as leading tones incorporated into applied dominants. They help create the intensification that supports the rising melodic line. Over the F♯ in 13 we hear V_5^6 of IV, in which the C♯ is another chromatic tone; the G♯ in the bass is the leading tone in V_5^6 of V; the A♯ in V_5^6 of VI. Again we see the difference between such short-range motions, which tonicize various scale degrees, and a long-range move such as the modulation to VI in 9–10, which gives the phrase its direction.

☞ Worksheet 21

59

Binary Form

80 through 87 have a number of things in common. Each is divided by a double bar into two approximately equal sections, and both sections are repeated; the same kinds of musical events take place in both halves of each piece; each piece has but a single musical idea, be it motivic or simply figurational; each piece moves to a cadence on or in V at the mid-point, then returns to the tonic either directly or by way of a detour. From these observations we draw the general description of binary form.

We might take note of the fact that while the

second half of the piece is a continuation of the first half and has no new material, it need not be a carbon copy. Indeed, it cannot be, since the tonal movement is bound to be different. This creates the possibility of varying the music in one way or another. Comparison of the first measures of both parts of a binary piece shows how the composer met the expectation of an exact replay, enhanced by the obligatory repeat of the first half, with music that is sufficiently similar to the opening to retain the sense of unity but different enough to make it interesting. The second half of the artfully simple *Bourée*, 80 , begins with music that makes the three implied voices of the first half explicit, changing texture and register and prolonging the dominant to prepare for the final return of the tonic. In 81 , the second half begins with the same chord that ended the first half, emphasizing continuity rather than contrast. We saw how the second (longer) part of 82 follows the cadence in V with a fresh start in III.

While most suites were written for keyboard, some were composed for orchestra and for various solo instruments and small ensembles.

The exercises or sonatas of Scarlatti are a special case. As you can see in 87 , freedom of registral movement is greater here than in most Baroque music. Scarlatti begins to explore the possibilities of using more than one musical idea in a piece, presenting two melodies or, rather, a line based on figuration as well as a more melodic line. We also hear two textures, two keys, two modes, and a short chromatic passage that contrasts sharply with the rest of the music, which is quite diatonic. While this music does not arrive at the clear duality that will characterize the Classic style, it represents quite a significant departure from Baroque monothematicism. Most striking is the fact that so much of the music grows out of the way in which the human hand meets the keyboard, and in the opening gesture, to cite only one instance, we are far indeed from the S.A.T.B. concept.

For study

Compare openings of the two parts of 84 , 85 , 86 , and 87 . In each, which is stressed—continuity or contrast? How is this done?

THE BAROQUE SUITE A favorite form of keyboard music, which reached the height of its popularity in the 1720s, was the suite. Written for amateur players whose level of proficiency must have been fairly high, the dance origins of the various movements gave them a popular touch. At the same time, the format gave composers an opportunity to work in their most artistic vein. The harpsichord suites of Handel and Couperin were among the best-known music of their time. There are four basic movements to a suite: allemande, courante, sarabande, and gigue. To these, other dances and similar pieces were added as desired.

For further study

Couperin composed what he called *ordres,* collections of a large number of pieces from which the player is to select those he wishes to perform as a group. Playing through any one of them will give you a good cross section of the composer's work. Rameau's suites or books of pieces are also more of a repertory than self-contained works. The suites or lessons of Handel are modeled after those of Couperin and Purcell and are quite unpredictable in their order and selection of movements. Bach's suites and partitas for harpsichord, violin solo, cello solo, and orchestra draw together many aspects of both French and Italian styles in a remarkable synthesis.

☞ Worksheet 22
☞ Worksheet 23

60

Comprehensive Analysis of *Allemande* from *French Suite No.1* by J. S. Bach, 83

BACKGROUND The *French Suites* were written before 1723, while the composer was living in Köthen. They are modeled after the harpsichord pieces of Couperin, and are contemporary with the suites of Handel. Considering that this music was written for harpsichord, it sounds remarkably good on the piano, perhaps because Bach concentrated not so much on tonal color as on the counterpoint.

OVERVIEW 83 is in D minor, in common time ($\frac{4}{4}$). There are two sections, each containing twelve very busy measures of music. Each section is one large gesture, for the phrases that comprise the sections are linked together so smoothly that the listener is hardly aware of cadences and phrase endings. The emphasis is on continuity rather than on contrast. Density of texture varies from two parts to six, but each line is so active and so filled with polyphonic implications that the ear has the impression of all registers being in play almost all of the time. The upbeat sixteenth note sets in motion a relentless rhythmic drive, pushing through cadences until it reaches the large punctuation mark that ends each section. No dynamic markings are found, nor does textural change imply any strong contrasts in the dynamic level.

LINE AND CHORD The chordal implications in this music are quite strong, yet the chords themselves have been dissolved in lines. Or, from another point of view, the lines flow together to generate chords at every moment. The balance between chord and line is truly extraordinary.

CONSONANCE AND DISSONANCE Bach does not rely entirely upon the sixteenth notes to propel the music on its way. On almost every strong beat (the first and third beats of the measure), there is a dissonance demanding resolution—that is, movement. The constantly changing dissonance-consonance relationship presents a rich variety of sounds,

combining with the unceasing rhythmic activity to keep that motion from becoming mechanical.

RATE OF CHORD CHANGE Another factor that lends interest despite the constant flow of sixteenth notes is the different rates at which the chords change. Most often there are two chords per measure. But some chords, most obviously those at the beginning and end of a section, go on for several beats. A few chords are of rather short duration, the shortest being an eighth note, as in 20.

MELODY It would not be very helpful to talk about themes or even motives in this piece. The melody is made of figuration, constantly changing and rarely repeating. A rhythmic figure of three sixteenth notes as upbeat, introduced in the first measure, pervades the entire piece. It is preceded sometimes by a sixteenth rest, sometimes by a tied sixteenth note, sometimes by another sixteenth note which skips to the figure. The result is that instead of hearing the sixteenth-note motion as strong-weak-strong-weak (contained within the beat and measure) we hear it as weak-strong-weak-strong (crossing the beat and the measure).

In the much simpler *Minuet,* 85, we saw the melody embodying both soprano and alto parts in one line, alternately with their sounding simultaneously. The Handel concerto movement, 91, had the first-violin part dipping down into the second-violin range and even into the viola's territory. Such expansion of line in musical space reaches a very high state of development in the keyboard music of Bach. In 83 the first ten notes of the right-hand part open up the soprano, alto, and tenor registers in one broad sweep. Less obviously, 5 shows the inner-voice note B♭ leapfrogging over the top line, which has worked its way down into the middle register. Then the E♭ that is heard on the second beat of 6 brings the top line forth in its normal position. The melody in 9–10 moves through both soprano and alto ranges, as it does again in 22–23 . All in all, the intricate weaving of the parts is made possible by the spatial expansion of the lines, one of the most important ways of elaborating the tonal structure.

TONAL STRUCTURE   The sketch below shows the framework within which the music moves. The structurally more important notes in the outside voices are written as whole notes, the main direction of the inner voices, in simplified form, appears as noteheads. Intervals noted between the staffs are those between middle voice and bass; those below the bass part, between the outside voices. In addition to these contrapuntal relationships, harmonic functions are shown by Roman numerals. Measure

numbers are written over the staff. Bar lines indicate phrases only. Tied notes mean SUS.

The piece begins with a short prolongation of I, bringing the voices into a position where soprano and bass are a 10th apart. This sets up the beginning of a long descent in parallel 10ths, occupying the first phrase up to the cadence. The descent is embellished by SUSs, and is detoured in 3–4 by a brief tonicization of IV. From this phrase we learn how an elaborate design can be built over relatively simple scaffolding, which is to be the procedure in the rest of the piece. The cadence in 5 is disguised by the SUS, whose resolution keeps the activity going into the second phrase. For a moment the inner voice leads with B♭, then the tritone A–E♭ sets off the upper voice. The tonicization of VI in 6 leads

106

to another descent in parallel 10ths, again embellished with SUSs. IV is tonicized again in $\underline{7}$. Both hands are involved with more than one line in these measures. The phrase ending, at the beginning of $\underline{9}$, passes by in a flurry of figuration, and the top line begins its motion to 2, the melodic goal in the first section. This third, shorter phrase plays upon an alternation of 6ths and 7ths. It ends with a dominant prolongation that strongly punctuates the first section. In the repetition, that dominant goes on to the tonic that begins the piece. The second time, the dominant is continued through the first measure of the second section.

There are but two phrases in the second half of the piece. The fourth phrase, after its initial concern with dominant and tonic, moves briefly through VI. E♭ again plays an important role, and it colors $\underline{15}$–$\underline{16}$. The strength of the emphasis on IV, with a full measure of prolongation of IV's dominant, makes a punctuation mark that ends the phrase. No sooner is G felt as a momentary tonic than the bass drops to C, which assumes the function of V of III. A stepwise motion out of the inner voice into the bass leads back to D, reminding us that although G and F have their own dominants, they are still IV and III of D. Another long descent in parallel 10ths is inflected by E♭, so that VI is tonicized in $\underline{21}$ and IV in $\underline{22}$. The left-hand part is particularly busy expressing both tenor and bass, which are finally heard together in the last measure and a half. The final dominant is only one beat long, but it has drawn all the other sounds to it, and its progression to the concluding tonic fulfills the listener's expectations and expends the musical momentum.

61

Longer Pieces Shaped by Tonal Movement

> A phrase or phrase group establishes a key, texture, and rhythmic and melodic character.

> Another phrase or phrase group moves to a secondary tonal center, using much the same texture and melodic shapes.

> Other phrases and/or groups may continue the same kind of activity in closely related tonal areas.

> A final group reiterates the opening, literally or with a variation, with emphasis on the tonic.

This, in brief, outlines the shape of longer Baroque pieces, such as the movements of a concerto, sonata, or cantata. These different genres have in common their dependence on tonal movement to organize large formal areas. What we might call the surface of the music is concerned with matters of texture, rhythm, figuration, and motivic development.

The movement from Corelli's trio sonata, 89 , illustrates the kind of piece outlined above. It is an introductory movement; more music is to follow. The texture may be described as an accompanied duet with background filling-in by the right hand of the *continuo* player; it does not change during the piece. Chains of SUSs between the two violins help create the expressive charm of the music. There are three phrases, each defined by tonal movement to a cadence. The first goes from I to V;, pausing after the dominant in a gesture that is typical of the composer. The second phrase begins on III and centers around that point for its entire duration, through the first beat of $\underline{11}$. This time there is no pause. The bass moves through the cadence in eighth notes, and the third phrase starts directly. The last, longest phrase begins with bass motion in 5ths, starting on the fourth beat of $\underline{11}$. Over that, the violins threaten to begin a sequence, but then avoid it. Both top and bottom voices gradually close in on the tonic. A strong dominant in $\underline{16}$–$\underline{17}$ reaches the tonic, but that is left behind immediately for a short extension which gives the ending enough time to expend the musical energy of the piece. Imitation among all three lines concentrates the final cadence and leads to a satisfying end.

The proportions of the Handel concerto movement, 91, are larger and there are more phrases, but the principle is the same as in the Corelli. The outline of the movement, shown below, indicates the layout of the phrases and their tonal goals. One phrase simply follows another, guided by the tonal movement. There is nothing special about this piece that derives from the concerto element; it is a piece for strings and *continuo*. But all the strings are not equal. As in the Bach *Air,* the first violin plays a larger role than the other instruments, extending its range over more than the "soprano" register.

Outline of 91

phrase	measure	tonal goal
1	1–3, second beat	I–V;
2	3, third beat–6	I–V; III
3	6–9, third beat	V–I III
4	9, last beat–12, third beat	V–I V
5	12, last beat–14, third beat	V–I IV
6	14, last beat–17, first beat	V;
7	17, second beat–20, first beat	V–I
8	20, second beat–22, first beat	V;
9	22, second beat–24, first beat	V–I
transition to next movement	24, second beat–end	V;

From this outline, and from listening for the sense of the punctuation marks of the music, we may learn about the overall shape of the piece. The initial phrase, by moving to the dominant, starts the motion of the piece and leaves it, unstable, unanswered by the second phrase. The second, third and fourth phrases continue the activity, each centering on a different scale degree, none satisfying the claims of the dominant that ended the first phrase. The sixth phrase does restore the local control of I, but it, too, ends with an open cadence. When the seventh phrase concludes with the harmonic cadence

the tonal voyage is complete—everything else is epilogue.

Since the melody dominates the piece aurally we should examine its nature. If we look for a motive, a single rhythm or pitch idea that is developed, we cannot find it. Rather, we hear a two-tone figure, simply the descending 2nd, as two sixteenth notes. Another figure involves a dotted eighth and a sixteenth, of which the first is a higher pitch than the second. With these two figures Handel spins out an elegantly flowing melody, against which is counterpointed a bass moving steadily in eighth notes. Second violins, violas, and the *continuo* fill in the four parts, although the strings complete all the chords and leave little for the keyboard to add. The piece breathes at the end of each phrase; but with the varying phrase lengths, the breathing places are also varied, creating an overall rhythm that has balance but is not predictable.

Like the Handel movement, the first movement of the Vivaldi *Concerto grosso,* 92, has a melodic line made up of a number of small figures repeated and elaborated. Unlike the Handel, this work groups together several phrases at a time into sections, making a more complex organization. Cadences, especially those ending sections, are strong and clear-cut, but their rhythmic activity moves through these cadences instead of pausing, as it did in Handel.

The first large section is in two parts. First the full ensemble (tutti) plays a five-phrase group that is rather more complex than most of Vivaldi's ideas. These sixteen measures will serve as a refrain throughout the movement since they are repeated in whole or in part at crucial points in the discourse and at the end. This recurring refrain is known as a *ritornello.* In the second part of the opening section the solo instruments, the concertino, introduce their own melodic material, answered by elements of the ritornello. The give and take between the large and small groups is the essence of the concerto principle. In this work it is particularly easy to follow because each group has its own musical ideas. Subsequent sections present little that is new in the way of melody, rhythm, or texture; tonal movement is the way in which sections can be defined. The following outline shows phrase groupings, sections, and the main outline of the tonal motion.

Outline of $\boxed{92}$

section	measures (indicating phrases)	tonal movement
first (tutti)	1–4 , 4–5 , 5–9 , 9–13 , 13–16	I
(solo versus tutti)	16–19 , 19–22 , 22–25 , 25–30	I
transition	30–36	modulation to III
second	37–39 , 39–42	III
	42–44 , 44–47	modulation to V
	47–48	modulation to IV
	48–51 , 51–55 (= 1–4), 55–62	IV
transition	62–65	modulation back to I
third	65–68 (= 16–19), 68–71 (= 1–5), 71–78 , 78–80 (= 4–5), 80–83 (= 5–9), 83–86 (= 13–16), 86–90 , 90–93 (= 13–16)	I

Miniature from a 1450 manuscript, showing Guillaume Dufay (c.1400-75) and Gilles Binchois (c.1400-60).

INTERLUDE TWO
A LOOK BACK

Even the simplest example of polyphonic music that we have studied thus far shows a highly developed tonal organization. All the sounds are related to the tonic in a network of interactions; the same intervals that control the vertical aspect also shape the horizontal; dissonance and consonance are used consistently to achieve tension and release; phrases have clear shapes that are molded by rhythmic and tonal impulses; phrase endings with varying degrees of closure enable the music to flow from one thought to another and to build overall continuity, while over the foundation of tonal movement the surface or design of a piece may take shape in infinitely varied ways, expanding into musical space to create variegated textures. Such sophisticated resources did not come into being overnight. Centuries of effort by countless musicians brought the art to the point at which we began the study of polyphonic music. Even a brief survey of their work will be of value at this point.

How polyphonic music first developed remains a fascinating, if largely unanswered, question. Here we can only point out that from the ninth to the twelfth centuries there was a period in which slowly and with great effort musicians learned how to combine melodic lines in relation to each other—that is, they learned how to write counterpoint. The earliest works discussed here belong to what is called the Notre Dame school, which flowered in Paris in the late twelfth and early thirteenth centuries. Even these are built on the results of the experimentation of the previous three centuries.

Before looking at any music, two points must be emphasized. First, it would be a mistake to consider any of this music as primitive, merely the precursor of later music which, being more sophisticated, must be better. Each piece is a work of art in its own right and must be heard on its own terms to the extent that the modern listener is able. Works of art, unlike works of technology, do not become obsolete. They become more remote, which makes it difficult for us to understand them; but only an impatient person would throw them away. No doubt we must make an effort if we are to get anything out of this music. This usually means suspending judgment for a while, exposing ourselves to the sounds in an open-minded way, and learning what we can about the context in which the music was created.

The second point is that the further back in time we go, the less certain we can be about the accuracy of the information on the page and of our ability to decode the symbols we read. Despite a good deal of thought and research, we are still not able to answer all of the questions that surround the notation of medieval music. Even the pitches are a problem since the plainchant notation used was not codified until the mid-twelfth century. More problematical is rhythm, which means that the coordination of parts is sometimes in doubt, too. Since there are no tempo markings, all we can do is make educated guesses about the speed at which the music is to be performed, taking into consideration such factors as the size of the cathedrals in which the music was first heard, the ritual function the piece served, and the forces for which it was intended. As for dynamics, it is generally assumed that there was little change of level in a piece. We know that the distinction between vocal and instrumental music, as styles of writing, did not exist. Most music appears to be vocal, but contemporary paintings, documents, and letters inform us that the same music that was sung could just as well be played.

From singing one melody to having two melodies sung at the same time is one of the great leaps of the human imagination, creating an entirely new dimension in music. Naturally, there is no written record of such a moment in our history; polyphony was improvised by singers long before it was written down. Just how polyphonic music began will always be a matter of some conjecture. But if you have ever listened to a group of untrained voices singing in what they thought was unison you may have observed that they were actually singing in parallel 5ths or other intervals. People are inclined to sing in the range that is most comfortable for them. On the average, high voices sing a 4th or a 5th higher than low voices. Singing two versions of the same melody is not polyphony, but it may well have led to polyphony as the singers began to put the difference between ranges to use. The earliest two-part music we have consists of a chant and a second line of music above the chant, moving more or less parallel to it. The interval between the voices is usually a 4th or a 5th. In time, musicians discovered other ways in which to move, that is, they discovered contrary and oblique motion.

When we look at medieval music, we realize that many of the pieces are built on pre-existing melodies which are chant or fragments of chant, and the texts, in most cases, are traditional ones. We may draw a parallel with medieval painters, who based their work on familiar Biblical subjects, returning to them over and over. Musicians of the Middle Ages did not seek originality or self-expression; they sought to glorify God by embellishing the chant, which was held to be divinely inspired. Medieval man saw the world as finite and bounded; tradition governed his artistic activities. Yet, within what may seem to us today as rather narrow confines, he built the cathedrals we still admire and created the music that filled them. A few examples of that music are discussed here. A complete analysis is not undertaken, but the factors that make for tonal coherence are surveyed, with comments on matters relevant to the course of study as a whole. Those interested in the performance problems in-

volved in these selections should consult Thurston Dart's excellent book *The Interpretation of Music* (1954).

The earliest type of two-part music is *organum*. It is a style of composition (of improvisation, before that) in which a second voice is added above or below a given melody, usually a chant. There are several kinds of organum, corresponding to the increasingly florid nature of the added part. The notes of the chant are usually held for a number of beats, and the voice that sings the chant is called the *tenor* (Latin: *tenere*, "to hold"). This means that the word *tenor*, in medieval music, does not indicate any particular voice. Usually it is the slowest, wherever it lies. The added part is called the *duplum*.

A short excerpt from a large organum, 94 , is by the first master of the Notre Dame school, Leonin. Considered the greatest composer of his day, Leonin wrote this music as the cathedral was rising, and may have heard or performed it within the still-unfinished edifice.

The tenor has the notes of a chant fragment, in large values. Over that, the duplum moves in phrases of varying lengths. For every long note of the chant the duplum has one or more of these phrases, each of which proves to be a prolongation of either one or two notes. The main note or notes of each phrase of the duplum form a 4th, 5th, or octave with the chant note, as the reduction shows.

It seems fair to conclude from this that Leonin took as stable intervals the octave, 5th, and 4th. These are the only intervals on the strong beats—that is, the beats that mark the beginning of each note in the chant. Often they are embellished with NTs, but those notes are decorative, not structural. Intervals used as dissonances include 3rds and 6ths as well as 2nds and 7ths. Of the consonances, the 4th is used least and may be taken as the least stable. Perhaps its later use as the least unstable dissonance may not have been as drastic a shift as it may seem at first.

While motivic development is still a long way off, each melodic bit is carefully shaped, and one grows out of the other in a natural way. The first three melodic units are similar, built on the same four notes centering around D. They are made from the Dorian family of melodic impulses. The next three pick up the skip of a 3rd with which the first group ended, striving upward against the F until the culminating G is reached. Then a different kind of melodic event is heard. The A-minor triad is unfolded melodically; is interrupted by the NT, F; and returns, leading into the final phrase. This is the longest, and brings together aspects of the earlier ones to conclude the section.

In what key is this music? The question implies that there is such a thing as a central tonality in the excerpt as a whole. But from our point of view there is no such thing. Each small unit centers around one note, but that is as far as tonal organization goes. There is a motion from D to G in the first four notes of the chant, after which G is prolonged. That is all. The final of the chant does not have the organizing power of a tonic in later music. Even a longer excerpt, or the entire piece, would demonstrate that the tonal unity which gives coherence to music on a large scale has not yet evolved.

From the point of view of texture, the anonymous two-part conductus, 95, is quite different from the Leonin organum. Originally, *conductus* was a style of composition used to accompany action or movement in the church service. Thus it did not have a liturgical text, nor did it have a liturgical chant to serve as its basis. Conductus were monophonic (one-voiced) at first, then came to include compositions in two or more parts. If there is more than one part, all voices move in note-against-note fashion. A long-short rhythm prevails, the long notes here represented by half notes and the short ones by quarter notes. This implies triple meter, the only meter used up to the fourteenth century for the reason that it symbolized the Holy Trinity. Once we are reasonably certain of the rhythmic values, we can discover what the composer construed as consonant and dissonant. The stable sounds are on the strong beats; not surprisingly, these are unisons, 4ths, 5ths, and octaves. The basic chord is an octave filled in with a 4th or a 5th, with no 3rd. Between the central sonorities the voices move through such dissonances as 2nds and 7ths, 3rds and 6ths.

What can we say about the tonality of this piece? In the first two lines, the lower voices relentlessly circle around D, while above, the upper voice moves back and forth between D and A. This adds up to a prolongation of the basic sound, D–A–D. The subsequent part prolongs the 5th F–C, ultimately returning to the original tonal center. Connecting links are few and short. The focus on the two 5ths, with D emerging as the controlling note, brings

a rudimentary kind of tonal unity to the entire piece.

Parallel, contrary, and oblique motion are used indiscriminately. None seems more desirable than another, and independence of voice is not a priority. Attention is focused, rather, on the melodies themselves, flowing within a loose framework defined by the basic consonances. Parallel 5ths, octaves, and unisons abound. We might think of them as the vestigial remnants of organum.

The grand style of the Perotin conductus, 96, bespeaks an advanced stage of musical development. The successor to Leonin at Notre Dame de Paris, Perotin was known in his time as *optimus discantor,* which tells us that he was considered the best contrapuntist of the day. His piece alternates between syllabic settings and long melismas. The elegant final melisma (see page 21) was known as the *cauda,* "the tail." It would be tempting to conclude that the syllabic sections were sung and the melismatic sections played. But there is no evidence to support such a conclusion.

The opening prolongation of a D-minor triad shows Perotin's method in a nutshell. All three lines move stepwise in strong and clear curves. *Optimus discantor,* indeed. Although all the parts are close together, voice crossing gives them room in which to move. The upper voice fills in the 4th from D to A, and reaches beyond for the NT, G, and its NT, F, circling around A as the center. The middle voice descends from A to D, goes beyond so as to surround the D, and comes to rest on the D after passing through it twice. The bass prolongs D with what we now think of as a SP, the skip of a 5th opening up the space in which the rest of the line will work. Each line is built around the 4th D–A or its inversion, the 5th A–D. The same interval that is set forth as the opening and closing simultaneity also guides the direction of each line.

The large and rather complex motet 97 is by Guillaume de Machaut, poet and composer of the late Gothic period. In the Middle Ages a *motet* was usually a secular piece for voice(s) and instrument(s). Each voice has its own words (French: *mot,* "word"). Although the text deals with courtly love, the tenor, here transcribed in the bass range, is based on chant. Medieval man simply did not make the sharp distinction between sacred and secular that other times have taken for granted. The bar lines are suggested by markings in the original.

A special feature of the motet, carried to its highest development in works such as this, is that one or more of the voices is *isorhythmic.* This means that a fixed sequence of rhythmic values is applied to the notes of the tenor part; other parts may also

113

use such rhythm rows. This rhythmic series is called a *talea*. At the same time, the notes of the tenor are in a pitch series, called a *color*. Talea and color for 97 are as follows:

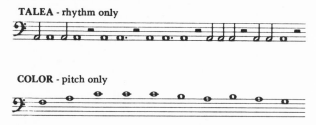

TALEA - rhythm only

COLOR - pitch only

Since the talea has more "notes" than the color, the pitches will appear in different note values as they recur during the course of the piece. Lengths of the two series are so calculated that three renditions of the color take the same time as two of the talea. Altogether, the talea is heard four times, the color, six.

The listener of Machaut's day was not expected to hear the talea and the color, just as a listener today is not expected to follow the tone row in a serial composition. The purpose of the isorhythmic structure was to give the composer a way of organizing his music. The logic of this kind of structure appealed particularly to French composers, of whom Machaut was the most renowned.

Indeed, the melodies are highly organized, but how do they work together? That question is not as decisive as it will be later, for the emphasis is still on the melodies rather than on the simultaneities. The fact is that although the parts move with a kind of fluency that was unknown a century earlier, the chords are much as they were. Octave and 5th are very much the prevailing consonances, but the 4th is losing ground. The triad is not entrusted with opening or closing a unit, but during the course of a unit it is heard frequently. Thus the 3rd begins to gain respectability.

The chant fragment on which the motet is built centers around F because of the 5th, F–C, but also centers around C because of the leading tone B. Short sections of the piece have their own tonality, but there is no overall tonal unity, and Machaut thinks nothing of ending the piece on G. When B is prominent in the tenor, F♯ may appear in the upper voices; when F is in the tenor, B♭ may be heard above it. Both of these cautious moves toward chromaticism are brought about by the avoidance of the tritone.

The two singing voices (they may have been replaced by instruments at times) move rapidly in varied rhythms. While they seem to be cut from the same cloth, there is no imitation between them,

and they rarely cross. The tenor has no text and is presumably instrumental. Again, the traditional element is the chant, in the tenor.

This music was meant for a small audience of knowledgeable aristocrats, and is much lighter in tone than the massive works of Leonin and Perotin. This motet is more like chamber music. It is meant to be heard in a castle, perhaps in a large room, but still in more intimate surroundings than a cathedral. Machaut's motet typifies the *ars nova*, in which such rhythmic novelties as duple meter and syncopation could be written down, hence, composed, for the first time.

If the French composers of the Middle Ages concentrated on erecting elaborate musical structures, the Italians, from their entry onto the scene in the fourteenth century, were captivated by the delights of melody. The exquisite ballata of Landini (also spelled Landino), 98, shows some of the same features as the Machaut, but many stylistic differences, too. The ballata, like Machaut's piece, is chamber music, a duet with instrumental accompaniment. The basic sonority of 5th and octave is the same, too. But the entire feeling of the music is quite unlike the courtly Machaut. All three lines are caught up in the lyric flow, and the instrumental part is no different from the voice parts. The symmetrical layout of the piece is readily perceived because both sections end with the same music, the rise to the high point (E) followed by the descent past the tonic (A), then a return to the concluding tonic. The elegantly shaped upper line has the melody throughout. Its first phrase circles around 1, the second prolongs 5. The next two work their way down through the octave to the lower 5, after which the rise to the peak is particularly expressive. The second half of the melody has a somewhat different shape, going as high as F♯. But it grows to resemble the first section as it progresses, and takes up the same concluding phrases to balance the piece in a lovely way. The instrumental part weaves in and out of the voice parts and is heard between them as often as beneath them. The emphasis is still on the lines, the simultaneities being worked out in a way that relies on the basic consonance of a 5th. Control of the chordal dimension has progressed somewhat but is still not as developed as control of the linear dimension.

The mode is Dorian, here transposed to A. At the end of each section a leading tone is heard, helping the punctuation. The particular melodic turn at the cadence, in which 7 steps down to 6 before arriving at 8 is often called the *Landini cadence*, although it was in use before Landini was born.

114

How did the triad become the normative sonority of tonal music? As the result of a long, slow process, no doubt, which was improvised more often than it was written down. From the English practice of adding to a melody a second part in 3rds and 6ths came the succession of what we now call $\frac{6}{3}$-position triads. The harsh sound of the 5th gave way in time to the more euphonious imperfect consonances; in three-part music, triads resulted. The style in which parallel $\frac{6}{3}$ chords predominate is called *fauxbourdon* (in French). The Dufay excerpt, 99, is written largely in fauxbourdon. Suddenly the music sounds "modern," much more like the music we are accustomed to. To be sure, sounds without 3rds are still present, but they are outnumbered by the triads.

The first note may be taken as an upbeat, followed by a bar line. The music will then fall into $\frac{3}{2}$ and $\frac{6}{4}$, moving back and forth between the two. The rhythmic vocabulary now includes both eighth notes and triplets. We may also observe that each voice has its own range, and that there is little voice crossing.

This brief survey leaves off somewhere near the point at which Renaissance music began. Its purpose has been to provide a framework for deeper study of the music and its historical context. Also, this overview may serve to create a perspective in which to see later music. It is important to realize that remote as this music is in time, it still has a great deal to offer today's musician and today's listener as well.

For further study

Aside from the complete works of a few medieval composers, the only readily available sources from which to learn more of the music are the excellent anthologies. For specific details, see the Reading List on page 147.

A valuable analysis of several medieval pieces is found in Felix Salzer's article "Tonality in Early Medieval Polyphony," *The Music Forum,* I (1967). The music of another medieval composer is discussed in Carl Schachter's article "Landini's Treatment of Consonance and Dissonance," *The Music Forum,* II (1970).

Why Study Counterpoint?

For centuries music students have been trained in the techniques of counterpoint. In a society that deeply respected tradition, that fact alone would have carried great weight in persuading music teachers to continue teaching the subject. But in today's world, mere force of habit is hardly a compelling reason for maintaining an educational practice.

Any intelligent answer must begin by defining the term. But writers on music are notoriously careless about terminology. We hear about sixteenth-century counterpoint, about Bach counterpoint, about harmonic counterpoint, about modal and tonal counterpoint. We hear about counterpoint as a discipline or as a means of expression, as training for composers or as irrelevant for composers but essential for theorists. Is there a definition that will guide us?

In the middle of the sixteenth century a distinguished Italian musician, Gioseffe Zarlino, wrote a treatise on music, *Istituzioni armoniche* (Venice, 1558), considered a milestone in the development of musical thought. The third section of the book, "Counterpoint," offers many insights into the musical practice of the time. Zarlino finds the origin of the word in the Latin *punctus contra punctum,* "a note against a note." More generally, he means line against line. Yet that definition is not complete enough to cover even the exercises in Zarlino's book, for nowhere does line move against line without regard for the sounds that are heard simultaneously. On the contrary, Zarlino himself gives the most careful attention to the matter of consonance and dissonance, by which the relationship between lines is governed. A definition of *counterpoint,* then, must include both the linear aspect and control of the simultaneities. It is the art of combining lines in relation to each other.

Composers and theorists after Zarlino built on the foundations he had laid. Not everyone agreed with all of his theories, but his approach to counterpoint was widely studied and emulated. Meanwhile, the language of music was changing radically. Only fifty years after the first edition of Zarlino's book, Monteverdi was talking about the older style, the "first practice," as against the new style, the "second practice." Before long, the invention (or rediscovery) of monody and the development of figured bass, the concerted style, opera, and the many innovations of the Baroque had made the music of Zarlino's time seem very old-fashioned. Yet counterpoint was taught as if nothing had changed since the death of Palestrina in 1594. In retrospect, the reason is not hard to find. Although the style of secular and some sacred music had indeed changed considerably, music in the Catholic church remained bound to the great traditions of the Renaissance and the Counter Reformation. Even composers who wrote for the Protestant worship felt obliged to study the "learned style." Composers who were busy writing operas and concertos still felt the need for training in the old manner of writing, and what was called counterpoint provided that training.

The classic formulation of the discipline saw the light of day in 1725, when Johann Joseph Fux published his *Gradus ad Parnassum*. A skillful composer himself, Fux organized the problems of combining lines in a systematic way, isolating the various techniques the better to master them. Breaking the subject down into manageable pieces had been attempted before, but Fux did it better. He put his exercises into a logical sequence, starting with the simplest and moving systematically to the more complex. As a result, counterpoint is everlastingly associated with his name. Identifying the relationship between consonance and dissonance as the critical element in the combination of lines and realizing that rhythm was closely bound up with dissonant usages, Fux defined five types or species of counterpoint exercises. They are:

first species: note-against-note consonance;
second species: two notes against one, using PTs;
third species: four notes against one, using PTs and NTs;
fourth species: SUSs;
fifth species: florid counterpoint, using all rhythms and all dissonant usages.

In each exercise Fux has the student write a melody or melodies against a given melody, the *cantus firmus*. The use of a given melody, in itself, was hardly new. As a compositional procedure, it dates back to the beginnings of Western polyphony. Zarlino was only one of many who had prescribed such an exercise, using chant as the given melody. But chant, no matter how beautiful, can pose many problems that confound the issues. Fux's instinct for proceeding from the simple to the complex led him to write short, clear melodies that are more appropriate for pedagogical purposes than chant, although they can be criticized on both stylistic and structural grounds.

By setting up specific exercises that organized the study of both pitch and rhythm, Fux was able to write a treatise of enormous value to students of the art. Bringing together teaching methods of proven usefulness, he presented them in a methodical way. His *Gradus* is a self-instruction book; written, like many such books in the past, in the form of a dialogue between teacher and student, it is still very much worth reading today.

For Fux, of course, the entire method was a means to a somewhat limited end. All he intended to do was to show a systematic way of learning how to write like Palestrina. One wonders how much of Palestrina's music Fux actually knew. The music of the Renaissance was largely unknown until it was rediscovered in the late nineteenth century, and whatever such music Fux heard, he heard through ears that were attuned to the late Baroque and the emerging *style galant*.

It is only a hundred years since the rise of the discipline of musicology, which has led to the discovery of so many buried treasures. Fresh publications of older music and much valuable research have made it possible to study that music in a more sympathetic way, which means that musicians have begun to make a serious effort to hear older music in its own terms rather than as something that could be dismissed as a "precursor." In the twentieth century the Danish scholar Knud Jeppesen defined the language and practice of Palestrina in detail in his monumental book *The Style of Palestrina and the Dissonance* (1927). Jeppesen was able to point out just how far Fux had been mistaken on many stylistic matters, and to show that the image of Palestrina's style that had been projected by Fux's 1725 book was wide of the mark. Subsequently Jeppesen wrote a counterpoint book which did, in a scholarly and thoughtful way, just what Fux had thought he was doing.

The remarkable thing, from our point of view, is that Fux actually accomplished something quite different from what he intended. In many ways it was something far more important. For in defining the species of counterpoint, in pinpointing the interrelationships of consonance and dissonance, in making specific the ways in which rhythm interacts with pitch structures, Fux articulated many of the basic factors that make tonal music work. The reasons that Haydn, Mozart, Beethoven, Chopin, Brahms, and many others found Fux so valuable had nothing to do with Palestrina, but had everything to do with their own music. In trying to explain how to write like Palestrina, Fux managed to explain instead some of the fundamental processes of musical motion. Therein lies his importance for us. In one way Fux may be likened to Columbus, who sought India and found the New World.

Most of what Fux formulated applies not only to the music of one composer or one period, but to all tonal music. The processes exemplified by the species can be seen at work not merely in the music of the sixteenth century, but in the music of the fifteenth century as well, and the seventeenth, and Fux's own eighteenth, and up to and including tonal music written today. What, then, is sixteenth-century counterpoint? It seems to mean the emulation of the personal style characteristics of one composer. But unless we are to study each great composer separately, it is essential that we define a counterpoint for all centuries. That will demonstrate what all composers have in common—which is to say that it will define the norms of tonal music. Without a clear codification of what has been the normative procedure, the study of music gets bogged down in a quagmire of details, devoid of underlying conceptual basis. With the aid of such a formulation, however, it becomes possible to approach any new piece of music in a systematic way; with specific tools and skills, one can both understand what gives the piece coherence and unity and relate it to other pieces.

The theorist who first saw the possibility of applying Fux's ideas on a broader scale was the Viennese Heinrich Schenker (1868–1935). A practical musician as well as a highly original thinker, Schenker assimilated the species concept into his own comprehensive theory about the structure of tonal music. As you have observed in one piece after another, beneath even the most elaborate musical surface the listener may project a framework, the tonal structure, which can be expressed as note-against-note consonance or something close to it. The structural framework is revealed by making a synopsis of the pitches, emphasizing the importance of the bass and soprano (because the music does), and using the process of reduction, one of Schenker's many contributions. That reductive procedure resembles nothing so much as the species, but in reverse order. The composer synthesizes while the theorist analyzes. Schenker applied the concept of structural levels to music, and also demonstrated how each level was elaborated—prolonged, as he called it—into the next. Schenker's work has been carried on by Felix Salzer, among others, who has successfully applied the concept of directed motion to music of both earlier and later epochs than Schenker. Salzer's *Structural Hearing* (1952) is an excellent exposition of Schenker's ideas in English. A more recent book by Salzer and Schachter, *Counterpoint in Composition* (1969), shows in rich detail how the principles of counterpoint can unlock many of the secrets of tonal music.

Counterpoint, then, is the art of combining lines in relation to one another. This relation is managed by the interaction of consonance and dissonance. The lines generate intervals that are heard simultaneously. These intervals make up the chords that are one aspect of the vocabulary of tonal music. Most chords in a piece are contrapuntal chords, whether the piece is a chorale or a fugue. The great difference between a chorale and a fugue is in the use of musical space—which is to say texture. But to call one "homophonic" and the other "contrapuntal" is to miss the point that they are both the product of lines moving through time. Our definition of counterpoint, taking a broad view, includes most of what is taught in courses called "Harmony." We maintain that to make sense, a pedagogical approach should start with musical motion, not with isolated moments frozen for purposes of labeling.

For music exists in time. Lines, melodies, rhythms, even chord progressions move in the temporal dimension, not on paper. A systematic and musically valid method of studying the way music moves through time is precisely what we have called counterpoint. The application here is broader in scope than traditional counterpoint, even though it is firmly rooted in that tradition. That counterpoint must be dry and meaningless is not an inevitability; it is simply a bad habit. If counterpoint is used to study musical motion, both broad and detailed, it becomes a two-edged tool. For it is both a key element in the analysis of music and also the basis for acquiring the skills of tonal composition. As such, it is essential to every person who is seriously interested in studying the art of music.

Music and the Rules

As a student you may have been told, "You have to know the rules before you can break them." What does this mean? What is a rule in music? How can you break it if it is a rule? Do composers follow rules in writing music?

Every music library is filled with books containing great numbers of dos and don'ts—mostly (it must seem to a student) the latter. On what authority can such directives be issued? The fact that a well-known writer or musician has stated a rule does not guarantee the validity of the statement. We maintain that the only authority is the music itself. We learn by observing what happens in pieces, then by generalizing about them. We hope our generalizations are inclusive enough and consistent enough so that we do not have to study every piece of music ever written before we can extrapolate the norms of compositional procedure. For composers do not follow rules; the rules are abstractions of what composers have already written.

Although these observations about how pieces work are called rules, they are actually closer to instructions of a "how to do it" nature. The term *theory* is often applied to this study; it consists, in fact, of a mixture of a little theory and a lot of practice. Much of the time it is a practical investigation of how sounds are organized into a coherent, artistic whole.

Rules fall into two categories. One category involves the basic operations that make a piece of tonal music intelligible, that govern the relation to the tonic, that shape phrases, sections, pieces. These are embodied in archetypes, which lie beneath the surface of every piece. The other category consists of rules that grow out of aesthetic choices. These choices express norms of melodic shape, the relation of dissonance and consonance, independence of voices. Since the norms of various styles may differ on some of these points, these rules may prove to be more relative than absolute. In tenth-century music the 3rd is a dissonance; not too much later, it is a consonance. The two lower voices in a Bach chorale will not move in parallel octaves, but in a Haydn string quartet they may very well do just that. If you want your piece to sound like Lasso or Bach, you should avoid parallel 5ths, but if you want your music to sound like Debussy or Hindemith, parallel 5ths are a means to that end.

If generalizations about a piece of music are accurate, what sense does it make to break the rules? None. The problem stems from the formulation of rules that have little to do with real music and that, at best, represent an attempt to keep beginning students from getting involved too soon with problems that are beyond them. This is part of the reason for the artificial distinction between harmony and counterpoint. What we are attempting here is to face the problem squarely by setting forth the basic principles of tonal coherence from the beginning, making no "rules" that have to be broken later on. One of the fascinating aspects of tonality is that the same principles work in the small detail and in the large view, in simple music and in the most complex. If the rules embody these principles, there is no way to break them. The statement "the exception proves the rule" is nonsense. The exception disproves the rule.

Composers do not follow rules. Nor do composers rely on sheer inspiration. Their minds are filled with ways of putting notes together, the norms of composition in their day. They use those norms in the same way that we utilize the norms of today in speaking and writing words. We think of what we want to say and we say it; the resulting sentence has a subject, an object, a verb, at the least. Composers also use their grammatical norms to convey their thoughts.

Finally, the fact that many rules derive from aesthetic choice makes us realize that different musics may have different sets of rules. We are studying the music of Western Europe and America since the Middle Ages. No less organized is the music of other cultures, which we are just beginning to study in the rapidly growing discipline of ethnomusicology. Anyone who has examined the art music of India knows that it is highly codified. The patterns of Javanese gamelan music are precisely arranged. The intricacies of African drum music bespeak an extraordinary degree of organization. Each has its own rules, which define the style and make it possible to hand down a living tradition from one generation to another.

MUSICIANSHIP
AT THE
KEYBOARD

PART ONE

1. Play all major and minor scales in two octaves.
2. Find any interval on the keyboard quickly and accurately.
3. Play on the white keys the scale of the Dorian, Mixolydian, and Phrygian modes.
4. Transpose those three modes up a perfect 4th or down a perfect 5th.

PARTS TWO, THREE, AND FOUR Six progressions are listed below. These are to be practiced in a number of different ways. The purposes of this work are:

to learn the basic chord vocabulary of diatonic music;
to practice hearing lines and chords at the same time;
to gain fluency in finding the notes of frequently used chord patterns;
to lay the foundation for improvisation.

How to practice:

1. Memorize a progression in block chords in any key.
2. Transpose to all major and minor keys. Remember that in the minor mode the leading tone is used in V.
3. Vary the position of the notes in the triads:
   a. soprano may start with root, third, or fifth; alto and tenor adjust accordingly;
   b. bass starts with tonic in either higher or lower octave.
4. Play in various meters, using repeated chords to create a rhythmic pattern.
5. Alternate hands: "oom-pah" in duple meter, "oom-pah-pah" in triple meter.
6. Use arpeggiation in one hand.
7. Add PTs, NTs, and SUSs.

PROGRESSIONS

1. I–V–I
2. I–IV–I
3. I–IV–V–I
4. I–II⁶–V–I
5. I–VI–IV (II⁶)–V–I
6. I–IV–II–V–I (major only)

Illustrations of some of the ways in which these exercises may be realized are given below. These are not models to be followed mechanically, but suggestions to show a few of the possibilities. Memorizing these illustrations is of no value. Rather use them to learn how to think at the piano.

Progression 1.

Block chords

Progression 4.

Using repeated chords

Progression 5.
Alternating hands

Progression 6.
Arpeggiation

PARTS FIVE AND SIX The following progressions are to be learned and played in the same way as those on page 12. Review the possible ways of using these exercises.

1. I–IV–VII–III–VI–II
   (II⁶)–V–I (see page 79)
2. I–V–VI–III–IV–I–V–I
   (see page 80)
3. I–IV (II⁶)–I$_4^6$–V⁷–I
4. I–IV–II–V–I (major mode only)
5. I–VII–III–IV (II⁶)–V–I
   (minor mode only)
6. I–VI–IV (II⁶)–V–I

{ V may be prolonged into V($_{4\ 3}^{6\ 5}$) or V($_{4\ 3}^{6\ 7}$) or may be V⁷

Memorize 80 and transpose it to E♭, E, and F major.

PART SEVEN Play 66, 67, 69, and 76 from the score. *More advanced:* play three parts and sing one.

Play the piano part of 70, 71, 73, 74, and 77, accompanying another person who sings the melody. *More advanced:* sing the melody and accompany yourself.

PART EIGHT Realize the continuo part of 79, accompanying another person who sings the melody. *More advanced:* sing the melody and accompany yourself with your realization.

Realize the continuo part of 88, accompanying the melody played by another person. *More advanced:* sing the melody, adding your own embellishments to the original line, and accompany yourself with your realization.

Realize the continuo part of 89, accompanying two performers.

Realize the continuo part of 90, accompanying the instrumentalist.

Realize the continuo parts of 93 and 62, accompanying two singers.

PARTS FIVE THROUGH EIGHT Improvise short phrases using the chords you have studied. Fix the tempo and meter before playing by counting one or two measures aloud. It is also helpful to decide beforehand whether the top line will circle around one note, descend to the tonic, or rise and fall. The following may serve as illustrations:

Top line descends 3–2–1.

The dominant appears as $V(\begin{smallmatrix} 8 & 7 \\ 6 & 5 \\ 4 & 3 \end{smallmatrix})$

Top line prolongs 5.

The dominant appears as $V(\begin{smallmatrix} 6 & 7 \\ 4 & 3 \end{smallmatrix})$.

Top line ascends from 5 to 1.

The dominant is prolonged with a $\begin{smallmatrix} 6 \\ 4 \end{smallmatrix}$-position triad.

A one-measure motive is used over a sequential progression:

INTRODUCTORY EXERCISES FOR SIGHT SINGING

1. Scales—major ($\frac{3}{4}$ and $\frac{4}{4}$)

124

2. I in major ($\frac{2}{4}$, $\frac{3}{4}$, and ¢)

125

3. Minor scales—and major

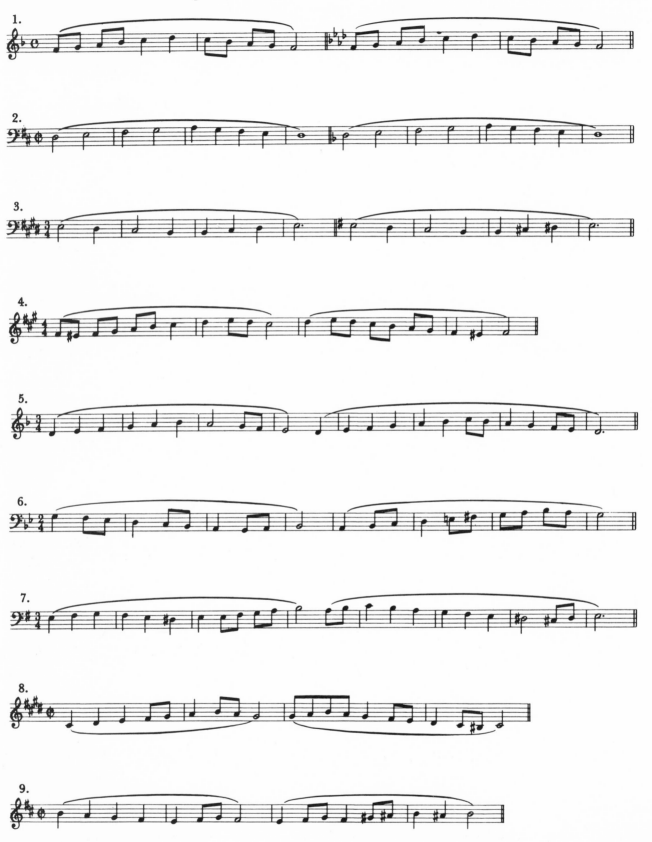

126

4. I—major and minor triads

5. NT (♩. ♪)

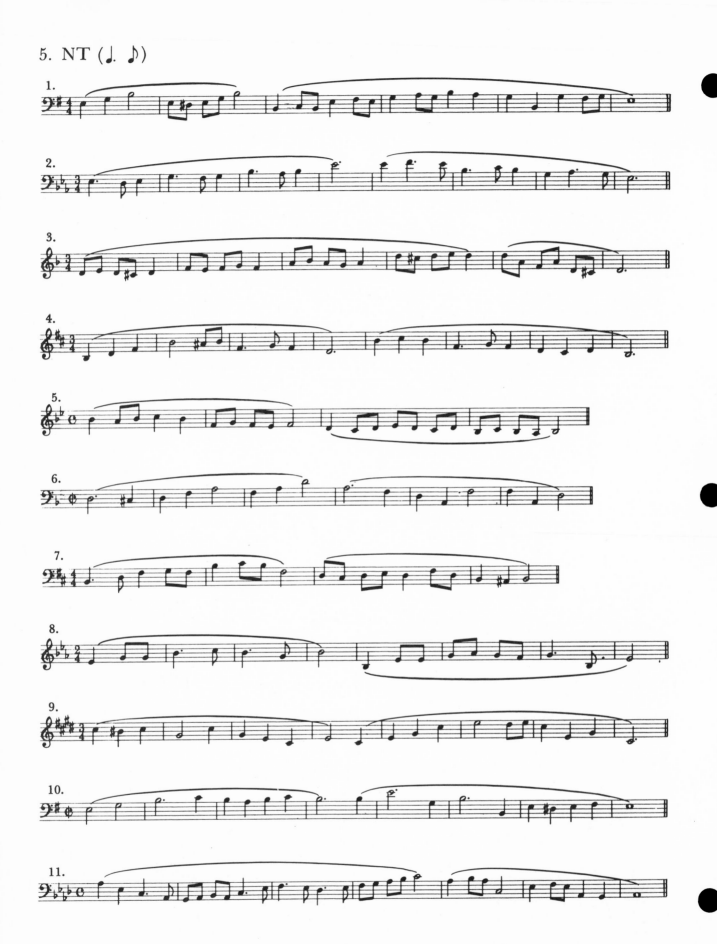

6. DN (♩. ♪ ♫)

129

7. SP and PS ($\frac{6}{8}$)

130

8. Skips to IN (♩. ♫)

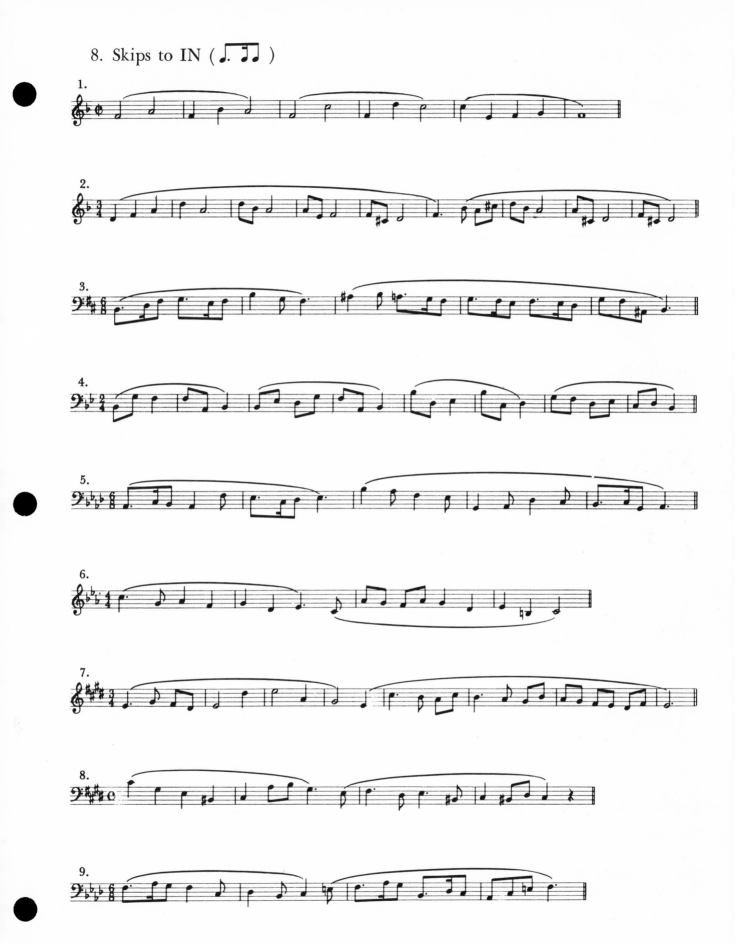

131

9. Skips in the V chord (♩. ♪)

132

10. Skips in the IV chord (♩. ♫♪)

11. Skips in the V⁷ chord (upbeats)

134

12. All triads

13. Octave displacement

14. Polyphonic melody

15. Interval studies

STUDIES IN MELODY
IMPROVISATION

1. Base your melody on a scale, ascending and descending:

Choose a tempo.
Choose a meter.
Beat time as you sing.
Sing up the scale from tonic to tonic, in the chosen tempo and meter.
Take the upper tonic or a note near it as your intermediate goal.
Sing down the scale, concluding on the lower tonic.
Notes of the scale may be repeated in your melody.
NTs may be used to elaborate scale notes.
The octave may be exceeded by one note in either direction.

Illustrations:

2. Base your melody on the progression I–X–V (or V⁷)–I, where X is II, III, IV, or VI:

Choose a tempo.
Choose a meter.
Beat time as you sing.
Use one chord to a measure at first.
When you have had some experience in this study, the chord outlines may be carried over the barline.
PTs may be used to fill in the chord outline.

Illustrations:

140

3. Base your melody on a pattern of structural notes on which you improvise prolonging notes:

Choose a tempo.
Choose a meter.
Beat time as you sing.
Sing the structural notes, one to a measure.
Sing a melody built on the structural notes.
Use NT, DN, IN, SP, PS, S, triads, and octave shift to elaborate the main notes.
Use one or two main notes to the measure at first.
With more experience, the structural notes may be used more freely.

Patterns:

    1–2–3–2–1
    3–2–1
    5–4–3–2–1
    3–4–5–4–3–2–1

Illustrations:

More advanced: Using any of the techniques of Studies 1–3, one student sings an antecedent phrase, with 2, 3, or 5 as the goal; in tempo, another student sings a consequent phrase ending on 1.

141

APPENDICES

Music Notation

Music notation is a means of communication. One person uses a set of written symbols in order to convey to another how to produce a specific group of sounds. Each symbol is an instruction, telling how to realize one or more attributes of the desired sound.

To make the communication as effective as possible, the symbols should be used as consistently as possible, and they should be written legibly. A neat, clearly written page transmits the writer's intentions far better than a page that distracts readers by forcing them to decipher a careless or inconsistent script.

Guidelines for music notation:

1. The notehead, ●, should be the size of one space on the music staff and oval shaped.

2. The stem, |, should be one octave long for a single note.

3. If two or more stems are connected by a beam the shortest stem should be at least one octave long. The beam should not cross more than one staff line, so that other stem lengths must be lengthened accordingly:

4. Sharps and natural signs should fill three spaces on the staff; flats, two spaces:

5. Stems should appear on the staff wherever possible:

6. The spacing of the notes should correspond approximately with their duration in time. Thus, not ♩. ♪ ♩ , but rather ♩. ♪ ♩

7. Slurs, ties, and legato markings should connect the heads of the notes, not the stems or flags.

8. In vocal music, dynamics and expression markings are written above the notes, the words below.

9. In instrumental music on one line, dynamics and expression markings are written below the notes.

10. In instrumental music on two lines, dynamics and expression markings are written between the lines.

Find at least one application of each of these guidelines either in this book or in music you are now practicing.

Instruments of the Orchestra: Ranges and Transpositions

Certain instruments sound pitches that are different from the notes being read. These are said to be transposing instruments. To find out what note is actually sounded, apply this rule: reading C, an instrument in X sounds X. Thus, reading C, a clarinet in B♭ sounds B♭. This tells us that all notes for that instrument sound a whole step lower than written.

Transposing instruments frequently used include:

1. piccolo: sounds an octave higher than written;
2. English horn: sounds a perfect 5th lower than written;
3. clarinet in B♭: sounds a whole step lower than written;
4. bass clarinet in B♭: sounds a major 9th lower than written if written in the treble clef ("French notation") or a major 2nd lower if written in bass clef ("German notation");
5. contrabassoon: sounds an octave lower than written;
6. horn in F: sounds a perfect 5th lower than written;
7. trumpet in F: sounds a perfect 4th higher than written;
8. contrabass: sounds an octave lower than written.

The Instruments of the Orchestra

English	abbreviation	Italian	abbreviation	French	abbreviation	German	abbreviation
Piccolo	Picc.	Flauto piccolo or Ottavino	Fl. picc., Otta.	Petite Flûte	Pte. fl.	Kleine Flöte	Kl. Fl.
Flute	Fl.	Flauto or Flauto traverso	Fl., Fl. trav.	Flûte or Grande Flûte	Fl., Gde. fl.	Flöte	Fl.
Alto flute	Alto fl.	Flauto in Sol	Fl. in Sol	Flûte en Sol	Fl. en sol	Altflöte	Altfl.
Oboe	Ob.	Oboe	Ob.	Hautbois	Hb.	Hoboe or Oboe	Hb., Ob.
English horn	E.H.	Corno inglese	Cor. ingl.	Cor anglais	Cor A., C.A.	Englisches Horn	E.H.
Clarinet	Cl., Clt.	Clarinetto	Cl., Clar.	Clarinette	Cl.	Klarinette	Kl.
Clarinet in E♭	Cl. in E♭	Clarinetto piccolo	Cl. picc.	Clarinette en Mi♭	Cl. en Mi♭	Klarinette in Es	Kl. in Es
Soprano clarinet in B♭ or in A	Cl. in B♭ / Cl. in A	Clarinetto in Si♭ / Clarinetto in La	Cl. in Si♭ / Cl. in La	Clarinette en Si♭ / Clarinette en La	Cl. en Si♭ / Cl. en La	Klarinette in B / Klarinette in A	Kl. in B / Kl. in A
Bass clarinet	B. Cl.	Clarinetto basso	Cl. b.	Clarinette basse	Cl. b.	Bassklarinette	Bkl.
Bassoon	Bn., Bsn.	Fagotto	Fag., Fg.	Basson	Bon.	Fagott	Fg.
Contrabassoon or double bassoon	C.Bn., C.Bsn. / D.Bn., D.Bsn.	Contrafagotto	Cfg.	Contrebasson	C. bon.	Kontrafagott	Kfg.
Horn or French horn	Hn.	Corno	Cor.	Cor	Cor	Horn	Hn.
Trumpet	Tr., Tpt.	Tromba	Tr.	Trompette	Tr.	Trompete	Tr.
Cornet	Cnt.	Cornetto	Ctto.	Cornet à pistons	C. à p., Pist.	Kornett	Kn.
Trombone	Trb., Tbn.	Trombone	Tbne.	Trombone	Tr.	Posaune	Ps., Pos.
Tuba	Tb.	Tuba	Tb.	Tuba	Tb.	Tuba or Basstuba	Tb., Btb.
Percussion	Perc.	Batteria	Batt.	Batterie	Batt.	Schlagzeug	Schlag.
Kettledrums	K.D.	Timpani	Timp.	Timbales	Timb.	Pauken	Pk.
Snare drum or side drum	S.D.	Tamburo	Tamb.	Tambour militaire or caisse claire	Tamb. mil.	Kleine Trommel	Kl. Tr.
Bass drum	B.D.	Gran Cassa	Gr. Cassa	Grosse Caisse	Gr. C.	Grosse Trommel	Gr. Tr.
Cymbals	Cym.	Piatti	Ptti.	Cymbales	Cym.	Becken	Beck.
Harp	Hp., Hrp.	Arpa	Arp.	Harpe	Hp.	Harfe	Hrf.
Violin	Vn., Vln.	Violino	Vl., Vln.	Violon	Vl., Vln.	Violine or Geige	Vl, Vln., Gg.
Viola	Vn., Vla.	Viola	Va., Vla.	Alto	A.	Bratsche	Br.
Violoncello or cello	Vc., Vcl.	Violoncello	Vc., Vcl.	Violoncell	Vc.	Violoncell	Vc.
Contrabass or double bass	C.B., D.B.	Contrabasso	Cb.	Contrabass	Cb.	Kontrabass	Kb.

146

Ranges of Orchestral Instruments *

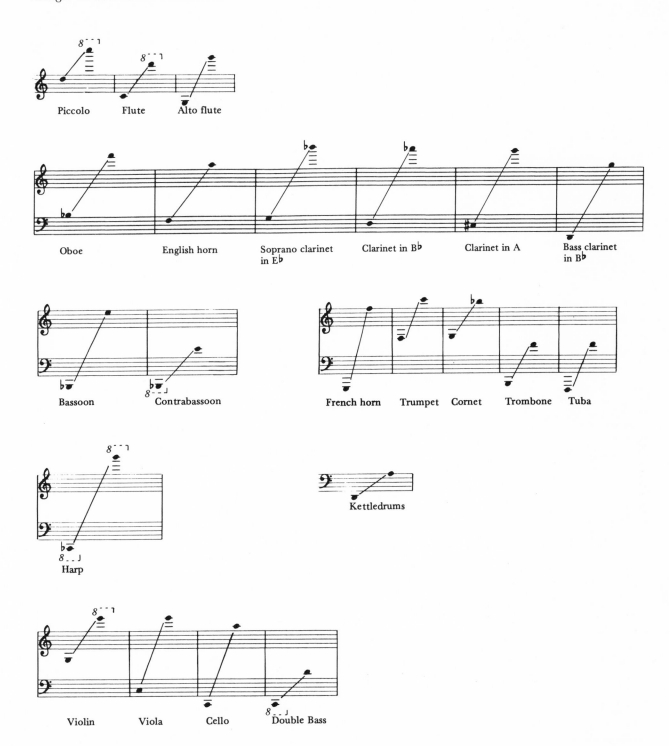

* Notes shown are sounding (transposing) pitches for all, including transposing, instruments (see below). In each case, the upper limit of the range is not to be taken as an absolute, since the extent of the upper range depends entirely on the virtuosity of the performer. The upper limits shown here are those normally found in the orchestral literature.

GLOSSARY

Words appearing in SMALL CAPS in the definitions are themselves defined in the glossary.

a cappella (It.): unaccompanied (choral music).

adagio (It.): very slow, slower than LARGO in the eighteenth century, not clearly distinguished from LENTO in later times.

affetuoso (It.): with tender feeling.

allegretto (It.): fairly fast, but not as fast as ALLEGRO.

allegro (It.): fast, lively.

allemande (Fr.): a dance originating in Germany; in Baroque SUITES, usually the first movement, in moderate TEMPO and $\frac{4}{4}$ time.

alto: (1) the lower female voice; (2) (Fr.) the viola.

andante (It.): literally, "walking" or "going"; a moderately fast TEMPO in the eighteenth century, taken somewhat slower in the nineteenth.

antecedent phrase: the first PHRASE of a two-phrase group that comprises a PERIOD.

aria (It.): air or song; used to denote a SOLO number in an opera or an instrumental piece in the style of such an operatic number.

arioso (It.): in the manner of an ARIA; in a singing style.

arpeggiation: a procedure in which the notes of a chord are played successively rather than simultaneously.

atonal: without a center of tonality or KEY.

authentic cadence: the V–I CADENCE.

ballata (It.): a late medieval Italian poetic form associated with the music of Landini; the term also applies to the music set to such poems.

bicinium (Lat.): in the sixteenth century, a two-part piece written for voices but often played by instruments as well.

bourée (Fr.): a French dance that appears occasionally in Baroque SUITES; usually in   , starting with an UPBEAT of two eighth notes, and faster than a GAVOTTE.

bransle or **branle** (Fr.): a popular dance of the sixteenth and seventeenth centuries, with lively TEMPO. The

branle simple is in duple METER, the *branle gai* in triple METER.

cadence: melodic and/or chordal movement to a goal at the end of a PHRASE. Any SCALE DEGREE that can support a CONSONANT TRIAD can be the goal of motion and of the cadence.

canon: literally, "rule"; a musical procedure whereby IMITATION is carried out exactly for an entire piece or section. The term is also used for a piece so written.

cantabile (It.): in a singing style.

cantillation: a term applied both to the practice by which the Old Testament is sung in the Jewish service and to the music itself.

canto (It.): soprano.

cantus firmus (Lat.): a MELODY which is given and may not be altered, serving as the basis of a composition or exercise.

cauda (Lat.): literally, "tail"; in medieval music, the very end of a piece.

cembalo (It.): harpsichord.

chaconne (Fr.) or **ciaconna** (It.): a Baroque continuous variation form based on a repeated bass pattern, like the PASSACAGLIA; usually in triple METER and slow TEMPO.

chanson: (1) in Renaissance music, a secular choral piece, often in less than four parts; some are chordal, others quite linear; (2) the French word for "song," although the proper term for "art song" is *mélodie*.

chant or **plainchant:** unaccompanied MELODY of the Christian churches.

chorale: the words and/or music of a congregational hymn associated with the Protestant church worship.

chromatic: literally, "colorful"; using the five PITCH

148

CLASSES that are not included in the DIATONIC SCALE of a given KEY.

circle of 5ths: a list of the MAJOR KEYS, arranged a perfect 5th apart, which may be diagramed as a circle. If the circle is read clockwise, the 5ths are seen ascending, with a progression through each of the MAJOR KEYS.

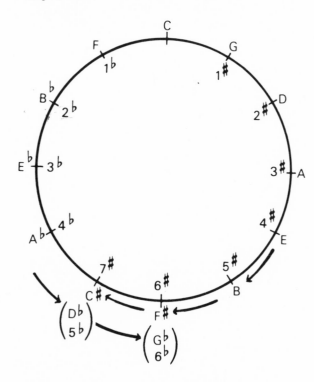

coda (It.): literally, "tail"; a concluding section of a composition.

color (Lat.): the pitch pattern that undergoes repetition in a medieval ISORHYTHMIC MOTET.

compound interval: an INTERVAL larger than an octave. A major 10th (a 3rd plus an octave) is a compound INTERVAL.

con anima (It.): with spirit.

conductus (Lat.): a medieval style of composition for one to three voices, not based on a pre-existent CHANT. In conductus of more than one voice, the voices move in rhythmic unison, a factor which distinguishes them from all other medieval polyphonic compositions.

consequent phrase: the second PHRASE of a two-phrase group that comprises a PERIOD.

consonant: consisting of two or more sounds which are in a stable relationship to each other.

continuo: short for *basso continuo* (It.); the continuous bass characteristic of Baroque music. The term refers both to the bass line itself, figured or unfigured, and to the instruments that perform it, a keyboard instrument and low strings or winds.

contrapuntal progression: a group of chords whose movement is controlled by the bass-soprano relationship, usually STEPWISE, rather than by root movements.

contrary motion: movement of two voices in opposite directions.

counterpoint: the art of combining MELODIES in relation to each other.

courante (Fr.) or **corrente** (It.): a dance movement, usually the second in a Baroque SUITE, in a lively TEMPO, with the METER written $\frac{3}{2}$ but often varying between $\frac{3}{2}$ and $\frac{6}{4}$.

diatonic: using the seven notes which comprise the SCALE of a given KEY.

diatonic semitone: a HALF STEP spelled with two different letter names—e.g., E–F or B–C.

direct or **similar motion:** movement of two voices in the same direction, but covering different distances.

dissonant: consisting of two or more sounds which are in an unstable relationship to each other. This relationship generates activity toward a more stable sound.

dolce (It.): sweet, gentle.

dominant: (1) the fifth degree of a MAJOR or MINOR SCALE; it is a more active note than the TONIC; (2) the RECITING TONE in a medieval mode.

Dorian: one of the medieval MODES, also used in folk song. It can be found on the piano by playing the white keys, starting on D, for one octave.

double (Fr.): a variation.

double neighbor or **DN:** a four-note group consisting of a main note, followed by lower and upper (or upper and lower) NEIGHBORS and the main note again.

downbeat: the strong, emphasized pulse that occurs on the first beat of a MEASURE.

duplum (Lat.): in ORGANUM, the part directly above the TENOR.

enharmonic: change of spelling without change of sound (in a system using equal-tempered tuning). Thus, G♭ is F♯ spelled enharmonically.

fauxbourdon (Fr.) or **falso bordone** (It.): originally, a performance practice in which the lowest of three lines would be sung an octave higher than written, turning what appeared to be a succession of parallel 3rds into a succession of parallel 6ths; a middle voice extemporized a 4th below the transposed voice completed the sonority of parallel $\frac{6}{3}$ TRIADS. In the later Middle Ages, a style in which parallel FIRST-INVERSION TRIADS are used as the predominant sonority.

first inversion: the 6 or $\frac{6}{3}$ position of a TRIAD, or the $\frac{6}{5}{3}$ position of a SEVENTH CHORD.

gaillarde (Fr.): a lively dance, usually in triple METER, popular in the Renaissance. It often forms a pair with the slower PAVANE, using the same material.

gavotte (Fr.): a Baroque dance type in   , in moderately fast TEMPO, usually beginning with an UPBEAT of two quarter notes. The gavotte is not one of the "obligatory" numbers in a SUITE, but is often added.

grave (It.): very slow, slower than LENTO.

149

ground bass or **basso ostinato** (It.): a repeated bass line on which a set of continuous variations is built.

half cadence: a term used by some theorists to describe a CADENCE on a SCALE DEGREE other than 1.

half step or **semitone:** the smallest INTERVAL in the tempered SCALE—e.g., E–F or G♯–A.

harmonic progression: defined differently by various theorists, but here taken simply as V–I or V⁷–I.

harmonic prolongation: the reiteration of I–V–I, stabilizing the TONIC.

harmony: (1) specifically, the V–I progression on any SCALE DEGREE in which the root movement is in control; (2) in general, an aesthetic term used to describe the way in which chords and progressions sound in a piece—e.g., "Wagner's harmony is rich and colorful."

hemiola: a rhythmic alteration in which two MEASURES in $\frac{3}{4}$ are performed as one measure of $\frac{3}{2}$.

heterophony: a performance practice characteristic of Far Eastern music, in which different versions of one MELODY are sung at the same time with little regard for the simultaneous sounds produced.

imitation: a way of setting forth the various REGISTERS by introducing a melodic idea successively on each level.

incomplete neighbor or **IN:** a two-note group consisting of a NEIGHBOR note either preceded or followed by the main note.

interval: the distance between two notes, derived from SCALE DEGREES (2nd, 3rd) or expressed by the number of SEMITONES contained.

inversion: (1) the procedure by which the lower note of an INTERVAL is raised an octave or the upper note is lowered an octave; (2) the position of a chord in which the bass is not the root—the $\frac{6}{3}$ position of a TRIAD is called the FIRST INVERSION, the $\frac{6}{4}$ position of a TRIAD is called the SECOND INVERSION; (3) a transformation of a MELODY in which all ascending INTERVALS become descending INTERVALS of the same size, and all descending INTERVALS become ascending INTERVALS of the same size; (4) a procedure used in ATONAL music in which a row or series is so transformed that each INTERVAL is replaced by its complement, found by subtracting the number of SEMITONES in that INTERVAL from 12.

isorhythmic: in medieval music, a piece that contains an extensive rhythmic pattern (TALEA) in the TENOR, which is entirely repeated at least once in the course of the piece, sometimes in conjunction with the repetition of an extensive melodic pattern (COLOR) as well.

key: "in the key of X" means that X is the note to which all other notes in the composition are related; X is the TONIC.

key signature: the array of sharps or flats that tells what the KEY of a piece is by showing a specific grouping of HALF STEPS and WHOLE STEPS. The key signature cannot show the difference between MAJOR and MINOR; only the music can.

koto: a Japanese stringed instrument, played by plucking the strings.

Landini cadence: the melodic ending in which the leading tone, instead of moving directly to the TONIC, is elaborated by moving to 6, then to the TONIC.

larghetto (It): not as broad (slow) as LARGO.

larghissimo (It.): literally, "very broad"; by implication, very slow.

largo (It.): broad, slow.

legato (It.): smooth and connected.

lento (It.): quite slow, but not as slow as GRAVE or ADAGIO until the nineteenth century, when the distinctions between these terms became less consistent.

Lydian: one of the medieval MODES. To find the Lydian mode on the piano, play a SCALE on the white notes, starting with E.

major scale: a particular configuration of steps with seven different letter names. The INTERVALS that spell out the major scale are WHOLE STEP, WHOLE STEP, HALF STEP, WHOLE STEP, WHOLE STEP, WHOLE STEP, HALF STEP. At the last INTERVAL, the initial PITCH CLASS returns, and the SCALE is complete.

measure: the unit of the predominant, regular grouping of pulses found in most music, so that we count two, three, or four beats as a unit. What we hear as such a unit is called a measure. Visually, the unit is represented by the space between two bar lines.

melisma: in CHANT, the group of notes sung to one syllable.

melismatic: a florid style of CHANT or, by extension, of melodic writing.

melody: an informal term used to describe a succession of notes which can be perceived as an aesthetic unit. We say that the melody of the piece is usually in the top line, voice or instrument, but bass lines and inner voices may also have melody.

meter: the grouping of pulses which we hear as a unit. The most common meters are two, three, and four beats: these are simple meters. Compound meters include six, nine, and twelve beats.

meter sign or **time signature:** the rubric which indicates the METER. The upper figure shows the number of beats in a MEASURE, the lower shows the value of the note that receives one beat. The only METERS whose signs are not indicated in numbers are   , which is the same as $\frac{4}{4}$, and   , which is the same as $\frac{2}{2}$.

minor scale: differs from the MAJOR SCALE in its distribution of WHOLE STEPS and HALF STEPS.

minuet: a dance in triple METER, the TEMPO moderately fast. Until about 1760 the minuet is in binary form; thereafter, it is in rounded binary form.

mode: a collection of pitches in a specific intervallic order.

mode mixture: the use of notes from more than one MODE over a given TONIC.

modulation: a change of KEY, meaning that a PHRASE ends on a different TONIC from the one on which it began. Large-scale tonal movement is often described as modulation.

motet: (1) in medieval music, a piece built on a TENOR derived from CHANT, usually in three voices; each voice may have a different text; (2) in the Renaissance, a setting of a sacred text for voices, often in imitative style.

motive: a short, clearly recognizable melodic idea used as the basis of a piece or section of a piece. The pitch and/or rhythmic ascepts of the motive are developed into the melodic material of the work.

neighbor tone or **NT:** an embellishing note a SCALE step above or below a main melodic note.

neumatic: in CHANT, a style in which up to four notes (represented in CHANT notation by one symbol or neume) are sung to one syllable.

obbligato: an essential instrumental part. In some eighteenth-century SONATAS for violin and piano, the violin is optional; when the composer wanted to ensure the participation of the violin part, he indicated it as "violin obbligato."

oblique motion: the relation between two voices in which one moves while the other remains on one note.

organum (Lat.): a compositional practice in which one or more voices were first improvised, later composed, against the notes of a CHANT.

parallel major: the major KEY built on the same TONIC as a given minor KEY known as the PARALLEL MINOR —e.g., the parallel major of C minor is C major.

parallel minor: the minor KEY built on the same TONIC as a given major KEY known as the PARALLEL MAJOR— e.g., the parallel minor of D major is D minor.

parallel motion: the relation between two voices in which both move the same distance in the same direction.

passacaglia (It.) or **passacaille** (Fr.): a continuous variation form built over a recurring bass, like the CHACONNE. The distinction between passacaglia and CHACONNE was apparently of no significance to Baroque musicians.

passing tone or **PT:** a note filling the INTERVAL of a 3rd with STEPWISE motion. A PT may be CONSONANT or DISSONANT, on a weak beat or a strong beat; if the latter, it is a P̃T.

pavana (It.) or **pavane** (Fr.): a dance of the sixteenth and seventeenth centuries, in slow TEMPO and duple METER.

pedal point: a note (point) originally played on the pedal of the organ, sustained while other voices move over it. By extension, a long-held note, usually in the lowest part of any piece.

pentatonic scale: a SCALE that has five notes to the octave.

period: a group of two or more PHRASES.

phrase: a complete unit of melodic and chordal thought, ending with a CADENCE.

Phrygian: one of the medieval MODES. To find the Phrygian MODE on the piano, play a SCALE on the white notes, starting with E.

piano (It.): softly, abbreviated *p*.

pitch class: a group of all pitches with the same letter name.

pivot chord: a chord that is used to make a transition from one KEY area to another, having a function in both. In this book, the abbreviation for a pivot chord reads "A major VI/E major II," ·meaning "VI in A major becomes II in E major."

polyphony: the art of combining two or more melodic lines in a coherent manner, relating each part to the others. The chords that result from the flow of simultaneous MELODIES are polyphonic chords.

prelude (Fr.): or **preludio** (It.): in Baroque music, a short introductory piece often based on a single melodic figuration. While Chopin's *Preludes* are not introductory, they retain the notion of a piece based on a single idea. The term is also used for a short introductory piece in an opera.

presto (It.): very fast.

quinto (It.): in Renaissance music, the fifth part. Usually, it has the same range as one of the other four voices, with which it crosses frequently.

recitative (Fr. and Eng.) or **recitativo** (It.): in opera and in genres derived from it, a style of vocal writing designed more for comprehension of the words than melodic interest: there is usually one note to a syllable, and the accompaniment is simple. Recitative accompanied only by a CONTINUO is known as *recitativo secco;* that which is supported by an ensemble is known as *recitativo accompagnato.* Both types may be found in the same work, as in Mozart's *Don Giovanni.*

reciting tone or **reciting note:** the dominant or tone of tension in a medieval MODE.

reduction: (1) the process of determining the main notes of a piece as distinguished from the embellishing notes, and thus defining the TONAL structure; (2) the practice of arranging a composition scored for a large number of instruments, such as an orchestra, for a smaller ensemble or for piano.

register: an informal term used to describe one segment of the total compass of pitches of a piece; we speak of "high register" and "low register" without usually defining specific notes.

relative major: the major KEY whose TONIC is a minor 3rd higher than that of a given minor with the same KEY SIGNATURE—e.g., C major is the relative major of A minor.

relative minor: the minor KEY whose TONIC is a minor 3rd lower than that of a given major with the same KEY SIGNATURE—e.g., D minor is the relative minor of F major.

rhythm: a term including all aspects relating to the flow of music through time. TEMPO and METER are important aspects of rhythm.

ritardando (It.): slowing. This should be abbreviated *ritard.*, but is often abbreviated *rit.*, in which case it may be confused with the abbreviation for RITENUTO.

ritenuto (It.): held back, slower. This should be abbreviated *riten.*, but is often abbreviated *rit.*, in which case it may be confused with the abbreviation for RITARDANDO.

ritornello: a recurring refrain, usually found in such Baroque genres as opera ARIA and concerto movements.

sarabande (Fr.): a slow dance in triple METER, usually found in Baroque SUITES.

scale: a STEPWISE arrangement of a group of notes. The DIATONIC scale of a given KEY is built on the TONIC of that KEY. Scales that imply no KEY include the CHROMATIC and WHOLE-TONE SCALES.

scale degree: the order number of a note that is part of a DIATONIC SCALE.

second inversion: the $\frac{6}{4}$ position of a TRIAD, or the $\frac{6}{4}{}_{3}$ position of a SEVENTH CHORD.

semitone: *see* HALF STEP.

sequence: repetition of a MOTIVE on a higher or lower SCALE DEGREE. Some theorists take the position that a single repetition of the MOTIVE does not constitute a sequence, and two repetitions are required.

seventh chord: a four-note chord built in superimposed 3rds over the root.

similar motion: the relation between two voices in which both move in the same direction but do not cover the same distance.

simple interval: an INTERVAL of an octave or smaller.

skip or S: disjunct motion—that is, melodic motion larger than a WHOLE TONE.

solo: literally, "one," "alone"; denotes a passage played by a single instrument or sung by one voice. The soloists in a performance are the leading performers.

sonata: a composition in more than one movement for one or two instruments. In Baroque music, a composition for one instrument alone (rare), one instrument and CONTINUO (the "solo sonata"), or two instruments and CONTINUO (the "trio sonata"). Later, a composition for piano or one instrument and piano. The term implies a seriousness of structure and concept.

sostenuto (It.): sustained.

stepwise: conjunct motion, melodic motion of a SEMITONE or a WHOLE TONE.

suite: in Baroque music, a set of stylized dance pieces, all in the same KEY. There are four movements which may be called "obligatory" movements, because they are usually present in suites of Bach, Handel, and Rameau: ALLEMANDE, COURANTE, SARABANDE, and gigue. Later, the term is used informally to describe a work in several movements that is more like a loose collection of pieces than a closely knit entity. Another term for suite is *partita*.

suspension or SUS: a dissonance technique which includes three stages—(1) preparation of the note to be suspended as a consonance, on the weak beat; (2) motion of another voice to put the suspended voice in a DISSONANT relation with it, on the strong beat; (3) resolution of the suspended note to a consonance, on the weak beat.

syllabic: in CHANT, the style in which one note is sung to each syllable.

talea (Lat.): in a medieval ISORHYTHMIC MOTET, the repeated rhythmic pattern of a TENOR part.

tarantella (It.): a lively Italian dance, usually in $\frac{6}{8}$.

tema (It.): theme.

tempo: the rate of speed.

tenor: (1) the higher male voice; (2) in medieval music, the part that holds (Lat., *tenere*) the notes of CHANT on which a MOTET is based.

tenore (It.): the tenor voice.

ternary form: three-part form, in which the middle part introduces new material and the third part repeats the first literally or in varied form.

time signature: *see* METER SIGN.

toccata: in Baroque music, a piece for keyboard instrument in a free, often improvisational style. In the twentieth century, the term is used for a brilliant or energetic piece for any instrumental combination.

tonal: applied to music that has a KEY center or TONIC.

tonic: the note in a piece that acts as the center of gravity, to which all others are related. It is the most stable note. Music that has no tonic is ATONAL.

tonicization: the process by which a SCALE DEGREE other than 1 temporarily functions as TONIC.

transposition: moving the entire body of a piece or group of notes higher or lower, while keeping their relationship intact.

traverso (It.) or **flauto traverso** (It.): the transverse flute —that is, the modern instrument, which is held horizontally, as opposed to the recorder, which is held vertically.

triad: a three-note chord consisting of two superimposed 3rds over a root.

tritone: the intervals of a diminished 5th or augmented 4th, both measuring six SEMITONES—e.g., F–B.

tutti (It.): all, the entire ensemble.

upbeat: an informal term for the weak beat preceding the strong or DOWNBEAT that begins a measure.

vers mesuré (Fr.): a French Renaissance poetic practice in which each line of verse follows a strict formula of long and short beats.

violone (It.): the lowest member of the viol family of instruments, used for Baroque BASSO CONTINUO parts.

volta (It.): time or turn, as in *prima volta*, "the first time."

whole tone or whole step: an INTERVAL made up of two HALF STEPS; a major 2nd—e.g., C–D.

whole-tone scale: one of the two SCALES made up of six WHOLE TONES to the octave.

LIST OF BOOKS REFERRED TO IN THE TEXT

Dart, Thurston, *The Interpretation of Music,* New York, Harper & Row, 1954.

Das Erbe deutsche Musik. Reichsdenkmale, 1935– .

Davison, Archibald T., and Willi Apel, eds., *Historical Anthology of Music,* 2 vols., Cambridge, Harvard University Press, 1946 and 1950.

Denkmäler der Tonkunst in Österreich, 1894–

Fux, Johann Joseph, *Steps to Parnassus,* Alfred Mann, tr. and ed., New York, W. W. Norton, 1943.

Green, Douglass, *Form in Tonal Music,* New York, Holt, Rinehart and Winston, 1965.

Grout, Donald J., *A History of Western Music,* rev. ed., New York, W. W. Norton, 1973.

Grove's Dictionary of Music and Musicians, ed. Eric Blom, 5th ed., New York, St. Martin's Press, 1954.

Hermann Keller, *Thoroughbass Method,* Carl Parrish, tr., New York, W. W. Norton, 1965.

Lang, Paul Henry, *Music in Western Civilization,* New York, W. W. Norton, 1941.

Liber Usualis, Tournai, Desclée, 1963.

Parrish, Carl, and John F. Ohl, *Masterpieces of Music before 1750,* New York, W. W. Norton, 1951.

Sharp, Cecil J., and Maud Karpeles, *Folk Songs from the Southern Appalachians,* 2 vols., London, Oxford University Press, 1932.

Strunk, Oliver, *Source Readings in Music History,* New York, W. W. Norton, 1950.

WORKSHEETS

Worksheet 1

1. Write all the As that you can find on the piano keyboard.

2. Write the key signature for each of the twelve major scales below. Start with C major. Proceed to the key that has as its signature one sharp, which is ——— major. Its tonic is a ——— higher than C. Continue the series by adding one sharp for each key. At the end of the line, the key signature of ——— sharps applies to the key of ——— major. Write the name of each key under the staff. These (except C) are sometimes called the sharp keys.

C major ———   ———   ———   ———   ———   ———   ———

Another way of spelling F♯ is ———♭. Start the next line with the key that uses six flats in its signature, ——— major. Continue the series with the flat keys.

———   ———   ———   ———   ———   ———   ———

3. What are the chromatic notes in the key of A♭ major? —— —— —— —— ——
   What are the chromatic notes in the key of D major? —— —— —— —— ——
   What are the chromatic notes in the key of F major? —— —— —— —— ——
   What are the chromatic notes in the key of A major? —— —— —— —— ——

4. Above each note write another note to complete the interval.

major 3rd	major 7th	perfect 4th	perfect octave	minor 2nd	major 6th	minor 6th	major 3rd	major 6th

5. Below each note write another to complete the given interval.

6. Above each interval write its name.

7. Starting from any note, write the following intervals:

8. Next to each interval write its inversion. Name the result.

9. Augment each interval two ways. Name all intervals.

10. Diminish each interval two ways. Name all intervals.

11. The three notes F–G–A may be scale degrees _____ in _____ major. They may also be scale degrees _____ in _____ major.

The two notes F♯–G may be scale degrees _____ in _____ major. They may also be scale degrees _____ in _____ major.

The two notes G–A may be scale degrees _____ in C major. They may also be (as many as possible)_____ .

12. Change each of the following simple intervals into compound intervals. Identify both.

13. Reduce each of the following compound intervals to simple intervals. Identify both.

14. In the first column is a list of simple intervals, named according to their tonal usage. Next to each write the number of semitones in the interval. Then write the inversion of that interval, first in tonal terms, then as the difference between twelve and the number of semitones in the interval.

interval	semitones	inversion	semitones
minor 2nd	1	major 7th	12 –1 = 11
major 2nd			
minor 3rd			
major 3rd			
perfect 4th			
augmented 4th			
perfect 5th			
minor 6th			
major 6th			
minor 7th			
major 7th			

Worksheet 2

1. Above each note write the note that completes the given interval.

2. Below each note write the note that completes the given interval.

3. Next to each interval write its inversion. Name both.

4. Write the scale of the Dorian mode, descending, starting on E. Add accidentals as needed.

5. Write the scale of the Phrygian mode, descending, starting on A. Add accidentals as needed.

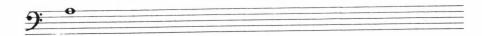

6. Write the scale of the Mixolydian mode, descending, starting on B♭. Add accidentals as needed.

7. Study these nine versions of a 6th.

Write as many versions of a 3rd as you can. Name each.

Write as many versions of a 5th as you can. Name each.

8. The relative major of G minor is _____; the parallel major is _____.

The relative minor of A♭ major is _____; the parallel minor is _____.

The parallel minor of D♭ major is _____; the relative minor is _____.

Name . . . . Date . . . .

Worksheet 3

1. Use consonant sounds only. Write in a note that results in

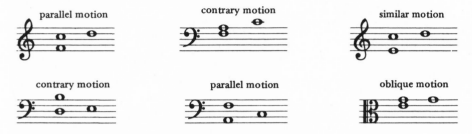

2. Describe each interval as PC (perfect consonance), IC (imperfect consonance), or D (dissonance).

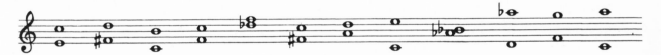

(Numbers 3 and 4 refer to 38 .)

3. Using the first phrase as a guide, write figures between the lines to show all simultaneous intervals. Circle all dissonant intervals.

4. Bracket one instance each of parallel, contrary, and oblique motion.

Worksheet 4

Write a counterpoint to each *cantus firmus*. Use consonant intervals only. Indicate each interval with a number between the lines as on page 32.

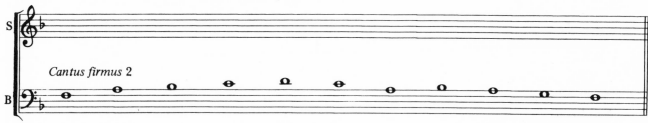

Cantus firmus 2

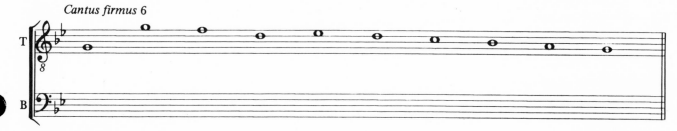

Cantus firmus 6

Cantus firmus 3

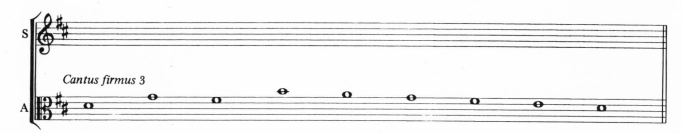

Cantus firmus 10

Cantus firmus 12

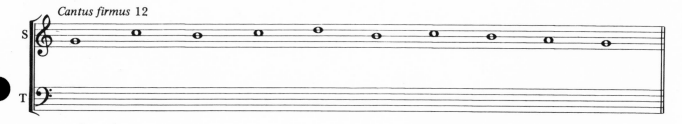

Worksheet 5

Write two parts against the *cantus firmus.*

Cantus firmus 3

Cantus firmus 6

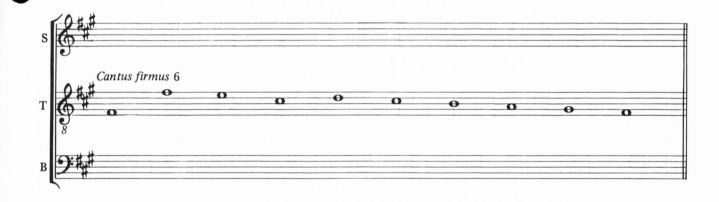

Cantus firmus 9

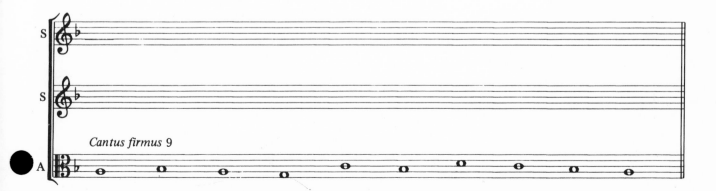

Name . . . . Date . . . .

Worksheet 6

1. Name the root, type, and position of each triad.
   a. Below each chord write the root.
   b. Below that write the type: M (major), m (minor), D (diminished).
   c. Below that write the name of the position: root or first inversion.
   d. Below that write the figures for the position: $\frac{5}{3}$ or $\frac{6}{3}$.

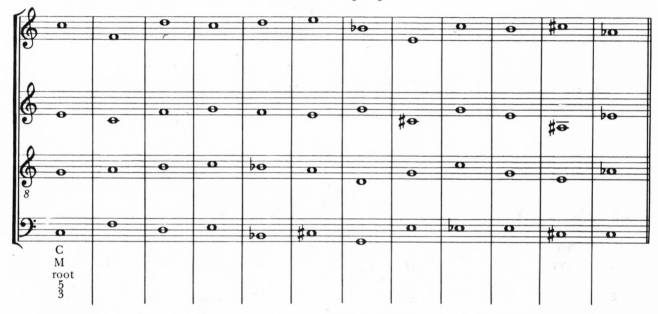

2. Write each of the triads described below in three different ways. The pitch classes are not to be changed, but their distribution is. Root, type, and position are given for each triad.

C	G	E♭	F♯	A	B♭	C♯	D	F	G♯
M	m	D	m	M	M	D	D	m	m
6	$\frac{5}{3}$	$\frac{5}{3}$	$\frac{5}{3}$	6	6	6	6	6	6

3. Take a recent four-part exercise you have written and describe the triads by root, type, and position.

4. Describe all the triads in ⃞41 by root, type, and position.

5. Examine ⃞42 for voice crossings. Mark each one X.

Worksheet 7

1. Write three voices against the *cantus firmus*.

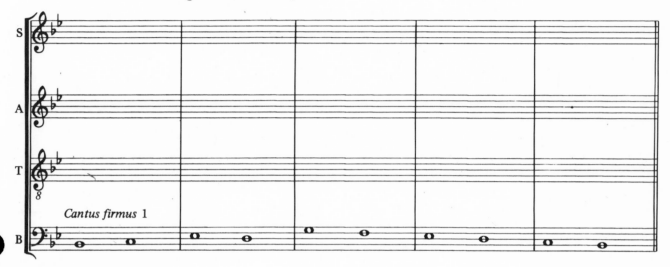

Cantus firmus 1

2. Do the same here.

Cantus firmus 5

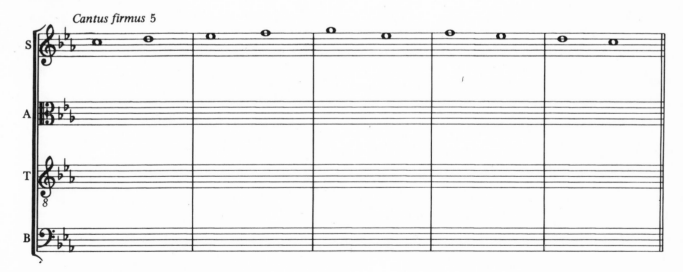

Worksheet 8

1. Write the key signature, then the triad. If no Arabic numeral is next to the Roman numeral, $\frac{5}{3}$ is implied; write the root position. If ^{6} is next to the Roman numeral, $\frac{6}{3}$ is implied; write the first inversion. Use the diatonic notes except for V♯ in the minor mode, where the leading tone is called for.

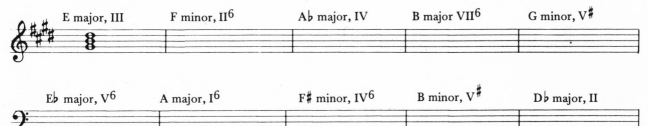

2. Next to each chord write its first inversion.

3. Next to each first-inversion triad write its root position.

4. Describe each triad as major, minor, augmented, or diminished.

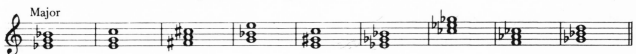

5. Write the major triad in root position, of which E is the root ⎰⎱═══, the third ═══, the fifth ═══.

6. Write the minor triad in root position, of which C♯ (D♭) is the root ⎰⎱═══, the third ═══, the fifth ═══.

7. Write an F-major triad, in root position, using at least four different spacings. Double root, third, or fifth.

Name . . . . Date . . . .

Worksheet 9

---

1. Find all of the PTs in [50C], *Sarabande 1*. Mark each succession of consonance-dissonance-consonance by writing the intervals, keeping in mind that dissonant relationships involve two voices at a time. Circle the numerals that indicate dissonant intervals.

2. Add a dissonant PT to follow the given consonance, and pass on to another consonance. **Do not** repeat half notes.

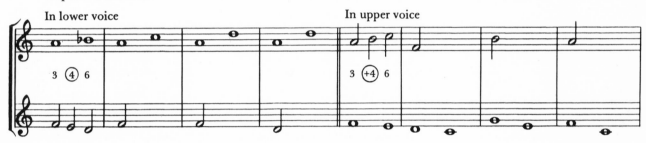

3. Set a counterpoint in half notes to each *cantus firmus*. Use consonant and dissonant PTs and consonant Ss.

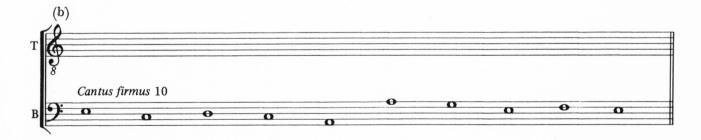

4. Add three voices in note-against-note counterpoint.

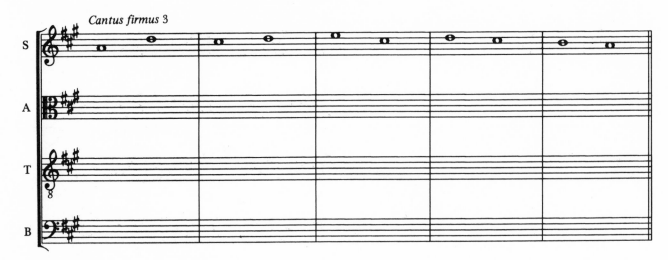

5. Use *cantus firmus* 4, 5, or 6 in the alto. Add three voices in note-against-note counterpoint.

Name . . . . Date . . . .

Worksheet 10

1. Write a counterpoint in half notes to each *cantus firmus*. Use PTs, NTs, and consonant Ss.

Illustration

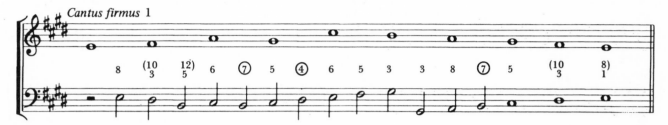

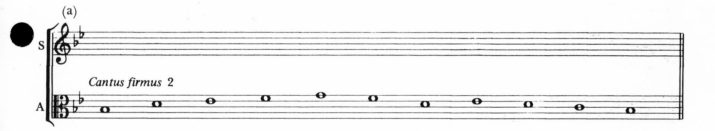

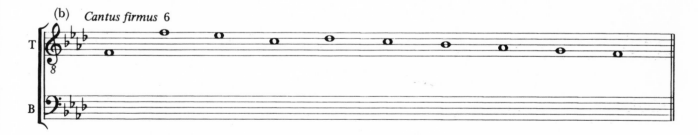

2. Write a counterpoint in half notes to *cantus firmus* 3, 4, or 7 (on page 33). Use PTs, NTs, and consonant Ss.

3. Add three voices in note-against-note counterpoint.

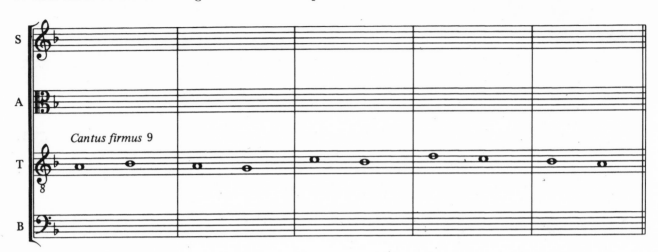

4. Use *cantus firmus* 11 or 12 in the bass. Add three voices in note-against-note counterpoint.

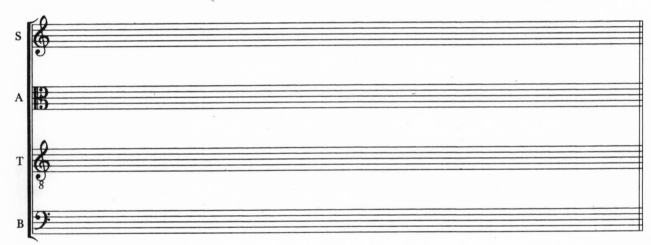

Worksheet 11

1. Find all the SUSs in $\boxed{38}$. Identify the dissonant and consonant intervals in each operation.

2. Elaborate each pair of dyads (chords each made up of two tones) with a SUS and show all intervals.

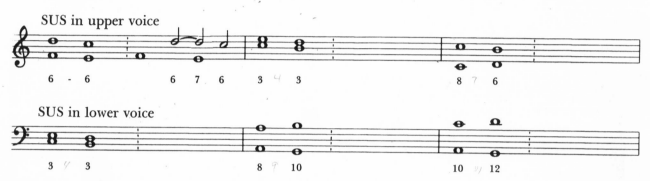

3. Using the techniques of Number 2 for the SUSs, write a counterpoint in half notes to each *cantus firmus*. In addition to SUSs, you may use PTs, NTs, and Ss.

Illustration

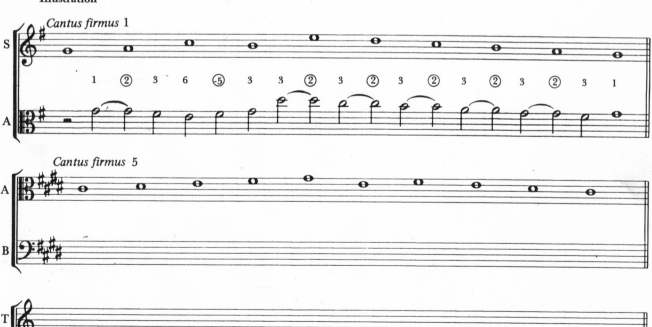

4. Use *cantus firmus* 1, 2, or 3 in the alto. Add three parts in note-against-note consonance.

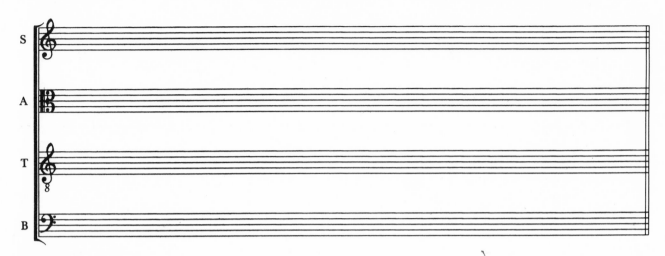

5. Use *cantus firmus* 4, 5, or 6 in the tenor. Add three voices in note-against-note consonance.

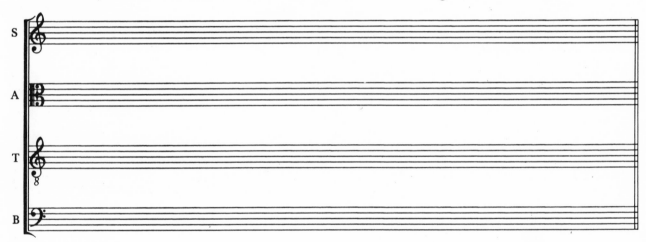

Worksheet 12

1. Add two parts: one in whole notes, one in half notes.

Illustration

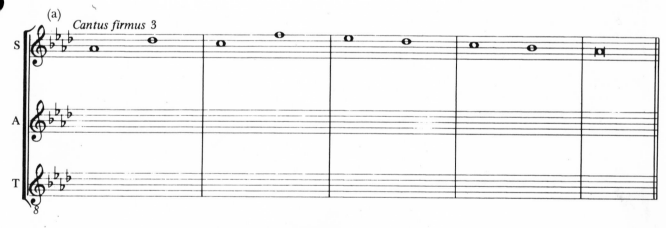

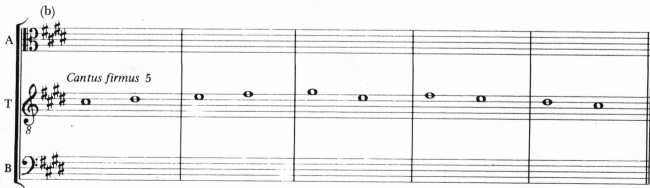

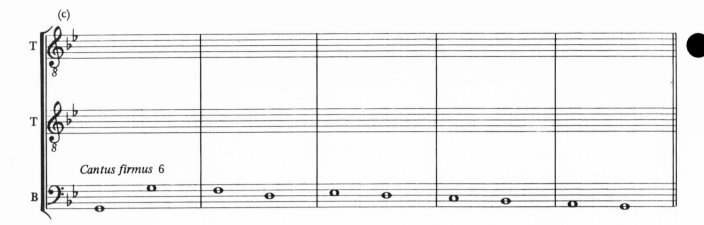

(c)

2. Add three parts.

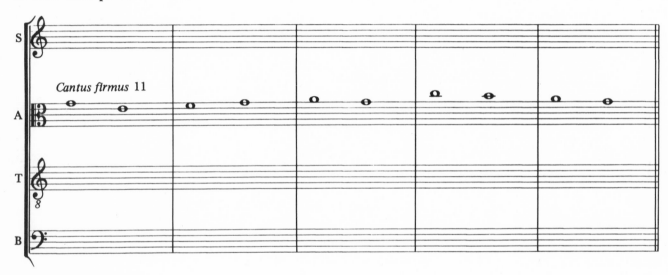

3. Add three parts.

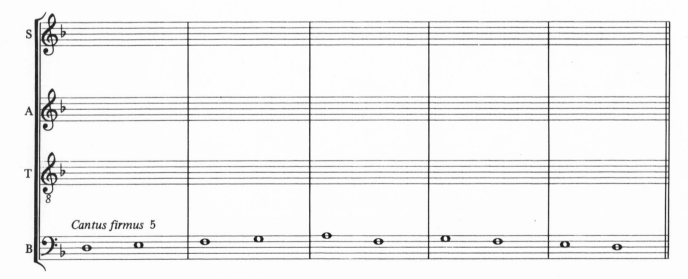

Worksheet 13

1. Write two lines in whole notes and one line in half notes against each *cantus firmus.*

Illustration

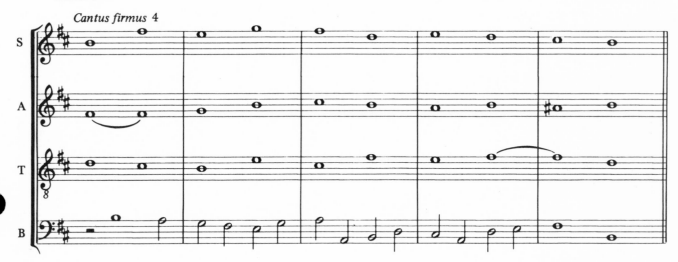

2. In each measure, elaborate at least one note with a NT. The other voices become dotted half notes.

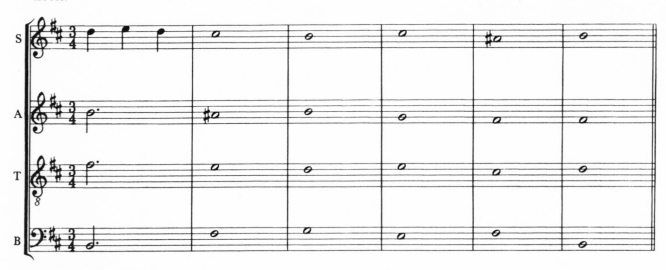

3. On the line marked S II write a second version of the soprano part, embellishing the consonant sounds of S I with dissonant SUSs.

Name . . . . Date . . . .

Worksheet 14

Connect each pair of consonant triads with one or more dissonant PTs.

Worksheet 15

We have seen three ways in which chords are grouped in musical phrases. They are:

a. prolongation of the tonic (less often, of other chords);
b. motion from I to V;
c. cadence, including the harmonic progression and 3–2–1.

Before composing complete pieces, we may develop more control over the tonal direction by doing short studies using the three motions. Consonance and dissonance are used as in the music studied. Work in two different ways:

a. improvise the studies at the piano;
b. compose the studies in your mind, write, then check at the piano.

llustrations

Worksheet 16

Illustration

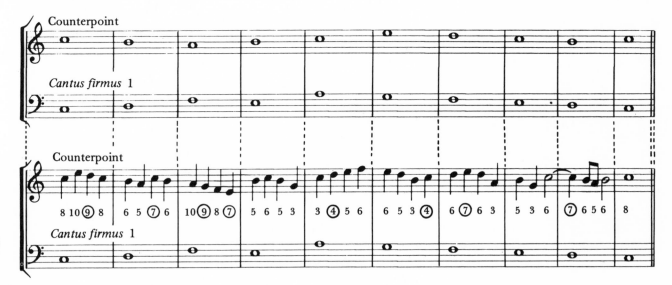

1. Given this example of note-against-note consonance,

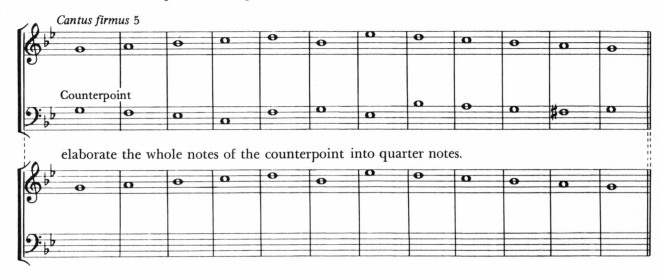

elaborate the whole notes of the counterpoint into quarter notes.

2. Write a counterpoint in note-against-note consonance.

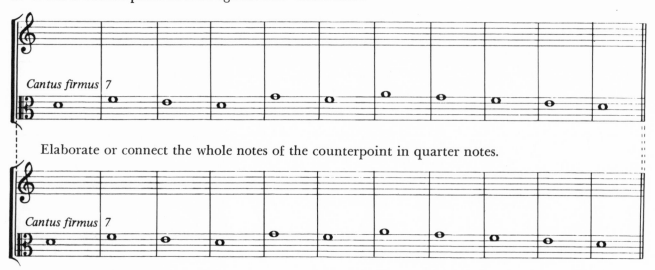

Elaborate or connect the whole notes of the counterpoint in quarter notes.

3. Without the preliminary stage, write a counterpoint in quarter notes.

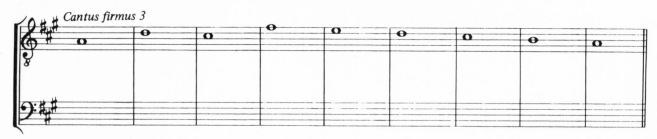

4. Use *cantus firmus* 2, 3, 4, or 8 in the upper voice (see page 33). Write a counterpoint in quarter notes.

Worksheet 17

1. The illustrations show five ways in which a two-part texture can be expressed as a single melody. In each the bass is unchanged. The specific technique used in each version is indicated.

Illustrations

I basic pattern   (a) arpeggiation

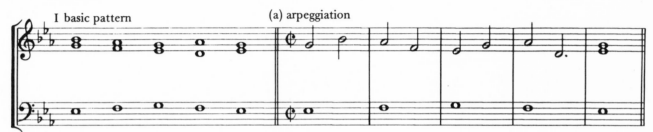

(b) connected with PTs

(c) NTs, chromatic and diatonic

(d) Inversion and NT

(e) Inversion, skips filled in with PT

2. Three progressions are given below. Write several elaborations of each, combining the two upper lines into a polyphonic melody. In each version, indicate what technique of embellishment you are using.

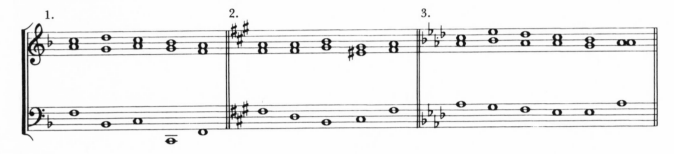

Worksheet 18

1. Study these brief tonic prolongations.

Write the Roman and Arabic numerals that describe each chord. Identify all dissonances as NT, PT, or SUS.

2. Fill in the chords in four parts, as indicated by the figures, over each bass note that is given. Add chords, dissonant where possible, in the beats between the given chords. Identify all chords that you add.

Worksheet 19

Make both a choral setting of $\boxed{1}$ and a version for voice and piano based on the same tonal structure. The tonal structure of the melody, by phrases, is:

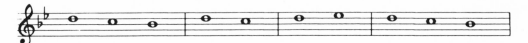

Write a bass line and outline the chords, using only I, IV, and V, in root position.

Use your bass to complete the two settings whose beginnings are given below.

smile, For they say you are tak - ing the sun - shine, _ That bright - ens our path - way a - while.

(b)

Voice

From this val - ley they say you are go - ing, _ We will miss your bright eyes and sweet

Piano

smile, For they say you are tak - ing the sun - shine, _ That bright - ens our path - way a - while.

Worksheet 20

1. 90A : The cadence in V, with 3–2–1 over IV–V–I, is in measure _____.

2. 90B : The V–I cadence in V is in measure_____.

3. 90C : The cadence in V is in measure _____.

4. 85 : The cadence in 8 is (*on/in*) V.

5. 93 (Aria): The cadence in 9 is (*on/in*) V.

6. 93 (Recitative): The cadence in 3 is (*on/in*) V.

7. 87 : Describe the cadence in 46–48 .

8. 88 : Describe the cadence that concludes this piece.

Worksheet 21

Give the complete figure for each applied dominant.

1. 80 : 15 , VII of IV.

2. 83 : 16–17 , first half, ———————.

3. 84 : 9 , first half, ———————; second half, ———————.

4. 86 : 3 , last beat, ———————.

5. 90B : 7 , last eighth note, ———————.

6. 90B : 12 , second beat, ———————.

7. 90C : 7 , third beat, ———————.

8. 90C : 13 (D minor), first beat, last eighth note, ———————.

9. 90C : 13 , fourth beat, last eighth note, ———————.

10. 90C : 19 , second beat, last eighth note, ———————.

11. 90C : 19 , fourth beat, last eighth note, ———————.

12. 90C : 20 , fourth beat, last eighth note, ———————.

13. 90C : 21 , second beat, last eighth note, ———————.

14. 91 : 7 (key is ———————), second beat, ———————.

15. 91 : 11 (key is ———————), last eighth note, ———————.

16. 91 : 21 , second beat, last eighth note, ———————.

Worksheet 22

Rigaudon

Kirnberger

Study this piece and answer these questions:
  a. How does the bass prolong D for four measures?
  b. Explain the use of the 4th in 2 .
  c. What are the main melodic notes in 5–8 ?
  d. In what register do they appear? Explain.
  e. What chord is heard in 9 ?
  f. Explain the dissonance at the beginning of 10 .
  g. What factors make for contrast in 9–12 ?
  h. What is the meaning of G♯ in 11 ?
  i. Write the right-hand part of 9–11 in a single register.
  j. Write a different right-hand part to the bass of 1–4 .
  k. Where is the bass motion of a 5th divided into two 3rds?
  l. What do the octaves in 13–14 accomplish?
  m. What do you think are the good points of the piece? The limitations?

Worksheet 23

Here is the first half of a keyboard piece in binary form. Study it carefully for its structure and its use of musical space. Then write a second half to match.

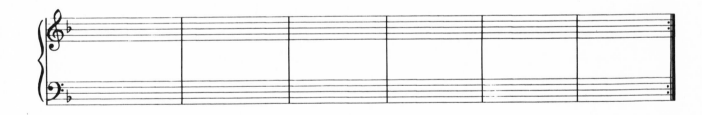

INDEX